To Will
&
To Do

For it is God which
worketh in you
both to will and to do
of his good pleasure.

—PHILIPPIANS 2:13, KJV

An Ethical Research
For Christians

To Will
&
To Do

Jacques Ellul

Translated by
C. Edward Hopkin

PILGRIM PRESS
Philadelphia   Boston

Christian Ethics
Morality

Translated from the French edition, published
by Labor et Fides, S.A., Geneva, Switzerland.

To Yvette

Foreword

When it comes to thinking and doing Christian ethics, the American layman—hardly more than his pastor—is bewildered. His conscience is confronted by an overwhelming array of moral perplexities. The traditional copybook answers from the Bible, church law, or Christian convention are remote and irrelevant to the demands of moral decision, especially in the area of social ethics. When it comes to right and wrong, nothing is for sure. Currently we have seen the rise of "situation ethics," opposing all fixed rules and principles, calling for Christian love to fit itself to unprecedented situations with infinite flexibility and go it on its own. An opposing counsel is given by the jackleg evangelist-preacher, who in the face of the tangled problems of the city, racial strife, international discord, fervently proposes that we should "come to Christ." "What we need is faith." But this answer is simplistic, nostalgic, and forlorn, offering really no more than a nostrum and an escape.

In such a situation, the thought of Jacques Ellul provides an intriguing kind of approach. Since he is relatively unknown to American readers—though several of his works have been translated into English—he more than deserves a word of introduction.

A professor at the University of Bordeaux, a scholar versed in history, law, and sociology, Jacques Ellul is a

Christian not by birth and inertia, the easy way, but by per-
suasion out of the torments of political turmoils in the
France of the 30's and his own careful reflection. He has
much of the ardor of a convert. His espousal of Christianity gives him a faith-standpoint from which his critical
study in the fields of law, history, and social analysis is illumined. His published technical works—*Propaganda, The
Technological Society,* and *The Political Illusion,* available
in English—are testimony to his sharp competence as a stu-
dent of the dynamics of Western society.

To Will and to Do is his major treatise on Christian
ethics. It fleshes out more fully the argument of his earlier
book *The Presence of the Kingdom.* A closely reasoned
statement of a conservative evangelical Protestant position,
it proposes "to search for the significance of biblical revelation concerning ethics."

It was not to the mother church of Rome that Ellul
turned in his prodigal pilgrimage. He has been sharply critical of the Catholic tradition (see *The Theological Foundation of Law: A Radical Critique of Natural Law*). Have
no doubt about it: Ellul is dogmatically Christocentric.
"Everything derives from the fact that Jesus is God." In a
manner reminiscent of the early Karl Barth (who with
Dietrich Bonhoeffer is often cited), Ellul stresses the radical break between God's revelation and man's reason, between faith and culture, between the Christian life and natural morality of the most refined and genteel sort.

At times the reader may be put off when Ellul speaks with
the stiff tone of voice of a biblical conservative. ("It is all
found in scripture, is a part of revelation, and nothing authorizes us to expurgate this or that text because it doesn't
please us.") Yet Ellul's position is not that of the Bible-
thumbing pulpit-pounder. His simplicity of assurance lies
on the other side, not this side, of sophistication. And he
avoids the peril of using the Bible as a moral rule-book, for
"morality of scripture is not made of rules but of a certain
manner of life."

His final position is somewhere quite beyond the thickets of natural law casuistry, the abyss of an anomic contextualism, and the escape of simple biblical piety. He ends with a paradox: the impossibility of and the necessity for a Christian ethic. It is like the paradox of a Saint Paul living "between the times," necessarily under the old law and yet in the new spirit. It is like Luther's paradox of life within the two realms.

Just how Ellul proposes that the Christian is to cope with this ambiguity of daily life, as justified by grace in the forgiving work of God in Christ, glad and free, yet perplexed and bound by the pressing hard choices of his political existence, the reader is invited to pursue for himself.

Waldo Beach
Professor of Christian Ethics
Duke University

Contents

Introduction

Lay the cards on the table. In order to write about morality, it is necessary to adopt from the beginning an attitude of intellectual and personal humility. All fabrication disqualifies the work, for it cannot be a simple intellectual construct when the search for the meaning of life is itself a search for a way of life. It would be useless to claim to pursue a moral quest without presuppositions. Such a thing does not exist, as shall be demonstrated. It is better to have presuppositions which are clear, and which one owns up to candidly, than to pretend not to have any when such a pretense would only be ignorance or a lie. "Here I wish I could wear a mask," said Stendhal; and doubtless anyone who writes about the conduct of life in its truth and in its reality will say the same thing, for he is writing about the most secret thread of his life. But he dare not go beyond the wish. He dare not wear the mask. The explanation must be given with the face uncovered. I therefore confess that in this study and this research the criterion of my thought is the biblical revelation, the content of my thought is the biblical revelation, the point of departure is supplied by the biblical revelation, the method is the dialectic in accordance with which the biblical revelation is given to us, and the purpose is a search for the significance of the biblical revelation concerning ethics.

This rigor in nowise implies that this is a book intended for Christians. To the contrary, I would expect all its value to come from a confrontation. Still less is it concerned with preoccupations peculiar to Christians. Every man in our decaying Western civilization is asking questions about the rules of his life. Still less, finally, is the biblical revelation limited to the narrow circle of the elect. It speaks first about all the others. We shall be dealing with the life and morality of men of the world.

Now that I have acknowledged the presuppositions with which I begin, and have taken a stance clear-cut enough to eliminate all misunderstanding, it remains for me to say that I have no competence to write this book. I am neither a theologian nor a philosopher by profession. I possess none of the specialist's qualifications, for in our day philosophy has become a technique, and one is disqualified if he has not climbed all the steps of that edifice in a university program. I am trying only to be a human being. I am trying to live fully in this age. I feel the anguish of those around me. I am acquainted with our general laxity in a society without structure and without rules. My trade is to reflect, and I have undertaken to do that as a man, nothing more. I shall run into many a problem which the specialists have studied hundreds of times. I approach these in innocence and with the fresh outlook of the incompetent. I shall take care not to give a definition of ethics. The reader will choose any one among the thousands available, since all these definitions are partly accurate, but only partly. The specialists will shrug their shoulders. Perhaps a man will pay attention . . .

I

Origins

Knowledge of the Good

1   The serpent said to Eve, "You will be like God, knowing good and evil." Such is the point of departure. Before this decision of man, Adam never raised the question of good and evil. He did not know about them. He was unaware that there was a good and an evil. He found himself in communion with the will of God, which he recognized directly in his relation of love with the Creator. His heart beat in rhythm with the heart of God, and his face was ever turned toward that of the Father which he reflected for the world and for the creation. He was free before God, which is to say that he could love God as well as cease to love him. He was free before God, but that freedom did not at all relate to some choice between doing and not doing, between a Yes and a No, after painstaking deliberation. To think in that manner about freedom shows clearly that we know nothing about it. We are distorting it, mutilating it, mummifying it. Freedom, precisely because it *is* freedom, cannot be defined in that way as an indetermination of choice. It is neither a consequence of the correct exercise of the reason nor of the independence of the will. Again, there is no test of freedom, because for the free Adam his freedom—which he was unaware of—was its own constant test and its own proof, the offering of a joyful life in response to the gift of life which had been given beforehand.

At this point is brought to pass, through Satan's intermediary, the awareness of an absence, of a gap, of the missing link in that suddenly glimpsed chain which bound Adam to God, and which when unknown was only a game but which when known becomes a question: the awareness of a forbidden domain which turns happy obviousness into tragic absence. Prior to that moment there is no moral conscience; there are no ethics. What is then proposed is not the possession of good and evil, as though good and evil were objects, things which Eve could lay her hands on. Adam and Eve do not take possession of good and evil. They only receive knowledge, comparable to that of Elo-him. They are going to know that there are good and evil, that there are obedience and disobedience, that there are love and hate. They are going to know, also, that there is a Yes and a No which they can say, and which someone can say concerning them. But does all this knowledge bear upon the content of good and the content of evil? The entire biblical revelation attests to the impossibility of that interpretation. In the Bible the good is not prior to God. The good is not God. The good is the will of God. All that God wills is good, not because God is subject to the good, obedient to the good, but simply because God wills it.[1] It is not the good in itself that determines the will of God. It is the will of God which determines what is good, and there is no good which exists outside of that decision. This point will be developed in chapter 2.[2]

Let us not say that this is a matter of simple, divine voluntarism. But to affirm that the good is nothing other than what God decides—that is, his commandment—means that from man's point of view the good is not *his* decision, nor a simple possibility; for that good has, as a matter of fact, an independent reality. The good is given, laid down by God—"He has showed you, O man, what is good" (Mic. 6:8) —and man is forbidden to discover it by himself. Man can only act well when he listens to the word of God; for "that which has been declared to man is clear, it is the good news of the free election by God, in Jesus Christ . . . man's good action resides entirely in the good action of God. It is determined by Jesus Christ. . . . To do good can only mean one thing; namely, to obey the revelation of divine grace." In all this, there is no question of metaphysics, nor any hint of the transcendence of the good. It is a matter of the affirmation of the gospel, of the very activity of the word of God which *alone* permits us to say, "No one is good but God alone" (Mark 10:18) ; for it is this God who defines the good *by doing it,* who designates it by sacrificing himself. "What God wants of us is always identical with what he wills and has done for us." Thus, it is indeed the "name of Jesus Christ" alone which makes legitimate the statement that the good is the will of God. "We should seek the commandment of God only in that place in which he has *ripped away the veil of opinions and theories concerning the divine will* in order to place himself clearly before us, in which he has made himself known as a grace." [3]

And that is also what permits us to understand (another departure from the theory of voluntarism) that there is never a divine requirement which is abstract, general, inherent, but only divine requirements which are concrete. Now Adam precisely is unable to have a knowledge of this good in the situation in which he finds himself; first, because such knowledge would mean that the will of God is set, immobilized in an objectively perceptible content, continuing without change, and that God, in the last analysis, is *relegated to the past* for man (who lives in time) : God *has willed.* I know this will which is the good. I know the good, and now God limits himself to re-willing ceaselessly the same thing (this good) , like a record playing the same groove over and over again. In other words, if man by himself knew the content of the good, that would mean that God is not free. The result, then, of man's disobedience interpreted as the knowledge of the good would be to give man a preeminent power, and to take freedom away from God. But it is necessary to go still farther: if such were indeed the sense of these words, that would mean that before his disobedience Adam did not know what God's will was; he fulfilled it in the spontaneity of love but he did not gain admittance to its lasting content, nor to the secret of its decision. Yet now, after the fall, Adam supposedly is endowed with this wonderful power to penetrate the mystery of God's decision. He supposedly knows how God determines what is good. What he failed to know in love and communion he now knows in disobedience and alienation.

Now that he has turned away from the face of God, Adam knows the mystery of the will of God! And he knows it by nature, by himself, autonomously, since the power in question is one which he took upon himself. It is patently absurd.

Finally, let us recall that this will of God is characterized throughout the Bible as a "holy" will; that is to say, set apart—in the last analysis, intimate, autonomous, now radically separated from man who is not holy. To call that will holy, is necessarily to say that Adam could in nowise know it. Only the holy can be in union with that will, but Adam does not answer that description. It will take Jesus Christ to teach us who it is that alone conforms to the holiness of God, and that the only way is, both by grace and also after man has dropped all pretention, to be brought into conformity with the will and the holiness of God. Man cannot know that will until he has been brought into conformity because it is a holy will.[4]

And how many biblical texts are there to tell us that such is not man's situation after the fall! Man is ignorant of everything about the will of God. He is ignorant of the whole mystery of the decision of the love of God—that mystery which Paul tells us the angels themselves would have loved to contemplate. And only in Jesus Christ do we discern it. How then could Adam have the power which the angels do not have? Because he ate of the fruit of the tree? What magic operation would have opened his eyes to the invisible; in short, would have given Adam a grasp of the revelation? But there was no magic in Eden. Because he disobeyed and separated himself from God's will? But we know that that will is not perceived except precisely by the person who fulfills it perfectly: Jesus Christ alone has known it. Well then? Nothing is left of the too obvious, too simple interpretation that Adam knew what was good and what was evil, that he received before Moses a sort of table of stone on which was engraved everything which he should do.

This knowledge of good and evil puts man in the astonishing position of living, in the final analysis, ignorant of the truth. That ignorance, to be sure, is not in the domain of intellectual knowledge. It has to do with the truth of the mystery of God. Now the mystery of God is not a body of information. The mystery of God concerns the whole of man's existence. The knowledge acquired by Adam hid this mystery of God from him in the very act of giving him the remarkable means of acting in the world; but, as Crespy has so well put it, "Ignorance is not a lack of knowing; it is a lack of living," [5] and indeed it is because it concerns the totality of human activity that it finally presents itself as in some way willful.

Again, it is with the very exact statement that the good is nothing other than the will of God, that one should connect the command not to judge, which we find throughout scripture. Man cannot judge his brother because he cannot know what is good. He cannot, of himself, decide what the good is. God alone can judge, precisely because there is an identity between the will of God and the good. Every time man claims to judge his brother he repeats Adam's fault, in trying again to be the one who declares the good—when his brother would be the one who does not know what the good is. As a matter of fact, judgment is the division between the person who has seized upon a good in and of itself, a good detached from the person of God, and the person who supposedly is dispossessed of that good. But scripture itself tells us constantly that he who is judged and rejected by

others is the one whom God accepts, loves, and saves, and
that on the other hand, he who pretends to judge others is
the one who is rejected by God.

The text of Genesis enlightens us on the true situation of
Adam: "You will be like God." Once again, if there had
been a good apart from the will of God (to which, of course,
the will of God should be subject), then one could understand that Adam, knowing that good,[6] would for all practical purposes be in the position of God who also knows it
and does it. But that would mean that God is not God, that
he is not sovereign, since he is determined by an excellence
higher than himself. If God is God, it is he who determines
the good. If Adam, after he has fallen, is confined to *knowing* a good determined by God, if God remains master of the
good, of which Adam is merely an investigator (the impossibility of which we have already seen), then the other part
of Satan's promise would not be fulfilled. Now the two
things go together. The ability to discern good and evil is
the very characterization which is here applied to God. And
Satan's entire promise is fulfilled, as God himself attests,
"Behold, the man has become like one of us." What does
that mean? Precisely that Adam, like the gods, now has the
power to *determine* what is good and what is evil.[7]

So far the reasoning in this discussion has been as though
the knowledge in question were of the intellectual order,
as Western man understands it. To know is to understand
with the intelligence what is good and what is evil. In that
case we could imagine that there is a good in and of itself.
But in Hebrew, "knowledge" does not have that meaning.
It has rather a living, active sense. Knowledge is a participation of the whole being, a commitment, an involvement.
It supposes a sort of creation in the very act of knowing.
And the source of the knowledge is a decision. When Genesis speaks to us about this knowledge, it is saying that
henceforth Adam is in possession of the decision concerning good and evil. He creates, so to speak, what is good and

what is evil by acting. Therein resides, now, his knowledge, which at the same time makes him like God. His will, like God's will, is going to settle the content of the good. But it is not the same content. It is not the same good. Henceforth, what Adam will call good is not what God calls good. This is the point at which the serpent's promise is fulfilled, and yet not fulfilled in truth, but only in a lie. The serpent is the father of the lie. It is indeed true that henceforth Adam will know that the good exists and that he will seek to define it by his own will. But the lie consists in the fact that Adam is no longer in communion with God, and therefore this good is not that of God. When God decides to prevent Adam from laying his hand on the tree of life it is an act of grace; for if that situation had been eternal for Adam it would have been beyond any kind of solution, and would then have been the very situation of the demons. Adam is like God, but he is separated from God. He is far from God's countenance. He has no more communion with God's will. Adam himself is alone—and alone as well in affirming what is good and what is evil. Moreover, the biblical text enlightens us on the significance of this knowledge when it describes for us what happened afterward as a result of the knowledge.

What is it then that Adam and Eve are about to know? What is the fruit of this information? What exaltation comes from this tree which is good for food, a delight to the eyes, and desired to make one wise? First of all, Adam and Eve knew that they were naked, they were ashamed in one another's presence.[8] That is to say that true love between them, together with love for God, had ceased; there was now shame, with a quite distinct quality of morality— a quality both positive and negative. It is positive in the sense that it reproves what is no longer permitted, but negative in that it recalls the original, lost innocence, by no means a useless defense, to be sure, in this world of concupiscence and confusion, but still a contemptible sign of the evil which has entered into the heart of man.

Subsequently, upon hearing God's footsteps, they hid themselves far from the presence of the Eternal. "I was afraid." There is the second knowledge: fear, springing from remorse. And again we are plunged into morality, remorse. One is now aware of the disobedience. What had been the law of love has become the law of restriction. This remorse, too, is positive and negative. On the one hand it is a legitimate warning, a debate with oneself in the midst of rebellious nature; but on the other hand it is a gnawing cancer which attacks the heart of man, undermining it, eating it away, and destroying it through the inability ever to receive a sufficient pardon. And fear! There you have moral knowledge as an instinctive knowledge of punishment. Whence did Adam acquire this fear, he who never before had known anything but dominion over the creation and mutual trust with his creator? Here he is, having discovered that God is a terrible and a vengeful God. And the question which God puts to him underlines derisively that exalted science produced by the fruit of knowledge, "Who told you that you were naked? Have you eaten of the tree?" Such then was the knowledge—knowledge of his nakedness, knowledge of his shame, but also of his loneliness (for it is true that a man who is no longer in communion with his creator is completely lonely), and again of his weakness and his destitution. The royal mantle that had covered him, the mantle of God's love, is torn to shreds. Oh, how naked, Adam!

Why is this weakness so tragic? Precisely because from this time forward Adam will have to decide for himself what is good and what is evil.[9] At that point, Adam's weakness takes on a terrifying character. God's sovereign power of discernment is indeed in his hands, but Adam's hands are not God's hands. Here now in this creation, the whole of which is cast adrift with Adam, it is he who will declare the just and the unjust, yet he himself is not just. Thus the substance of all the promised knowledge is reduced at the very beginning to the discovery of his nudity. And when his

eyes are opened, what does he see? Not the unfading absolute of a total good which he thought to possess, but the
deadening ridicule of his nudity. And in this account in
Genesis the discovery of morality is completed by accusation. The man accuses the woman and the woman accuses
the serpent. The law of love is indeed broken. But the moral
law is brought to light, one of the characteristics of which, in
fact, is this parceling out of responsibilities, this capacity to
detect who is guilty and the degree of the guilt, this screen
which one puts up in the face of accusation: I am just,
Lord, it is not I, it is the other person. There you have the
last of the results spoken of by this first passage, the discovery of good and evil by fallen man.[10]

From this moment on we are caught up in a very strange
venture! For the very act by which man wants to decide
what is good, wants to know the good by himself, constitutes the sin. Thus, sin is not the failure to obey a morality.
It is the very desire to determine that morality independently of God, a desire which is, at the same time, concupiscence, the will to power. Consequently, the most virtuous man who at the cost of prolonged asceticism cries,
"There is the good," is the very one who reproduces for
each person, and in each person, the sin of Adam.[11]

Without pressing the texts too far, perhaps the last verse
of Ecclesiastes is aimed at this good and evil established by
man and which God calls into judgment. In fact, if we
take Neher's translation, which seems to this writer to be the
most true to the original, this verse reads, "It is God who
will bring every deed to judgment concerning everything
which is eternalized, whether good or evil." From this it
seems one might say that the deed is not good or bad,-but
that man's work is the good and the evil. This is also confirmed in Isaiah 41:23: "That we may know that you are
gods; do good, or do harm." Here, to do good is clearly a
divine attribute. And man pretends to carry this good and
this evil to eternity, to eternalize it. And God calls this

creation of man into judgment. The judgment of God, in fact, is not a distinguishing of good from evil according to the criteria which man has looked at and chosen. God's judgment is aimed at the good as well as at evil, at what man calls good, which is confronted with judgment and measured against God's good as expressed in his will.

That is the situation. Man knows that a good exists. He knows that from now on the choice has to be made. Finding himself in a state of disobedience, of alienation from God, he grasps the existence of the good in the form of an accusation, and he aspires to the good as a way of escaping the accusation. But he is ignorant of that good because he does not know the counsel of God. He is ignorant of the eternal decision of God, at the same time that he is ignorant of God's will, *hic et nunc,* for him. He cannot rely upon anything absolute for perceiving the good. Yet he is the recipient of the terrifying and derisive gift of saying, by himself and for himself, what the good is. Here he is, then, armed for the battle, in which he relieves himself of his anguish and at the same time overburdens himself with futile requirements. Through this recall of the biblical account, one can see how far we are from the interpretation of the early theologians. According to them, fallen man retained intact his knowledge of good and evil. The entire domain of the conscience and of the intellect supposedly was maintained, while only the will was fallen. Man, they said, knew the true good but no longer had the power to perform it. This explanation, of course, can be sustained if one starts from certain philosophical premises; and in fact it is on the basis of philosophical presuppositions that Thomas Aquinas builds his system. One can offer any of the possible explanations, and the most diverse, merely by a change in the metaphysical standpoint; but none of that is biblical.[12]

What the Bible tells us is much more radical. First of all, before the alienation, Adam had no *knowledge* of the good. It is expressly in order to have that knowledge that he eats of the fruit desired to make one wise. Adam did have an existential communion with the good, which is quite another thing. Now he will have a duplicating awareness, knowledge in separation from that something which now becomes an object, and which at the same time is a complete stranger to him. Hence, across the barrier of the disobedience, Adam did not *retain* something which he had previously had. More than that, we have seen that he had no knowledge of the true good, of the unique, intimate will of God. This consideration would have led to absurdities which the theologians have avoided by covering up the reality of the problem. The error surely stems from treating the good the same as any other object, a thing to be known among other things. And since man was capable of knowing the stars and of knowing himself, since that science was exact and led to right action, it became a certainty that man had kept intact his capacity to know. And why would he not *also* know the good among all the diverse objects to which he applied his reason? The Socratic experience showed clearly that man was capable of discerning a good, precisely by an appeal to the reason. Each person's experience also revealed the possibility of feeling a call to something which he considered good, and that only the failure of his will stood in the way of its fulfillment. But all of that rested upon ignorance of the biblical revelation, or rather upon the primacy bestowed upon philosophy or on experience, thanks to which the interpretation of revelation was colored.

The biblical rebuttal is easy. The texts are numberless in which God, having revealed his will to *his* people (and his alone), concludes: "See, I have set before you this day life and good, death and evil. If you obey the commandments of the Lord your God, . . . then you shall live" (Deut. 30:15–16). If every man had the knowledge of the good, how could God call his will revealed? What gift would he be giving his people, and to them alone, if all peoples had the knowledge of the good instinctively? What need would there be for a revelation if the good were registered in nature? What can the expression "this day" mean if since the fall, and even before, man found himself with that choice?

The debate over the possibility of man's natural knowledge of the good according to God is obviously inconclusive. Everything depends upon the point of departure which is selected. If one adopts a strictly biblical reference, then it would seem that one could hardly do otherwise than to follow Karl Barth on the subject of the impossibility of the natural knowledge of God by man, which leads to the same impossibility for the knowledge of the good.[13] If one adopts some other point of departure, then all the interpretations become possible. Either one feels the necessity for an intermediate power whereby man may lay hold of the good (conscience, reason, as in Thomas Aquinas or even Augustine) ; or one points to the evidence for a human reality which demands a return to the good, which assumes that the good is known [14]; or one lays a foundation in anthropology, however Christian, and deduces from that a power resident in man for knowing the good by himself [15]; or the good appears as a counterpart to the obvious effects of evil upon man [16]; or again, with Brunner, the law of natural "orders" constraining us to a life of community with men causes us to discover the Christian truth of love for one's neighbor, for it is the God of love who has given us life in these orders. In any case, whatever man recognizes in these orders as just, according to his own nature, is in conformity with the will of God. In the last analysis, all these attempts have their source in the impossibility of man's accepting his own incapacity to define the good by himself, to grasp the good by himself, and in his injustice in wanting still to exercise the discernment of good and evil.

In scripture, there is no possible knowledge of the good apart from a living and personal relationship with Jesus Christ.[17]

In reality, however, man has even less knowledge of the true evil than he has of the good. Man learns what is evil;

that is, discovers himself as a sinner, at the time of the revelation of the good as the will of God—a revelation which is granted not as a condemning justice, but as a justice of love. He learns it at that time only. He can have no true natural experience of it whatsoever; because all natural experience of evil will necessarily be ambiguous, and will be all the more falsifying since its overall point of reference is a good defined by man. He cannot be convinced of sin by confrontation with a good, a morality, a more or less abstract principle, but only when he is confronted by God.[18] Human transgression goes so far that unless the divine demonstration intervenes to prevent him, man can always listen to the thousand and one truths which will be told him on the subject of morality and the commandment of God.

That is why we cannot agree with Ricoeur when he sets forth the penitential experience of Israel as a point of departure for all the notions (symbols) of guilt, of sin, and of all the mythical constructs stemming from them—a penitential experience presented as a human experience, located at the human level. To liken the fear of the most holy God to the negativity of the transcendent,[19] to say "the conscience, no longer finding in real suffering the manifestation of the law of retribution, looked for that satisfaction in other directions," [20] that "the consciousness of sin increases and becomes limitless in proportion as historical insecurity increases," [21] etc., is to reduce to a natural experimentation on the part of man, and to its natural deepening, that which only exists in consequence of the revelation and in the presence of the revelation of the good (justice and grace). In the latter case, sin is no longer a symbol for explaining an experience, but an objectively existing reality only to be discovered by revelation, by the placing of man in confrontation with God.

Hence, since man is separated from God and in that situation defines the good for himself, he is radically incapable of discerning, loving, and willing God's good. That is why man is guilty whenever he pretends to do good, and why he is idolatrous whenever he pretends to be religious. We can only conclude that either the revelation of God is meaningless or there is no natural knowledge of the good. And God's greatest witnesses know it well. After the word addressed by God to his people, let us consider the prayer addressed to God by his servant. When Solomon accedes to power and addresses God, what does he ask for? "Give thy servant therefore an understanding mind to govern thy people, that I may discern between good and evil" (1 Kings 3:9) . What meaning could that prayer have had if Solomon had been born with that discernment, if the fruit of the tree had really opened his eyes to the good? Now, indeed, Solomon asks for that discernment as the leader of the people *of God,* as the one in need of the true knowledge of the true good, of the will of God for which he is responsible on earth. And he who asks that of God is Solomon! Solomon, the wise, the just, received the unusual discernment as a gift, as a grace.

For a man so to know the good is a miracle. To be sure, in Solomon's case, more than in the case of some others, we can see that the will fails to match the knowledge! How often this wise man disobeyed the good! But for him the problem was not a problem of the will alone; for if he knew the good which he failed to do, that was because the revelation of God had enlightened him, because God had opened his mind, had caused the scales to fall from his eyes, had bestowed upon him the wisdom and the vision of the good. But a prayer and its answer were required. There had to be the submission of a man, who far from pretending to know the good, acknowledged before God that he did not know it, that he was incapable by himself of discerning good and evil. Moreover, it is just when man acknowledges that incapacity that he can have a revelation of the good from God. Indeed, as long as man claims to know the good by himself, as long as he can declare himself the master of that wisdom, every revelation from God only produces a situation of conflict. God reveals a good which is not the one that man pretends to proclaim. From then on the very nature of sin is set forth. And that is indeed why the Bible directly links the moral problem to the intention of sin. That is when, in point of fact, covetousness, the source of sin, bursts into view; for that covetousness of which Genesis speaks is not so much the desire to possess the forbidden fruit as the pretention of becoming like God, of possessing the knowledge of good and evil. Covetousness played up that possession. The point is that from the moment one possesses that discernment, one also possesses the power to justify oneself.

It is because man has become the master for declaring good and evil that at the same time and by the same action he claims to give himself his own justification. Man's thirst for justification rests on his capacity to settle the good for himself. But just as this thirst for justification is nothing other than the desire to flee the judgment of God,[22] so also the settling of the good by man is nothing other than his refusal to be in communion with God. Those are the two aspects of the same revolt and of the same "fall." That is why man puts such stock in knowing the good: prodded now by sin, he can justify himself by invoking the good, by invoking the law, whether he be Jew or Christian. Here is where the conflict with God is the most obvious. This is also why only the man who acknowledges that he is incapable of that knowledge can find grace with God. God indeed answers the prayer of Solomon the wise man, who is wise by the very fact of humbling himself like that, of praying like that, already enlightened by that light which comes, but who alone learns, because it is the light *which comes,* that he is in the night—the man already wise, who knows that all wisdom is vanity. It is no accident that tradition places Ecclesiastes under the name of Solomon. It is precisely the wise man who knows that he is not wise, and that unless God gives him the knowledge of the good in his revelation, he knows nothing, and is living in folly.

The Good

2 What is the good according to the Bible? Thousands of books have been written on this subject by theologians. Our presumption will encourage us not to analyze these extraordinarily diverse theses, and not to venture into that labyrinth which has become hopelessly involved for reasons not always connected with purity of faith. The biblical teaching seems comparatively simple. A preliminary remark is called for: practically all the texts (with the exception of a very few which we shall examine at the end) are addressed to—and are speaking about—the people of God; that is, the people of Israel in the Old Testament and the people of the church in the New. Consequently, it is a question of people who have received the revelation of God, for whom the word of God is a word of life and a living word. It is a question of those who know *already* that the good refers to God. Therefore, whenever these texts speak quite simply of "good," they cannot do it abstractly and in an unspecified manner. Tell an average Christian today, who is not a theologian but who has a living faith, to do good, and that will immediately evoke for him ideas and images referring in one way or another to Jesus Christ, however diversely and imprecisely.

Hence we should interpret these texts in relation to those to whom they are addressed, since they are neither a philosophy nor a cosmogony. They always claim to carry a personal revelation, and they have meaning only for those who believe and who already accept the will of God. Every time there is a question of the good in the Bible it is because God is speaking.[1] When Cain is told to "do well," that is not an objective and impersonal formula. It is God who says to him "do well," and hence who initiates the dialogue; and it is only in this dialogue that Cain learns what is the good for him. It is also in the dialogue that Cain learns the possibility of doing the good because God is present in his word, and adds all his power to the possibility which is given to Cain *at that moment*. So it is in the many similar texts in Isaiah 1:16–17: "Cease to do evil, learn to do good." It is God who speaks to this people—his people—who because they have been chosen by God have henceforth the possibility of doing the good, and who are awakened to that possibility by this word *hic et nunc*. In that situation only, and at the same time, the good receives its content. Biblically speaking, the good only has content because God makes it known: "He has showed you, O man, what is good" (Mic. 6:8). Consequently it is not an instinctive knowledge, intuited a priori. God must intervene, must make known, must reveal and be revealed, before man can have that knowledge, which is exactly the opposite of the knowledge obtained by Adam. Nor is it a man acting on his own who acquires and wins that knowledge,[2] "He has showed you . . ." It is an action which comes from outside the man, a movement toward him. In fact, whenever God speaks, and by that fact acts upon man, he speaks the good (Numbers 24:13), and on the subject of the good and the evil the prophet can only repeat what the Eternal might say. Thus the knowledge of the good is linked to that of the will of God. The two are always bound together, and even identified:[3] "He has showed you, O man, what is good; and what does the Lord require of you . . ." says Micah. With the Jewish people this notion is developed in terms of the identification of the good with the law, the latter being the totality of God's will revealed and decreed.

Biblically speaking, an action is not good because it achieves values, nor because it conforms to a moral regulation, nor because it is motivated by good intentions. It is good whenever it is the very work of God. As Soë says, "Man is never a star, he is always a planet, without any light of his own." [4] Man only reflects the good that comes from God. Surely, if the good were distinct from the will of God, man could perform it himself and possess himself of it. Nowhere does the Bible open up that prospect. If Jesus says, "You are the light of the world," it is *because* he says "I am the light of the world." And no disciple can reverse the relationship and say for himself, "I am . . ." Karl Barth says, likewise, that the action of man is good in the degree in which it is sanctified by the word of God.[5]

We shall not develop this well-known theme further. Numerous texts remind Israel that in abandoning the law it is abandoning the good (Hosea 8), or again, that it is in learning to know the law that the children learn to know the good (Deuteronomy 1:39). But once again it is not a matter of the objective law and *erga omnes*. It is a matter of the law as the word of God addressed to his people. We find this idea also with Paul, for example, when in chapter 2 of the letter to the Romans certain expressions seem to imply an objective knowledge of the true good. In verse 10, we read, "Glory and honor and peace for every one who does good, the Jew first and also the Greek," but the whole context shows that it is not a question of all men but only of those to whom a revelation has been given. In verse 5, the expression "hard and impenitent heart" is reserved for those who reject the revelation of the word of God. In verse 7, we have reference to "those who by patience in well-doing seek for glory and honor and immortality."

For Paul, these three expressions have a content which is very precise and directly related to "his gospel." They do not have a vague, disputatious sense, rooted in human concepts. Finally, verse 32 in chapter 1 is also very clear. There it is entirely a matter of men who *know* the *judgment* of

God concerning the things of which Paul has just spoken. This knowledge is precise, rigorous, circumstantial, not intuitive and evident. It bears upon the judgment of God; that is to say, it is in fact a word of God which no man can carry directly within himself, which is the most awful and the most intimate aspect of his relationship with God. Of this, a man has knowledge only when he knows God's love, since it is from the standpoint of that love that man can learn to know what God detests and rejects, and from that standpoint alone. Thus Paul confirms perfectly the point of departure which we saw in the Old Testament—God who reveals himself in his love thereby teaches man his will, and then it is that man knows what is good.[6]

Let no one object that if the good is nothing other than the will of God the moral life becomes unadulterated incoherence, actions which succeed one another disconnectedly, blind and contradictory obediences. To say that is to form a strange concept of God! I well know that one can sometimes get that feeling from a superficial reading of the Bible, and of the apparently disordered series of commandments, but God is one. There is no division or change in him, no contradiction. It is because he is one that his will is coherent, and our moral life is coherent. It is because he is one that these commandments form a whole without contradiction. It is because he is one that our obedience is not absurd, and our lives are not made up of disconnected moments. And all of that is true even if our tangible experience does not teach it to us.[7]

This will of God which gives content to the good is not arbitrary.[8] God does not call evil good in forgiving our sin, for God cannot lie. But God renders good that which is evil in itself, healthy that which is sick in itself, glorious that which is wretched in itself, living that which is dead in itself. We present ourselves to God bad, and we come away good. That is the forgiveness of sin, but God never says that evil is good.

God's decision has nothing to do with caprice; and what he ordains for man to do, or not to do, is not related to the fantasies of a tyrant whose rights coincide with his power. The movement that regulates the relationship between God and man in the history of the covenant of grace, during the course of which God is faithful and steadfast, and therefore in the final analysis the good, is not an incoherence. It is within the framework of the history of the people of Israel, of the history of Jesus Christ, that all the ordinances of God are placed, all his prohibitions, which are not to be generalized and which presuppose the coincidence of the good with the will of God.[9]

The good, whenever God speaks, does not remain a word and a notion. It receives, we might say, a content, but it receives it from God. The story of Cain's revolt is significant: "Why are you angry, and why has your countenance fallen? If you do well, will you not be accepted?" (Gen. 4:6–7). In this passage, to do well is to stop being angry, to put an end to despair, to master evil. But that is not a good *in itself*. Anger and despair are not the evil. Why is Cain angry and in despair? That is the important question. The answer is easy: because Cain did not accept God's decision to recognize Abel's sacrifice and not that of Cain. Cain did not accept the will of God expressed in that decision. He cannot believe that God loves him anyway. He thinks that God is unjust. Therefore, it isn't anger and despair in themselves that are the evil; these are evil as aspects of Cain's attitude toward God. The good, then, is to accept the decision of God, to believe that God loves him anyway, to acknowledge the will of God whatever it might be, including the will which gives preference to Abel. The good is to be in agreement with that will, and in the strength of this agreement to master anger, despair, evil, since it can only be done by loving that will of God without judging it. This is to say that anger, despair, evil, are products of an external knowledge of God's decision which one does not love. All the other descriptions of the good derive from that one.

The good, according to Deuteronomy 30:15–16, consists of loving God, walking in his ways, adoring only him.[10] According to Psalm 14, it is to seek God, to pray to him, to call upon his name, and because of that to respect others and not destroy those whom God loves. Successive phrases of Amos are also significant: "Seek me," "seek good" (Amos 5:4, 14). At bottom, that identifies the will to do good with seeking God. But at the same time it is to have a fear of the Eternal (which is mentioned repeatedly), to set forth the truth (of God), to seek peace (with God) (Psalm 34:14), to put one's trust in God, to have faith and hope in him, to be faithful to his love, and in his love to find one's joy and to delight in his will and in his presence (Psalm 37:3). Thus the good is a certain relationship with God, and only with respect to God can it be set forth. Nowhere is there a good foreign to this attitude of man before God. And if the good is determined by the word of God, to do the good is to believe in this word of God and to carry it out. Only that attitude toward God leads inevitably to a given behavior with regard to men, which behavior, likewise, is never taken in and of itself, independently of faith.

Thus the good, at one and the same time (but never separately) will consist in praying to God for others; interceding for one's enemies (Psalm 35:12–13); bringing about justice for men; defending the poor, the humble, the oppressed (Isaiah, Amos, Micah). We are familiar with the duties set forth by the prophets and also the virtues stated by Paul that go to make up the good—the good behavior before God. It is needless to persist in describing them. The important thing is to remember that none of that is to be understood except inwardly, within the good itself, which is the will of God. We can recapture, then, this notion of the good through the astonishing passage in Micah (6:8) : "He has showed you, O man, what is good; and what does the Lord require of you but to do justice, and to love kindness, and to walk humbly with your God?" The three requirements summarize all the rest: to walk before God (in his presence, in the light of his revelation and with faith) humble and subject to his will—to practice love of neighbor—to do what is just,[11] such is the good.

The New Testament, which is more reserved in the use of this word, can tell us nothing to the contrary. In this connection Paul often returns to passages of the Old Testament. James defines the good as love of neighbor, and as faith in God put into practice. To a certain degree he emphasizes the ethical character of the concept. In fact, the strongly theological tone set by the Old Testament can convey the feeling that the good is an inward, mystical affair, and a matter of intention. That, obviously, would be to misunderstand the realism of the Old Testament, but the misunderstanding threatens to arise nevertheless. The letter of James brings us back to the heart of the moral problem by insisting on the practical nature of the very ingredients which constitute the good (chapter 2). Moreover, none of this changes what we have learned.

The third letter of John takes another step in advance: "Beloved, do not imitate evil but imitate good. He who does good is of God; he who does evil has not seen God" (3 John 11). This verse puts us in a clearly christological situation. "Imitate the good": that formula presupposes that the good is not an abstraction, not a mere attitude on the part of man. Now there is (and this is a new fact in contrast with the Old Testament) a model of the good. But this model is not a formula, not a congealed idea, a fixed object. The imitation implies the concept of "following," so commonly met with in the Johannine writings. To imitate is to follow someone who is walking ahead of you. If we put this text back into its Johannine setting, the imitation of the good must be related to the imitation of Jesus Christ himself. That it is indeed Jesus Christ whom the author of this letter calls the good is confirmed by the continuation of the same verse: "He who does good is of God." John has just defined the one who is of God as the one who confesses that Jesus Christ has come in the flesh. Likewise we read at the end of the verse: "He who does evil has not seen God." John says that one can only see God in Jesus Christ. Hence there is a close relation between the performance of the good and the person of Jesus Christ. That should not surprise us! But we must also grasp the fact that there is here no contradiction with the Old Testament.

We might sum up the progression thus: the good is that which God speaks in his word; it is, in consequence, a certain attitude of man toward God, as a result and as a function of that word; again, it is a certain attitude of man toward man, as a result and as a function of the relationship with God. But on the one hand, the word of God is fully expressed, explained, and revealed in Jesus Christ, and only in Jesus Christ, who is himself, and in himself, the Word. Thus Jesus Christ is truly the good. On the other hand, the attitude toward God and toward man is put forth as a requirement, a call, and a promise in the Old Testament, while in Jesus Christ this good is totally and fully incarnate and fulfilled. The good, then, is a something already accomplished into which we are to enter, but which does not on that account do away with the call and the demand addressed to each one individually. This can no longer be the cause of anguish and despair. We, and we alone, are no longer totally responsible for bringing to pass the good on the earth. It has been brought to pass. But we are always spurred on to fill up anew the measure of the good, for the sake of him who has brought it to pass.

This amounts to the same thought as that expressed by Bonhoeffer,[12] according to which the good has become a reality in Jesus Christ. While in all our thinking there is a dissociation of the good from the real, the two cannot be dissociated in the fact of the incarnation. But that is the only place in which they do coincide. Everywhere else man is unable to lay hold of the good because he is hemmed in on all sides by the real. The word of God which spells out the good is pronounced in Jesus Christ, and nowhere else. To hear and to practice the word of God is to receive holiness as a member of the Body of Christ. Holiness is a living relationship with Christ.[13] If it be true that Jesus Christ alone is indeed the whole good, then we learn three truths which are decisive for our life before God, three truths which we need to take in and to meditate upon. The first is that the voice of Jesus Christ is the voice of the holy God himself. But since it is the voice of Jesus Christ, it is not only the voice of a God who would limit himself to giving orders and making promises, who would be only a transcendent and a distant God. We could never hear or take in the command of that kind of a God. We would only be confronted with nothingness and despair. The voice of Jesus Christ, at the same time that it is the voice of God, is also the voice of man. It is near at hand, but it is the voice of a holy man, a man sanctified in our place, who speaks the good in our place, and who accomplishes in obedience to his Father what Adam wanted to accomplish in disobedience.

The second truth brings us to the heart of the dilemma of faith and of the good: man always looks for a good which will determine a "deed"—whereas in Jesus Christ it is always a matter of a "being." [14] This runs counter to everything being taught today under the influence of Marx; namely, that man exists only in a "deed." But that is not the voice of the Lord.

The third truth brings us back to our powerlessness for accomplishing the good. If any good whatsoever could be resident in man, or could be accomplished by man apart from God, that good would have appeared in Jesus Christ. Now in Jesus Christ himself the love of God finds nothing worth the trouble of being loved.[15] Jesus Christ himself has nothing to put forward in the presence of God, nothing to show except our sin and our transgression. Man in his person only exists as a renegade. The only just man has no justice to present in our name.

This conception of the good, which seems to us to be rigorously biblical, permits us to answer very quickly three classical questions of morality.

1. The first question is one of indifferent actions (controversy of the adiaphora). Between what is "commanded" and what is "forbidden" there is supposed to be a broad domain of actions which concern neither salvation nor the good. In reality, this is unacceptable from the Christian standpoint. All of life should be obedience, and consequently there is no act which is foreign to God's will.

A life does not consist of a series of separated acts, each one isolated from the others, but of a continuity of which each act is an expression. This unity of life is what Jesus Christ indicates when he says, "Either make the *tree* good, and its fruit good; or make the *tree* bad, and its fruit bad" (Matt. 12:33). The fruits are only consequences. Therefore fruits are not to be separately judged. None of them are indifferent. And Paul says it explicitly: "Whether you eat or drink, or whatever you do, do all to the glory of God" (1 Cor. 10:31). Hence the smallest act has meaning. There are no "optional" acts, no "negative" or "positive" accommodations. There are no distinctions between a time of peace and a time of war.[16] All is embraced in the determination of the good as the will of God. Man is called upon to realize that all his life concerns God and that his work is judged in its global sense. "We cannot envisage any human action which would not be dominated by the command of God. . . . No act exists that is free or neutral in the sense of man's being dispensed from making a decision in the face of God's command. No neutrality on man's part is possible."[17]

2. The second question is closely related: Are there autonomous *domains* of activity which do not concern the Christian life? Scientific, technical, and economic problems do not seem to give rise to Christian ethics. A portion of these areas is purely intellectual and hence involves no "moral" judgment. If economics, politics, and sociology are

phenomena of the same order as physics, if there are "laws" of these activities, where can one find room for moral decision? Another portion of these domains is purely "natural," in which there could be no necessity for discerning a good and for looking to a "revelation." A natural morality suffices. All theologians who believe in a natural law attempt to answer that question, and the same is true to a certain extent of the theologies of the moral conscience (even with Luther). But in reality the problem vanishes the moment the Bible convinces us that the good is the will of God, for all the domains in question are part of the creation of this God. He is the Creator of politics, as of economics, and consequently nothing escapes his judgment or his grace, and everything finds itself included in this decision of God, which is the good. There is no domain so scientific or technical as to escape this determination of the good, because the latter exceeds by far the reduced moral categories of our evaluations. "The good is life." Still less are there any domains in which natural morality would suffice, for it is sin itself which defines that natural morality.[18]

3. Finally, the third classical question is that of the autonomy of morality. Is the latter a domain in itself? If we adopt the biblical vision of the good, we are obliged radically to reject that idea. On the one hand, the world (and morality which is of the world) wants to be autonomous, and all philosophical morality must declare itself autonomous, but in the very degree in which it is in revolt against the good of God. On the other hand, revelation teaches us that if one takes the creaturely condition seriously it is impossible for man to lay the foundation of his own ethics independently of the lordship of the creating and redeeming God. No ethics in accordance with the will of God can be autonomous.[19]

It was necessary for the Son of God himself to bring about the fullness of the good, for man could never succeed. The biblical teaching is clear and cruel: "The Lord looks down from heaven upon the children of men, to see if there are any that act wisely, that seek after God. They have all gone astray, they are all alike corrupt; there is none that does good, no, not one" (Ps. 14:2–3). Nowhere in scripture is that terrible judgment diminished. It is, to the contrary, often upheld. The situation is presented as a universal fact. "Surely there is not a righteous man on earth who does good and never sins," we read in Ecclesiastes 7:20; and Paul uses this observation as one of the foundation stones of his theology. He cites Psalm 14 to the effect that the whole world is guilty before God (Romans 3:10–12). This radical incapacity is true of all men without distinction. Of course the "impious," who does not believe in God, does evil *necessarily* (Psalm 36:4). This is a continual lesson. It is obvious if one thinks of the concepts of the good which we were indicating above. Now it is no less obvious that the authors of scripture were not stupid, and that they knew very well that those who did not worship Yahweh, or later Jesus Christ, were capable of doing good. A lot of good was being done in Egypt, in Greece, and at Rome; and they knew it. What man calls good was being more or less accomplished, but at least accomplished. One must not, then, speak of a blindness or an ignorance in these declarations. Still less should one speak of a partisan or sectarian attitude. It is simply a different concept of the good.

Likewise, according to the human concept of the good there are degrees; a more good and a less good, a greater or a less evil. And this, in fact, corresponds with the judgments which man can make from the point of view of his concept (which he creates). But the Bible instructs us, to the contrary, that there is a holy and a not holy. There is no degree of the holy, no border zone, no approximation, since that which is holy is, in point of fact, that which is separated. In the same way, when Jesus declares that whoever has violated the least commandment has violated the whole law, he rejects the more and the less. Now that cannot be understood if the good is an objective reality, in and of itself, which man might come to know by his own efforts. It is only to be understood if the good is brought into correspondence with the absolute of God's will.

All of that boils down to saying that what man might define and perform as good is not the good before God and according to God. The impious man who rejects God can know nothing of the good. He cannot have the slightest knowledge of it and hence, before God, he can only do evil. But we are not confronted with a sectarianism! The reason is that it is not a matter of dividing some men from other men *in this connection,* of dividing the impious who do evil inevitably from the believers who do, or who can do, the good. Alas, revelation is more rigorous and less simplistic than that! The Jews, even though recipients of the revelation, are no more *capable* of doing good than the others. Every time Israel, taking itself as the knowing subject who is aware of the revelation given to it, thinks to fulfill that revelation itself, every such time Israel commits evil before God.

Consider the extraordinary provoking of God set forth in Isaiah 41:21–24. Israel pretends *to be* in and of itself (apart from its Lord) and to do good by itself (apart from its Savior). God says, "Set forth your case. . . . Tell us what is to come hereafter, that we may know that you are gods" (always the pretention of Eden . . . and Israel, because it had received the revelation, could indeed take itself for a god!). "Do good, or do harm, that we may be dismayed and terrified. Behold, you are nothing, and your work is nought." This Israel of God, then, is placed on the same footing as the others, and Jeremiah reminds the people of Israel of it: "Can the Ethiopian change his skin or the leopard his spots? Then also you can do good who are accustomed to do evil" (Jer. 13:23).

Thus, although knowing in what the good consists, Israel is no more capable of performing it than the impious. Israel's situation is even worse than that of the unbelieving because Israel *knows* what the good is and the other does

not. This knowledge is the great difference between them;
but Israel, who knows, is fully responsible on that account.
Israel is called into judgment before this very good. But
there is more. Israel has the possibility of filling up Adam's
sin to the full measure, because the pretense of being like
God can take root in Israel and in Israel alone: the pretense of naming good and evil autonomously in spite of
the fact that God has revealed what is good. That is the
meaning of the outstanding passage of Isaiah: "Woe to
those who call evil good and good evil, who put darkness
for light and light for darkness, who put bitter for sweet
and sweet for bitter! Woe to those who are wise in their
own eyes, and shrewd in their own sight!" (Isa. 5:20–21)
Man wants to know good and evil by himself, wants to define them. So be it. But the serious thing about Israel is that
Israel hangs on to this claim in spite of the fact that God
has revealed what is good in his sight, and Israel heaps the
pretense to overflowing by defining what Israel *itself*, man,
decrees to be good and decrees to be evil in relation to and
utilizing the very revelation of God. And hence Israel goes
so far as to decree as evil that which God has revealed as
good. This is obviously the most serious thing that could
happen, and which did happen, and which was carried
through completely when Israel was to say that the Son of
God is sacrilegious, that the innocent is guilty, that the
Messiah is an impostor, and that the incarnate God does
evil.

Should we take this to be a Christian interpretation, so
that the frontier between the good and the wicked would
henceforth be drawn between Christians and non-Christians? Emphatically, no! With respect to the good, Christians receive no better treatment in the Bible than the others. "I do not do what I want, but I do the very thing I
hate. . . . For I know that nothing good dwells within me.
. . . For I do not do the good I want, but the evil I do
not want is what I do. So I find it to be a law that when I
want to do right, evil lies close at hand. For I delight in the

law of God in my inmost self, but I see in my members another law at war with the law of my mind and making me
captive to the law of sin which dwells in my members.
Wretched man that I am! Who will deliver me from this
body of death? Thanks be to God through Jesus Christ our
Lord!" (Rom. 7:15, 18–19, 21–25). Paul is talking about
himself, but what he says *should* be said by every Christian
for himself. There we find once more, as for the Jew, the separation between the knowledge of the good derived from
revelation and the power to perform it. Here and here alone,
and for the man who has received the revelation, the distinction between knowledge and power is validated.

This distinction, then, has a place in the life of the Christian and not, as in the interpretation of some theologians,
in the life of every man, of the natural man. Moreover, this
knowledge of the good reveals all the more the incapacity to
perform it; for the pagan can delude himself. Ignorant of
the good according to God, and determining it for himself,
he can to a great degree perform it and be satisfied. On the
other hand, he who has received the revelation of the good
according to God should no longer delude himself. He
should realize his incapacity in spite of all his efforts, judging himself by the absolute and not the relative standard,
and he will discover his captivity to evil.

Thus, the fact of the fulfillment of the good by Jesus
Christ (and he alone fulfills it, and he fulfills it completely)
does not in any sense make things easy for the Christian.
What he has in Jesus Christ is both the revelation of the
good and the correlative revelation of his sin, and at the
same time the proclamation of the joyful gospel of grace
which has been made to him! But that does not give him
any intrinsic capacity to do by himself the good which God
has set forth. There is no permanent transformation of his
being which would consist in this ability to perform the
will of God by himself. He has no intrinsic possibility which
would be self-sufficient and new and which would become a
second nature.

Certain biblical texts, however, seem to project another notion of the good, a notion based on nature and which would be every man's possession. From time to time there crops up the formula "render good for evil," which is applicable to anyone whatsoever. Thus Joseph reproaches his visitors for having repaid him evil for good (Genesis 44:4). But this formula always bears a very concrete meaning: a man does good to another and the latter is quite capable of experiencing it as such. I do not need a revelation to know that when I am hungry and someone gives me bread he has done me good. All the Old Testament texts relating to a good recognized as such by the natural man refer in greater or less degree to this practical, pragmatic, experiential meaning. Also, there is in the Bible a whole thread of realistic thought concerning the good. It probably represents *all* that the natural man can *legitimately* identify as such.

Perhaps a group of texts in the letters also should be similarly interpreted. "Repay no one evil for evil, but take thought for what is noble in the sight of all" (Rom. 12:17). "For we aim at what is honorable not only in the Lord's sight but also in the sight of men" (2 Cor. 8:21). "Would you have no fear of him who is in authority? Then do what is good, and you will receive his approval, for he is God's servant for your good" (Rom. 13:3–4). "For it is God's will that by doing right you should put to silence the ignorance of foolish men" (1 Peter 2:15). These four texts have in common the idea that the good practiced by Christians can be perceived and understood as good by non-Christians, but they contain different teachings. Nevertheless, the first and the second enjoin seeking what is good in men's eyes; that is, not only doing what God wants but also what is called good by men, at a given time in a given civilization. We shall come back to that later on.[20] But it is important to point out that the second text explicitly contrasts two kinds of "good," that which is good in the eyes of the Lord and that which is good in the eyes of men. Christians cannot limit themselves to one of the two, while despising the other.

They must *also* do what men consider good, although that is in no way confused with the good according to God. On the latter point, let us note that these words confirm the teaching brought out above, which declares that the good according to God is not the good according to men. Scripture is very reserved on the good according to men. It is aware of it and recognizes it, but it throws hardly any light on it which is not directly concerned with man's salvation.

The last two texts emphasize a quite different aspect. The Christian in doing good (and here no indication is given as to which category of good is intended, so that the habitual biblical sense would seem to be taken for granted) would receive the approval of the authority, and would put to silence the ignorance of foolish men. These two cases refer to pagans who become capable of perceiving the good done by Christians. This obviously is part of the witness which Christians are to bear before men. Alongside of the witness by word of mouth there should be the witness of life—of works and of action. The two are inseparable, necessarily bound together, as Jesus Christ taught ("Let your light so shine before men, *that they may* see your good works"), and one is not valid without the other. That pagans might be able to approve the good according to God which Christians practiced may be conceded, whether on the ground that that corresponds to their concrete understanding of the good, which we have discussed and which is absolute, or on the ground that this act corresponds to the norm of the good in a given society. There can be a coincidence, either accidental or volitional (in "Christianity") between what a society calls good and the good according to God, in which case there is no problem. But there can also be opposition between two concepts of the good, two contents which differ. It is not inevitable or certain that pagans would recognize the good done by Christians. It is not inevitable that the state would approve the Christian attitude, as history has indeed demonstrated. In any event, we are here on extremely ambiguous ground.

If men approve the good done by the Christian because that good corresponds to the current notion, there is no witness. It is not the good according to God, the work for God, which is perceived. It is the confusion of the humanistic idea. It is very possible, and even probable, that this is what Paul is alluding to when he speaks of authorities. The latter will accept and ratify the conduct of Christians because on many points (such as do not kill, do not steal, do not commit adultery) the good revealed by God recalls a certain notion of the good current in the Greco-Roman world.

On the other hand, if men find themselves confronted with a behavior attempting to express the good according to God which they find surprising or shocking, a great ambiguity reigns once more; for there is nothing which can, of itself, warn them that this is the good according to God. They do not have some hidden sense, some intuition, in the presence of a given act, to say, "This is the good of God!" In and of themselves, their eyes are closed to good works, and what is good does not directly concern them. If they are capable of discovering that good behavior (and on what basis will they find it so?), even so they cannot directly receive from it a witness concerning God. Their judgment of the good cannot enlighten them on the source of the good. That is exactly why the word is indispensable. It is the light which informs these good works. Without the accompanying word the works remain obscure and incomprehensible for the outsider who observes them. They need to be explained. Their ins and outs, their origin and reason, need to be carefully set forth. Thus these two texts remind us that the practice of the good is a necessary part of the witness, but it does not suffice of itself, and it does not presuppose that the good is directly perceived by man as a manifestation of God.

Everything we have just said about the good in the Bible, about that which bears that name in the revelation, brings to light an extraordinary contrast with the origin of morality; that is to say, with man's capacity to decide between good and evil. The good according to God is not integrated with a human morality, and perhaps we shall see that it cannot be the object of a morality at all. The latter is of men. It does not amalgamate with the good of God. It belongs to the category of the fall, and to the category of necessity.

Morality Is of the Order of the Fall

3 We retain the term fall because it is current and practical, but we know that it has some unfortunate and inaccurate connotations.[1] Ricoeur's criticism is undoubtedly true, but if one questions the term one must not lose sight of the fact to which it refers; namely, the loss of communion between man and God. It is not our intention to enter into a discussion of the hundreds of doctrines put forth as interpretations of what the Bible describes for us as an event. We adhere to the most traditional one, which seems to us best to fit the biblical account and the indisputable certainty that the broken communion with God totally changes the life of the creature. Either the communion with God is the very ground of one's being, of life and of good, in which case the rupture of that communion changes the whole, or else the change is only partial, which implies that the communion with God was only secondary and not decisive. We cannot agree with those who try to minimize the importance of this event.

In any case, all such theories really aim at setting an artificial price upon man, at preserving a greatness for him, a good, a self-sufficient dignity and, in the last analysis, an autonomy before God. All these theories distort the clarity of scripture, often by subtle and apparently legitimate means, the purpose being to justify man's being what he is.

They presuppose the validity of what man is and does, apart from the sole grace of Jesus Christ. The last attempt of this kind consists in drawing conclusions which seem to us to abuse the hypothesis (merely nominal perhaps) that the Genesis account is a myth. One then denies that there was a before and an after, that there was a transition from one situation to another. (I shall reject Ricoeur's terminology—a passage from innocence to sin; because that is not what the text says. These formulations are anthropocentric and "essentialist." Surely it is a passage from a communion to a break.) One then denies that there was a particular moment when evil was initiated, and describes the situation as one of perpetual beginning, a state of innocence and a state of sin superimposed on one another (and not succeeding one another in time). I am created in an instant; I fall in an instant. There is no prior and posterior state, but two states existing simultaneously, which means that man is not radically lost and bad. To the contrary, man is naturally good. Innocence is primary and evil is only contingent.

Problems remain that are beyond solution in spite of the subtlety; apart from the question of the unity of the biblical thread which one picks apart cleverly in order to minimize the strands, and to explode the unity into fragments of "blemishes," of "worthlessness," of "guilt," and of "myth." Here are some of the problems.

1. *Is* the world with which we are familiar the world created as God willed it? Ricoeur explains the nonexistence of the fall for man, but the Bible tells us about a total damage to the creation (things and animals). We find no answer in Ricoeur. Now if the world is not the one which God created, there must certainly have been a before and an after.

2. Ricoeur tells us that man himself initiates evil (and that there is no original sin) but, however, that from the beginning of his and action he finds himself confronting an "evil already there, an evil already proposed." I cannot take that path. The dialectical form of the idea has

great possibilities, but there are limits. It seems to me that here we are faced with an intellectual impossibility.

3. To say, "I am created at every instant, I fall at every instant," presupposes a solution to the problem of continuous creation; and on the other hand, one should ask, *why* this necessity for falling? If indeed there has been no transition to the state in which man is a sinner, must one suppose that it is possible for a man not to be a sinner, that in some instant he might not fall?

4. The whole doctrine of Ricoeur, like all the doctrines which minimize the seriousness of the fall and of man's evil, minimizes the work of Jesus Christ by the same token. If man, created in every instant, falls in every instant, then Jesus Christ is nothing more than a man who in that instant did not fall.

But if, contrary to that, Jesus Christ is indeed what scripture teaches us that he is, then we must come to grips with the question: If the fall and evil were not totally serious, would God have gone to the extreme of this unthinkable sacrifice of his Son, of this incomprehensible self-deprivation? For the work of salvation to be as great as that, the alienation in the fall must have been fundamental. The *whole* must have been shattered for the *whole* to have been restored. The *whole* must have been lost for the *whole* to have needed to be saved by grace.

Hence, there is no longer any antecedent innocence remaining in existence, for that kind of innocence permits some economy in God's work.

The Bible shows us clearly that the origin of morality is bound up with disobedience. Henceforth it forms part of the order of the fall.[2] Just what does that mean? It is indeed a matter of a category, of an order. It is neither nothingness, nor the absurd, nor incoherence. It is an order, an organization, a stability, embracing whatever is necessary to maintain life (relatively) and creation (also relatively). Morality constitutes part of those things. Hence it is need-

ful. We shall speak about that again. But it is an order of
the fall; that is to say, of the separation from God, in a
world whose prince is Satan, and where sin reigns alone
over the heart of man. Morality is not of some other essence,
some other order, some other nature. There is no order of
sin, and then a miraculously preserved morality which
would judge sin and make possible the denouncing and
combating of it. In point of fact, morality is in that order
of sin exactly in the degree in which it is a knowledge on
the part of sinful man. Morality is part of the world. It
goes to make up part of the world of sin. It is within that
which is sin. It is not a judge of it, in the position of an
arbiter who stands above the conflict. To suppose that morality, enunciated by man, or felt by him in his conscience, or
obeyed by him in his behavior, could, when all is considered, be the will of God, is to suppose that man has not lost
all in the fall, that a little something is still in the Eden
situation.

We are not trying to reexamine the question of the
"imago Dei." Whether some of this more or less remains in
man, whether it is existent but shattered or disturbed, we
shall not settle that, nor even what the *imago Dei* is, for we
do not need to resolve that problem in order to resolve our
problem. It is sufficient to notice that whatever it is of the
imago Dei which survives, that cannot in any case be the
moral sense. In fact, the temptation and the fall were occasioned and motivated by the desire to become like God
and the will to discern good and evil. It is indeed certain
that that is the very thing which could not have been retained for man. He could have kept all of the *imago Dei,*
but he surely could not have kept that which was the bond
and the heart of disobedience.[3] Otherwise it would, in the
final analysis, have been a victory of man over God.

Man can have neither a true religious sense, a direct
knowledge of God, nor an unblemished moral conscience,
because these are the products of revolt and autonomy.[4]
Hence we do not need here to go into the question of what

the *imago Dei* was composed of, or what it might still be composed of. For our purpose we need only be sure that it cannot be composed of the moral conscience, and therefore that what man calls by that name cannot be a reflection of God, a remainder from man's initial integrity. It is, to the contrary, an additional sign of his belonging to the world of sin. It is a way of being in this present world and not a souvenir of a past Eden. That which man assumes to be the good and that which he condemns as evil undoubtedly make some sense and have some value. We shall be looking into that, but it has no validity of life and of salvation before God. It is a good included within disobedience, within sin, and therefore it is not a good of and for God. It could, in some sense, be said that this good is no nearer to God than evil (so called by man), because it is man pretending to be God who has decreed "this is good," and in doing that he exactly repeats the step taken by Adam. He would know the good—that is to say, would define it—because he cannot know the true good which is in God.

The whole moral procedure of man is, in reality, contradicted by the gospel. Nowhere is there a ratification of human morality by Jesus Christ. The gift of God in Christ is redemption, the restoration of the life of man, the initiation of a life which is new; that is to say, founded upon novelty and not upon the perpetuation of a prior good or upon the coronation of an instinctive knowledge of the good. If the situation of Christians is described to us so often as that of strangers and exiles, it reflects the fact that there is nothing which truly attaches them to this world, that *all* of this world is foreign to them, including the good determined by morality. And nothing in the life of these Christians corresponds to what men call good. The Christian life is not characterized by good, but by salvation. It is not well doing, but being well received by God. The gospel establishes no moral distinction, but proceeds to a revelation of grace. There are no normative ethics of the good, but there are ethics of grace, which are quite the opposite.[5]

Therefore the gospel, far from confirming the morality of
the world, overturns it and contradicts it in what man designates as good just as much as in what, in his pretention, he
judges to be evil. Hence, the fact of the revelation of Jesus
Christ sets up a tension between grace on the one hand and
human morality on the other. From that point on, morality
defining the good is not a kind of bridging of the gap between man's world and God's. The good and virtue, which
Plato was able to make into a superhuman ideal, are indeed
of man and in man.

The carrying out of what man calls good does not bring
him closer to God. Nothing can bring man closer to God.
Let us recall that after Adam is rejected he leaves Eden, and
at the gate of the garden there are henceforth placed the
cherubim and a flaming sword, guardians not to be de-
ceived. The search for Eden, like the search for the Holy
Grail, is impossible, but for a different reason. The Grail
was still on the earth, but nothing can make it possible to
negotiate the absolute gap that separates Adam from Eden
—nothing can appease the wrath of the guardians. "Remember, God is in heaven and you are on the earth." There
is no more pitiless word than that. And the good that you
do, no matter how ideal, is nothing but the good of the
earth, in no way commensurate with the requirement of
God, with that which he calls good. Of course that good
exists, but it is beyond your reach.

God's requirement is holiness. Now the accumulation of
all the virtues in the world, all the good works, all the high
ideals, all the honest intentions, does not constitute holiness. Even the Roman Church, with all its propensity for
mistaking exceptional moral purity for holiness, does not
fall into total confusion here. Holiness is of a different
order. It is never a succession of righteous and pure acts,
and the latter do not necessarily show it forth. All the good
that man can do remains man's good, and never becomes the
holiness of God. Now it is the latter which God expects of
man: nothing less. There is an impassable abyss between

the two. No value established by man, no accumulation of values, takes into account the holiness of God, which is not a morality carried out to the nth degree, nor a *perfection,* but the very life of God.

Moreover, that refutes the reasoning of those who look to the good either in support of or against Christianity. "Christians do more good than others"; or, inversely, "What is Christianity? You don't have to be a Christian in order to do good." In fact to take the measure of the Christian life, whether in support of it or against it, by the standard of what men have decreed as the good leads only to frustration. We shall refer later on to the extreme diversity in man's concept of the good. And that which is accepted as the universal scale of values for the good, to which the Western adversaries of Christianity resort, is precisely a concept stemming from Christianity itself in its distorted and secularized version. No, that good in no way permits us to smuggle ourselves into paradise. There is no bridge for raising man up to God. Glory and thanks be to God: he has come down toward us. He has come upon the earth. He has crossed the abyss, and there is where we meet him, while he deigned even to enter the domain of our morality and to submit to its judgments, he whose condemnation judged our morality, and our justice!

Does man, nevertheless, possess a morality? Does natural morality exist? [6] First of all, let us not misunderstand. It goes without saying that a natural morality does exist. The problem arises from the desire of some to see in that natural morality a morality which is just before God—or better, an expression of the will of God in nature, again a bridge to Eden. Let us note that in the Bible the word nature is very often taken in a neutral sense. There is a natural order of relations between a man and a woman; that is to say, dictated by biology. Similarly a woman's long hair conforms to nature. Here again it is a matter of biology. One can deduce absolutely nothing from these various texts. Whenever the Bible speaks of nature in a sense which involves a moral or spiritual evaluation we are forced to admit that the testimony of the Holy Spirit expressed in scripture is not at all encouraging. Nowhere are we told that nature conforms to the good or is capable of producing the good. To the contrary, all men are by nature children of wrath (Ephesians 2:3) ; that is to say that conformity to our nature destines us to undergo the punishment and the wrath of God. There is even an antinomy between nature and grace. Far be it from us to enter into theological debate! We confine ourselves to what is strictly necessary to our ethical question.

Paul, then, reminds us (Romans 11:24) that nature never merits grace. Even if nature brought us to the point of doing what we call by the name of good, that would be of no use for receiving the grace of God. When man remains natural man, we know of a certainty that he does not receive the Spirit (1 Corinthians 2:14) , and that is also what Jesus tells Peter who has just confessed his faith. And Peter is very enlightened about nature when he writes, "like irrational animals, creatures of instinct" (2 Peter 2:12)— granted that this letter is probably not by Peter, but that is of minor importance. We might multiply the citations. The important thing is simply to understand that from the biblical point of view it is not because it is natural that a thing is good. Quite the contrary! We are here at the opposite pole from modern thought which considers an act legitimate the moment it conforms with nature.

The Bible reveals to us that nature has nothing to do with the good (according to God) and that the fact that a morality is natural is no guarantee that it correctly defines the good and is a sure guide. To the contrary once again! From the biblical point of view, to speak of a natural morality is in fact to speak of the same thing that we do when we describe the morality of the fall. Natural morality does not define a good and an evil "from before the fall," by a sort of miraculous knowledge from east of Eden. It defines a good and an evil within the fall, pertaining to disobedience, and consequently foreign to the will of God. We need to note, moreover, that nowhere does the Bible which speaks to us about nature allude to a natural morality. Such a thing never comes into question. It is an invention of theologians and philosophers.

At the same time, it is necessary to examine the one text in which one might think to see an allusion to that infused knowledge of the good, which according to Catholic theology and Protestant liberalism belongs to man by nature— the one text on which is based the whole concept of natural morality, the moral conscience, natural right. That is a great deal to pin on a single biblical text which is not confirmed anywhere else with the meaning that some have wanted to attribute to it. It is the celebrated text which reads: "When Gentiles who have not the law do by nature what the law requires, they are a law to themselves, even though they do not have the law. They show that what the law requires is written on their hearts, while their conscience also bears witness" (Rom. 2:14–15). This is interpreted in a rudimentary fashion by saying that natural man (the gentile) by following his nature can perform instinctively the commandment revealed by God in his law, which proves that there is no need for the revelation since this law is written on the heart of man and the latter has only to listen to his conscience. Even Calvin allows, in the presence of this text, that natural man retains a certain bridle of justice; a certain natural glimmer of the good; an opinion and a judgment which make it possible for man to distinguish between right and wrong, between uprightness and foul play. To us, this text does not appear as certain and convincing as all that. I suppose it will be an unwelcome remark to make that it is the only text of its kind. And yet that has to be said!

The harmony of the biblical texts is essential. Each text should be interpreted by the consensus of the others, and no text carries decisive weight wrested from its theological and historical context. On the other hand, of course, there can neither be a question of brushing it aside, nor of twisting it to make it fit in with the rest. Contradictions, or opposite trends of inspiration, are possible in the Bible; but it is doubtful that such contradictions would be found in one and the same writer—and almost impossible that they should be found in one and the same book. Now, in the letter to the Romans, we see Paul first of all assert with respect to gentiles that they are totally perverted (Romans 1:18–32). Man is given over to his dishonorable passions, and there is no exception. Then, all men are under the power of sin (Romans 3:9). The whole world is accountable to God (Romans 3:19). Our text is found exactly in that frame of reference! What worse contradiction can we imagine! In chapter 2, Paul says that the gentiles do the will of God instinctively, in chapters 1 and 3, that they are incapable of doing so! That is hard enough to accept.

First of all, let us consider this text taking the word gentile in the obvious sense. Now one can observe right away that it does not say that there is a law of nature written on the heart of every man. For one thing, it is the *work* of the law *(ergon)* which is written; that is to say, not the very will itself of God, but a work, a consequence. There is no instinctive "forensic" knowledge of the law itself. There is simply a performance of the work required by the law, and this putting of it into practice, this carrying out of the work, for motives which may be very diverse, proves only the coincidence between the revealed will of God and the action of man, who might be entirely ignorant of the fact that he is doing God's will. But when they do this work they show by that that they are a law (just) to themselves. Paul's formula is quite clear. He does not say that they have the law of God in them, but that they *are a law to themselves.* In short, they themselves were transformed into law by the work which they accomplished. That has nothing to do with a natural law written by God on the heart of every man. To the contrary, it makes one think of the parable of the man who had two sons (Matthew 21:28–31) in which the one who says "I will not" does what the father asks and still more to the point, of the parable of the last judgment (Matthew 25:31–46), in which the righteous are unaware of what they have done, and have performed the work of the law without there having been any law for them, either revealed or natural. And it is true that this combination can occur and that, for various motives of the natural order, sometimes bad, man can perform a work which corresponds to the will of God, or again, a work which God in his love adopts as his own.

On the other hand, it is not said that "man" has in his heart, as part of his nature, a law coming from God. It is only said that *when* perchance it happens that the gentile carries out the will of God *then* he shows that he *has* the work of the law written on his heart. Thus this text is doubly restrictive. In the first place, it is never a question of all mankind, but only of those who fulfill the law. Hence one cannot conclude that all have the law written on their hearts whether they obey it or not. Then second, whenever this act is performed it shows that the law is written on the heart: not "the man had the law on his heart" (and he obeyed it, understood), but "he has . . ." beginning with the moment when he carried out this will of God. This corresponds to the formula: "They are transformed into law for themselves." Therefore, in all this there is no question of a universal natural law coming from God and integrated into the natural consciences of all men, or of mankind. Finally, we should emphasize that the law of which Paul speaks is not some moral law or other, but the law of justification. Our text follows Romans 2:13: "The doers of the law . . . will be justified"; and it precedes verse 16: "On that day when, . . . God judges the secrets of men by Christ Jesus."

All the teaching of Paul affirms that the performance of moral works, the practice of the law, cannot save us. We are saved by grace in Jesus Christ. It is a matter of this sal-

vation, of this justification. How could we think that the
law which justifies would be written on the heart of each
man, as part of his nature, from the very beginning, without conversion and without grace? There is never any giving way in Paul's theology. Jesus Christ alone justifies. The
law only condemns. How could we imagine that here he
would want to speak of a justifying law? This brings us,
then, to the very powerful and well-known interpretation
of this passage by Barth in his *Epistle to the Romans*. According to him, the gentiles here in question are the gen-
tile-Christians. It often happens that Paul calls these Christians of gentile origin by the shortened term gentiles, in contrast to Jews (for example, Romans 11:13; 15:18–19). The
notions of the "heart" and of nature are to be understood
in that perspective. The heart on which is written the work
of the law is precisely the transformed heart, which has
been turned from a heart of stone into a living heart, the
heart on which God has written his will according to the
prophetic promise of Jeremiah 31:33 and Ezekiel 11:19. But
it is no longer the natural heart. It is that from which grace
itself has uprooted sin and has planted life in Jesus Christ.

The nature according to which these gentiles fulfilled the
will of God is not the nature of the flesh. It is the new nature, not that of the flesh destined for death, but the new
man destined for life. It is the nature of the olive tree
which has been grafted onto the elect olive tree. So there is
no natural moral law. The gentile converted to Christ has
no need to learn the Jewish law or to be circumcised. That
is the meaning of the passage. The parallelism between the
law and circumcision which Paul establishes in Romans
2:15, 25 is very enlightening in this connection. Just as the
gentiles do not need to be circumcised in order to be saved
in Jesus Christ, since they have the circumcision of the
heart, so also they do not need to learn the law of Moses,
since now—by reason of their faith in Jesus Christ—they
have the work of the law written on their hearts. They are
in fact, then, a law to themselves. God gives them his Holy

Spirit, and by that very gift a new heart which knows the divine will, so that these gentiles, too, can live according to that will. This is written large in the whole general thesis of the letter to the Romans concerning the relation between Jews and Christians. The Jews, for their part, know the law explicitly and intellectually, but they resist grace. They fail to fulfill the work of the law. They do not obey the will of God. The gentiles converted to Christ are not very knowledgeable concerning the law. They have not learned it, but they fulfill the work because Jesus Christ has sent them the Holy Spirit.

This interpretation in depth of these verses seems completely convincing to us because it follows the general line of Paul's thought, and it does that in the exact context of chapters 1 to 3 of this letter. We are aware, however, of the reservations expressed in this connection; and we would call attention to the fact that even if one does not accept this interpretation, and prefers to hold to the idea that Paul is speaking purely and simply of gentiles, without qualification, that would not at all lead to our seeing here an allusion to natural morality. The entire first portion of our argument still holds good. Consequently, no matter which meaning of the word gentiles is adopted, the result is the same with respect to the concept of a natural morality, taken in the sense of a knowledge of good and evil infused into nature, and in the sense of a natural power in man to discern and to carry out the good.

The theological concept of natural morality is based on a philosophy. It is a drive to find some accommodation between the data of the world and theological data. This attracts or assumes several serious errors. In all the formulations of natural morality it is not a question of Jesus Christ. It is hard to see what purpose the work of God fulfilled in Jesus Christ can have in this construct. Neither the incarnation, nor the death, nor the resurrection have anything to do with the theory of natural morality. So one is confronted with a Christianity without Jesus Christ; for if man is able to compensate naturally for sin by his good conduct, if the fall is merely a "weakening," then there is in fact no need for Jesus Christ. Buddha, Socrates, or Nietzsche will do just as well for lifting man into moral or religious conformity with his nature.

We are thus brought to observe the second error. One is led to the abandonment of the doctrine of justification, for that is the very doctrine which destroys every claim of man to know justice naturally and by himself; even more, the claim to carry it out. If God is the only just one, and if he does not bestow his justice on man except in justifying him, and if he only lets man know his work of justice by revealing it to him, then that means that man knows nothing about justice otherwise, and that he has no justice written in his nature. The doctrine of natural morality is an aspect of heresy cropping up incessantly, by which an accommodation is sought between grace and nature in the process of settling a value upon nature.[7]

The third error is an error of method. It is the transposition of the theological to the philosophical; that is to say, the transformation of the living event of love and grace into a principle of systematic construction, of elaboration and explanation. It is a utilization of the revelation for man's satisfaction, which has the effect of crystallizing and immobilizing that revelation in order to make it fit the system, thereby emptying it of all value.

Finally, it is necessary to bear one question in mind. The supporters of the doctrine of natural morality believe in the existence of a human nature. They speak constantly of "the essential nature of man." Whence do they deduce this? Who has made it known to us?[8] If it is a matter of a philosophical concept (which is, in fact, at the bottom of the idea of natural right in Aristotle and the Stoics), it has to be admitted that modern philosophy (existentialism, phenomenology) rejects that concept, and there is need to restate the question. If it is a matter of a concept drawn from the sciences (psychology, history, sociology, for example), there, too, one must be very careful, for precisely these same sciences which a half-century ago affirmed the existence of this human nature, contest the idea today. Modern psychology, like contemporary history, scarcely acknowledges the notion of a permanent, stable "nature" of man. If, finally, one claims to find this idea in the Bible, we have already examined that question. Moreover, if we accept the standpoint of these authors we shall be bound by the principle that the Bible is here taken as the decisive court of appeal. This implies that one must accept it also in the other domains; to wit, in the domain of morality. Now the Bible tells us nothing about a natural morality. Consequently, if we base our idea of a human nature on the Bible, we certainly cannot infer the existence of a natural morality.

In any case, it can be asserted that the desire to construct a natural morality corresponds to the settling of a value on man and a devaluing of the work of Jesus Christ. There is a fundamental conflict between the inherent content of revelation and natural morality. For the church, the latter is always a way of conforming to the world.

Does the moral conscience, nevertheless, exist? [9] It is true that the New Testament, principally Paul, occasionally mentions conscience.[10] Again, we must be clear about the meaning of this term. The Greek word which is used, *syneidesis*, means "consciousness of these thoughts and of these actions." This denotes the fact that one is aware.[11] Most of the passages in which Paul uses this word clearly have that significance: "My conscience bears me witness" (Rom. 9:1); "conscience, being weak" (1 Cor. 8:7); "my liberty . . . determined by another man's scruples" (1 Cor. 10:29); "the testimony of our conscience that we have behaved, . . . with holiness" (2 Cor. 1:12). And even the texts which speak of "conscience' sake" (Romans 13:5; 1 Peter 2:19) should also be understood in the sense of being aware of, being conscious of. Thus conscience, here, is not a moral quality. It is rather a clarity; and the majority of the passages show that there is a relation between faith, knowledge, and conscience. Faith, in effect, gives us a light which enlightens us with respect to Jesus Christ in whom we believe.

The knowledge of the gospel gives us the means of being aware (conscious). It is a matter of being conscious of what one does, of one's passions, of one's sin, of one's acts—and also of one's intentions—also, indeed, of one's holiness. The conscience is a clear-sightedness, which makes it possible, for example, (but not exclusively) to make one's examination of conscience! A weak conscience is not a weak disposition for doing good, but an insufficient knowledge of the gospel, which is not able to bring a true judgment to bear (for example, all that Paul says on the subject of meats offered to idols is very clear about this). When Paul exhorts to keep the faith *and* a good conscience (1 Timothy 1:19), or "to hold the mystery of the faith with a clear conscience" (1 Tim. 3:9), he implies that the faith should be linked to a conscious deed, to an act of conscience, to the examination of one's life in relation to faith. And the "good conscience" spoken of by Peter or by Paul (Acts 23:1; 1 Tim. 1:5) is the consciousness of doing good; that is, of living in Christ.

This is what M. H. Roux reminds us of in his commentary on the Pastoral Epistles, as follows:

It is the totalitarian character of the Christian faith which causes it to create a good conscience in man. The liberation of man by Christ and in Christ implies that he acquires a new awareness of his entire existence, especially of his relations with others. He is called upon to see, hence to know and to understand, himself first of all. It is this new awareness of himself which is truly good for the Christian, for it does not spring from its own ground, nor from a natural light. It proceeds from him who, by coming into the world, enlightens every man. The Johannine theme of sight and of the light surely, in its way, conveys the close relation between faith and the new moral conscience, which is a true discerning of the conduct of life. Such a good conscience, assured of judging rightly and of choosing God's will, can only be maintained in faith; that is, faith in Christ. Finally, it is this good conscience which remains the touchstone of the faith, which allows faith to be kept sincere and without hypocrisy. It is this good conscience which alone can inspire to good works, and can produce a love, a justice, and a holiness whose authenticity is guaranteed by Christ himself.[12]

On the other hand, the author of the letter to the Hebrews shows us that the conscience is also a consciousness of man's sin (Hebrews 10:2), in pointing out that if the sacrifices of the Old Testament had really purified man he would no longer have any consciousness of sin. Moreover, we must stop and look at this letter, for it contains quite a remarkable teaching. It teaches us, on the one hand, that the worship prescribed in the law, in the sacrifices, cannot render perfect in respect to the conscience. It is a question of worship. It is not a question of the *moral* conscience. It is a spiritual conscience. It is also a question of a conscience more or less great, made more perfect (or not). Hence it is not in any sense a natural conscience. It is not in man's nature to have a conscience of that order. This conscience, and all the letters demonstrate this, is a product of faith, a consequence of the revelation. One can lose it in losing the faith (1 Timothy 1:18–19).

The letter to the Hebrews tells us that Jesus Christ purifies our consciences from dead works. It is a matter of works of the law. This latter was a revelation of God; hence it aroused a conscience. But it committed man to a sterile path of works, of practices, which precisely exercised the conscience in relation to false criteria, involved it in false judgments. The total revelation of God in Jesus Christ, for its part, brings fullness of light, true clarity. This makes it possible for us to see ourselves in the love of God, which fills us with joy, and at the same time with shame. Then we no longer have to suffer the application of conscience from the standpoint of our works, as required by the law; instead, it is from the standpoint of the love of God revealed in Jesus Christ crucified. It is at the foot of the cross that the conscience becomes true and that, eventually, it can be good. Everywhere else it is perverted and can only be bad. Thus, if we try to sum up this teaching, we shall say that the conscience is first of all the fact of being aware of what one is. Hence this conscience can be a neutral quality of man, but ordinarily the act of conscience includes a judgment, or at least serves to form a judgment. Only, the judgment to which the conscience proceeds depends upon the criteria which it applies.

In this dialogue, the natural conscience never uses any but human elements. It can be said that there are tensions among these various human tendencies and influences. One can hardly say that there is a "better" which judges the "less good" on the basis of fixed and sure criteria. Present-day psychology tends to negate such an idea.[13] And whenever we judge ourselves it is always in accordance with our own criteria, which gives us a decided advantage. Hence the validity of Paul's declaration: "I am not aware of anything against myself, but I am not thereby acquitted. It is the Lord who judges me" (1 Cor. 4:4). Here we have a second element of the act of conscience, that of the criteria in relation to which one is called upon to judge. If you wish, we shall say that the conscience applies itself to reality (the first element) and to truth (the second element). That can only take place when the conscience, enlightened by revelation, receives from God a knowledge of the truth. Again, since it is that kind of knowledge which the conscience makes use of, the individual must add faith. In that case we see that the conscience will lead to a self-criticism, to a consideration of one's acts and works in relation to revealed truth. It is indeed an instrument of judgment, but only in a secondary way. This, then, allows us to reject most of the moral definitions of the conscience. The latter is not the place in man in which the good is naturally registered.

The doctrine of grace eliminates the possibility of the value of a moral conscience. The conscience is neither the reflection of God (who only reveals himself in Jesus Christ), nor the place where God speaks (for one cannot separate the encounter with God in scripture from the encounter within the person by the Holy Spirit); nor is it the voice which judges us (for it is God, in the moment in which he gives himself, who reveals to us our true guilt), nor the receptacle in us of a hidden truth which revelation merely brings to light (without grace we cannot believe the gospel, so how could it be preexistent in us?). Conscience holds no knowledge. The Holy Spirit entering into us sets up a dialogue other than that of the conscience. To pretend to validate the moral conscience is, in the last analysis, to empty out the entire doctrine of grace.

There is no voice of conscience identical with the voice of the good. It is not a discernment of good and evil as objective and independent entities. It is not a natural capacity of man to lay hold of the good, and to judge himself in relation to the content of the conscience. To be sure, all these notions can be sustained, and often have been. They are respectable, but there is nothing of Christianity in them. For the Christian faith there is no moral conscience. Karl Barth emphasizes, as follows:

> The notion of conscience belongs to the eschatological, not the anthropological, class of notions. It is in the light of the mutual belonging of our existence with the existence of Jesus Christ, in the light of future perfection, that the conscience can be understood as the organ of our participation in the good (revealed). Of itself the conscience is nothing. It is not an autonomous voice of God. Hence the conscience does not make possible the judging of good and evil, but simply the bearing of witness to a judgment to which we are subject.[14]

Up to this point we have been speaking basically of the conscience of the converted man; and that, obviously, is what the apostles are most concerned with. Still, two texts speak of the conscience of unbelievers. It goes without saying that this capacity for an act of conscience is not limited to Christians! The first of these texts is quite categorical and harsh: "To the pure all things are pure, but to the corrupt and unbelieving nothing is pure; their very minds and consciences are corrupted" (Titus 1:15). The unbelievers here in question either are Christians who have fallen away from the faith, or Jews, as is shown by the preceding verses. Here, then, the conscience is perverted; that is, incapable of bringing to bear a just evaluation of conduct, since, separated from the truth (from the Christian point of view), it no longer has an authentic criterion. This conscience is corrupted because it makes use of criteria other than the gospel, participating necessarily in evil. Hence the judgment of the conscience will involve the whole man in evil, the act of conscience as such being absolutely useless.

The other text is the celebrated one in Romans 2:14–15. We have already studied it in connection with the question of natural morality. Let us take only the passage having to do with the conscience. The gentiles "show that what the law requires is written on their hearts, while their conscience also bears witness and their conflicting thoughts accuse or perhaps excuse them." Basically, this does not shed any further light on the conscience. Here, no more than elsewhere, is there any question of a moral conscience. The work of God's law is written on the hearts of these people. That is what the conscience bases itself on, and proceeding to the debate of judgment and of the act of conscience it bears witness, in effect, to the fact that they have a just action with respect to this work of the law. Hence the meaning is exactly the same as that which we saw above. Manifestly the biblical thought knows nothing of this so-called moral conscience. The conscience is not an integral part of man, in recollection of heaven.[15]

Morality Is of the Order
of Necessity

4 Brought about by the fall, necessity is introduced into the world. Determinism, mechanism of history, scientific law, destiny, *ananke,* whatever name is used to cover it up, whatever be the form in which man accepts it, necessity is always the same. There is no great difference between the profound meaning of the implacable fate which hung over the family of the Atridae, the type of all mankind, which ran its inevitable course through the ignorances, the repeated unawareness, of the supposedly free decisions of each of its members; and the law of large numbers hanging over modern throngs, which is fulfilled by man in his seemingly free decisions, and which in his spontaneity reduces him to the common model. There is no great difference between the unshakable blind *ananke,* which imposes its standard even on the gods, and scientific law, carried out and fulfilled over and above all our claims to freedom, which causes us to say, "Therefore God does not exist." When that happens, we are confusing God's creation with the order of the fall.

It was a creation which had been made for the love and the joy of God. It was the very place of freedom, for nothing could be the expression of God except the freedom of his creation. Nothing could have responded to God except the spontaneous free gift. Nothing could have loved God except the free play of the creature turned toward his Creator. There is neither duty, nor restraint, nor organization. There cannot be any necessity in that creation because God is not subject to necessity; and that which he creates is not the fruit of a torturing and implacable will, but of love. Everything in that nature is spontaneous because it is all a response to the spontaneity of God. Everything has a function, but that is a free observance of a word which God proposes to all. It is all a free gift because it is a response to the free gift of the creation (God, in creating, obeys no necessity but a pure freedom of giving) and of God's love. If God loves, it is not because . . . He loves gratuitously. There is no account to be made, drawn up, and rendered. There are no restraints and no duties to perform. Truly there is the play of life which gives itself because it has been received, which has a meaning because it is in the presence of God. But, no less truly, Adam's break with the Father brings about negation, chaos; and everything is in danger of returning to nothing—whenever this freedom is no longer in love, it is a great confusion. Once love has disappeared through the will to power, the significance of everything changes. The order established by God ceases to be a free gift and becomes an external restraint.

Now the creation would disappear if it were not relentlessly maintained. The function set forth in the word ceases to be a spontaneity and becomes an obligation. Life ceases to be play, and becomes pain and travail. Man bows to this necessity through not having known how to live in the freedom of love. Thus the same creation enters the order of necessity,[1] and from that moment on man knows indeed that he is subject to fate, that there is registered in nature around him and in him a destiny from which there is no escape. Everything is written. Indeed it has to be for the world to endure. The tiniest atom of liberty threatens the very existence of the world. The slightest *real* political liberty is an immediate threat to society and to the state. After the fall, man's true choice is no longer "liberty or death," but in fact "liberty or life." Life can only be maintained thanks to the total and finely woven network of restraint, from the unknown restraints that control matter and the worlds, to judicial and social restraints. All is maintained by the prisoner's iron collar which holds it. Freedom leads to destruction because henceforth it is located outside of love. If the planet no longer follows its orbit, if the animal wants to be free with regard to food and reproduction, if man wants to be free with regard to law, then necessity from the top of the scale to the bottom is the condition for preserving the world of the fall. When, in fact, some freedom or other asserts itself we might say that it brings death.

The achievement of the slightest liberty involves immense sacrifices, as we well know—the martyrs of freedom! —and when this freedom is achieved (I mean in this illusory domain of politics and economics) it immediately degenerates into new restraints, while those who fought and who knew the momentary liberty inscribed in their combat are dead. Dead, that is, reduced to the most complete necessity of all; for death is the ultimate point at which necessity is registered with its most absolute trademark, its most irrefutable presence. The way wherein one might have claimed to be free, becomes a thing. At that moment, destiny's victory is inexorable and whoever pretends to escape it through freedom inevitably finds it again in death. Such is the order, which is not that of God's love but which God maintains anyway because it is preferable to nothingness, the negation of God.

Located in the order of the fall, morality is registered in the order of necessity. What are we to understand by this? [2] Undoubtedly that morality itself already constitutes a part of the restraint. Morality always presents itself as a system of duties and obligations, without which society, or any group of people, would not be able to live. Of course there is a hierarchy of importance in the determinations. Not all are on the same necessary and inexorable footing. Morality is situated among the less rigorous, even below the law of the courts; but it still very obviously represents a claim to govern man by imposing on him a certain quality of feeling and action. So the consequence of man's decision to be like God is, among other things, his being subject to a certain good that is not the will of God but that forms part of the order by which the world lives. The fact that it implies less necessity than, for example, scientific law stems from its supererogatory character in the order of the preservation of the creation. If man fails to obey the rules of life biologically and chemically, if he thinks to avoid them, he dies and disappears inexorably.[3] If he disobeys the moral rules of his group, the necessity is not ratified so immediately and implacably. There are delays and ambiguities, a hope of escaping the sanction. Man can pretend to be free with respect to this moral law. He does not die in consequence. He will, perhaps, experience some unpleasantness, remorse, in his "conscience," or other people's judgments against him in his social relations. What is brought into question by his disobedience is not himself directly, but his group. The moral law is not a necessity for the individual's survival. It is a necessity for society.

Biblically, and this reflection is absolutely essential, the observance of morality is in no sense a condition for individual life or for the individual's success on earth, any more than it is a condition for salvation and eternal life. The book of Job reminds us that this very performance of the good is not related to individual preservation. On the natural plane, morality concerns the preservation of the group.[4] Each person is to respect certain taboos, perform certain acts, cultivate certain feelings, participate in certain operations, share certain relationships, react with the right kind of indignation, give voice to this approval or that disapproval, because these are basic principles of the world in which he lives. If he disobeys in this area he weakens the inner spirit, the unity and the equilibrium of that group. This is true even if the disobedience is inward, for the group requires an interior allegiance which shows itself in a moral dimension of behavior. What kind of a soldier is it who fights without patriotic enthusiasm? What kind of a workman who works without a pride in his craft? What kind of citizen obeys the law outwardly, without a sense of community responsibility? What is marriage without loyalty? The outward appearances of social life require the inward, effective, and active involvement of the individual, without which the appearances are stripped of all efficacy and strength. The group can only endure by means of the perpetuation of virtue; and it is not without significance that the word *virtus* can have the dual implication of courage, strength, power, and then of moral virtue. Thus we can see morality's share in the necessary order of preservation.[5]

But to say that morality's share constitutes a part of necessity is to go much farther yet. In reality, the good which morality affirms is a good determined by necessity. It is not a good within the scope of liberty and the free gift. In spite of all his pretentions—intellectual, spiritual, and moral—man is remarkably predetermined. When he calls such and such an act good, when he develops this or that ethical system, he is in no sense taking a stride into the absolute, nor bursting out suddenly into the domain of freedom. He continues to be conditioned by his heredity, by his biological life, by his environment, by his education, by his human relationships. What he achieves as good, what he defines as evil, are completely relative and essentially variable notions. For it to be otherwise would mean that man had retained part of his original freedom, which he has not retained, or that he had direct access to the absolute will of God, which is even more contrary to the truth. Henceforth, the morality that man formulates is never an act of his freedom.

The moral structure, the defining of the good, are ideological expressions of the social and biological determinants with which the individual lives. The good is determined by historic, geographic, and psychological circumstances. But, of course, that is not all it is. It is not only the mechanical translation of these necessities. It is also a protest against them, a refusal to acknowledge that one is determined, an assertion of human liberty. But we should never forget that it is just when man is the most predetermined that he insists on declaring his freedom! Morality, of course, does express the will—or at least the claim—of man to transcend his material situation, and to achieve precisely that absolute which escapes determinism. But in the very process of developing, as he thinks, this means of controlling his situation, man constructs his ideal world in, and in relation to, the situation. The determining action of conditions and circumstances weighs upon morality not only positively but negatively as well.

Morality is directly conditioned by the environment, by the economic and social structure, not only in its expression and choice of values, but still more in its protest against the conditions. It sets up a counterpart, a counterpoise, a reverse image; but it is with respect to *this* known disagreeable weight, with respect to *this* disagreeable image, that morality is developed, so that man still does not escape from necessity. He limits himself to voicing a protest, which is itself conditioned by that against which it is protesting. It never manages to formulate a good in itself, free of these concrete conditions. It never gets to the point of formulating an eternal, immutable, universal good.

Look at the greatest systems of moral thought and it will easily be evident how dated they are, the extent to which they belong to a time and to an epoch. To grasp them once again requires an effort. Never do they speak directly and openly to us as they were able to speak to their contemporaries. Only by extracting certain happy expressions, a few rare pearls out of the whole superseded mixture, can we still follow Socrates or Confucius. But whenever we thus take apart, whenever we sort out a few strands from thread to which they properly belong because they especially appeal to us for their strength or brilliance, and which on that account we call "eternal values," we are acting out of our own necessity and our own conditioning.

An Indian thinker probably would not select the same pearls, and two hundred years ago or two hundred years hence a Western thinker might treat as negligible what we consider essential. Because two thousand years ago a wise man spoke a sentence which still speaks to us we praise the permanence, the freedom, and the absolute quality of those values. But did that statement speak to medieval man? To a fifteenth-century Inca? Our choice is just as arbitrary as theirs, not merely arbitrary in the sense of an uncontrolled freedom in the formulation of values, but arbitrary in declaring the eternity and fixity of a given value. There, too, our moral attitude and our moral choices are determined by circumstances. When we forget that fact we easily mistake ourselves for gods, and right there is where sin resides. Moreover, necessity soon becomes apparent whenever it is a matter of carrying out this proclaimed and formulated good; for man, confronted with the good which he ought to do, always, in reality, fulfills an order of necessity. When morality expresses that necessity directly there is no disharmony, and man in obeying his own determinations does good by that very action.

For a citizen of a Western country to obey his summons to selective military service is in harmony with the morality of his country, which has made the fatherland into an absolute value and military sacrifice into one of the highest of virtues. But when an ethic is evolved in protest against necessity, then man is caught up in a conflict,[6] not a conflict between moral freedom and moral necessity, nor between the ideal imperative and the sordid interest, but between the two necessities of social and historical pressures on the one hand and of psychological refusal and resentment on the other. The same citizen, upon receiving his summons to report for military duty, might feel in his heart, "Thou shalt not kill" (assuming that this would be accepted as a working morality in the country in which he lives, which is not the case, for example, in France today!). Most frequently, following the psychological rule of the economy of means, the individual will obey whichever necessity is the most urgent, because he inevitably seeks to avoid conflicts and tensions. Thus, at all levels of the moral problem we find determinants in the ascendancy. That does not

mean, of course, that morality is without value, but only
that it belongs to the world of the fall characterized by
necessity.

Morality is always an ethic in a situation of necessity.
Ricoeur has recently shown that the morality of our time is
a morality of anguish. In reality, every morality is one of
anguish, because man is always confronted with situations
which are beyond him. This is not only true today. Morality is one of the means employed by man to defend himself
against anguish. It is a refusal to admit that the game is lost.
In this line of development, morality does not usually confine itself to expressing necessity. It seeks to integrate it.
One of the greatest incentives for the formation of morality undoubtedly is man's attempt to control necessity by
submitting to it—by making a virtue out of it. Like technology and politics (in a very different direction and by
very different means) morality is an art of the possible.
That is what it expresses when it is not a theoretical construct. The necessary becomes the good.

It has to be admitted that in a situation of necessity man
is not free merely to take note of the conflict. He must integrate it. He has to translate it into such terms as will make
life possible to him. To make a virtue of necessity is to face
up to a situation which has gotten out of hand. It is to recover man's superior dignity, which consists in naming the
nameless. What was a purely blind occurrence takes on
meaning and value because man has given it a name. He
has integrated it into his system. He has qualified it. But it
is also a knowing how to bear the determinism that crushes
us, the burden that destiny has placed upon us. In point of
fact, it is an ability, buttressed by a declaration of values,
not to give in to that which obligates us except by integrat-
ing it; and the ability to declare proudly (but in quite a different sense from that intended by the Roman jurists)
coactus voluit, sed voluit. The will has integrated constraint.
Constraint has not subjugated the will. Morality always

claims this transcendence, but it never fails to embrace necessity while taking its stance with respect to it.

Thus it is that all morality takes into account the limitation of human nature. No morality can maintain that its commands are absolute or that its rules are unbreakable. Popular wisdom is good at finding methods of conciliation, but the moralists also have worked out countless casuistries to this end. We know that a strict moral rule is impractical. Once a rule is set forth in luminous rigidity someone comes along to explain it, to comment upon it, to adapt it. It is a question of knowing when and how it can be carried out, and to what extent. One then begins the slow work of elaboration, in which ambiguity is introduced from case to case. No great system of morality escapes this: that of Christianity, of Judaism, of Confucianism, of Islam. The work of the moralists has always consisted in the extenuation of principles because the latter are inapplicable; and a morality *should* be applied, otherwise it is nothing. If one insists upon the purity of the requirement and of its formulation, then it will remain a gratuitous and illusory intellectual system. If one wishes to have it applied he must make it applicable, which means that he must bring it down to the fair level of human capacity. Moreover, this adaptation can take place without the participation of schoolmen. It often happens spontaneously. Thus the morality of Kant was perfectly adapted to circumstances by the Western bourgeoisie of the nineteenth century who probably had never read Kant.

If a morality remains intact, it is simply and always because it has never been applied by anyone. So it is with that of Nietzsche and that of Aristotle. Adaptation—but to what end? The answer is easy: adaptation to man's possibilities and to his weakness—a concession which should not be made and which one deplores, but which is part of morality itself because man is feeble. In reality, one should not be speaking of weakness, but of necessity. This adaptation, this extenuation, is always the integration into ethics of social, biological, economic, psychological, and historic necessity. The "limitations of human nature" that one must indeed take into account are, in reality, limitations due to the conditions of man's life, to the conflicts in which he is involved, to the burdens which come in upon him from all directions. It is because one knows in advance that he cannot overcome this conditioning that he is called upon to adapt the principles of life and action to the conditioning; in other words, to insert the latter into the very imperative which was designed to regulate action and life. To fail to take these necessities into account is to elaborate an inapplicable system. But it must also be remembered that an inapplicable (and unapplied) morality *is not an ethic*.

The fixing of pure values in and of themselves, contemplated but not lived, can be a metaphysical endeavor but it is never the work of a moralist. If the latter creates a perfect but unapplied morality he is only the victim of an illusion, for a morality only has importance and weight in the greater or less degree in which it informs the life of man. Ethics presupposes conduct, whether the latter be in the realm of act, of intention, of remorse, or of hope. The moral claim should be incarnate in at least some human reality, for it contains as well an intention to provide meaning and direction to the individual. Divorced of applicability that intention can, at most, be an empty protest on the part of philosophers and visionaries. Now this requirement of applicability assumes that morality is taking account precisely of the limitations and necessities of human life. If it fails to integrate the determinants it faces man with a discouraging, unusable absolute, and man turns aside from the excessive effort of an incommensurate perfection that he cannot even strive toward, knowing too well, though perhaps subconsciously, his limits and weakness.

In the same line of consideration is the fact that, in all morality, necessity tends, more or less, to become justification. At first sight such a thought seems scandalous! Are not the good and virtue precisely a rejection of necessity? Do they not say that we should obey justice and not determinism, and that to drift with the tide is not a moral act? And yet, every morality in accepting man's conditioning (and it cannot do otherwise) turns this conditioning into a justifying value. Is it conditioning by work? The work becomes a justifying value, so likewise, for example, one's native land, education, science. In reality the process is that of an evolution which leads to labeling as "good" the necessity imposed upon man, to declaring necessity a value (which of course is not done arbitrarily or theoretically; not arbitrarily, for it is not a matter of just any necessity but only of the most urgent—not theoretically, for it is not a matter of proclaiming philosophy but of a kind of unanimous consent, of collective knowledge).

It is at this point that necessity becomes justification because it has taken on the aspect of obedience to a value. It has to be that way, otherwise man would forever be the defendant before his own court of law through a scale of values foreign to his life, an intolerable situation which would cut off every action at the root. But when, between the great military coercion of 1792, such as the world had never seen, and the keen desire to avoid the army (which was traditional), there slips in the value of one's native land, then the desire to escape is conquered by the value of country, and even he who accepts armed service through compulsion is enthusiastically justified. In one way or another, on different planes of activity, in all systems of morality, necessity ends up as a value, and then displays its extraordinary efficacy for allowing man to declare himself just.

However, we must look at the counterpart of this integration of necessity into morality. The latter suffers the fate of everything which is of the order of the determined. Subject to necessity it goes the way of all flesh, toward the supreme necessity, toward death. The death of morality, of moralities, of ethical systems, of values, is both the sign and the consequence of their radical, essential, and inevitable belonging to the order of necessity. Every morality dies. Everything that man proclaims as good today is laughed at and flouted tomorrow or it merely collects dust, becomes anemic and collapses of itself. The successive collapse of ethical values is the best proof from experience that, when all is said and done, morality is of *this* world of the fall, where tragic destiny reigns. Subject to the usual course of history? Inscribed in civilizations? And on that account transient and mortal? Yes, of course, but not only that. That is not all there is to say about it. One must see more clearly. If morality is mortal, that is not only because it follows the usual course of history, with a budding, a flowering, a zenith, a decline, and a death. In the last analysis it is because there is nothing in morality capable of defending itself against this deterministic process, nothing which transcends this course of events, nothing that endures *in spite of* the fact that everything around it changes. There is nothing in morality which is free of the general law of absolute destiny: death—the work of man.

Morality has raised a protest against this destiny. It has declared its escape from this destiny, an illusory declaration which experience thus far has failed to ratify. It is not my intention simply to conclude that all morality is relative. We shall deal with that later on. Here, I intend a different clarification; namely, the undeniable, inevitable character of this evolution, its certain end. These ideas are taken, at this point, only as testimony to the fact that morality is of the order of necessity. Ethics are never a proof of man's freedom. At most when they claim to be that, they are a flight to the unreal, and a lie which death will uncover. It is of no use to say that the just, the good, and the beautiful are proclaimed anew. That is true. But their contents differ according to the place and the moment. As modes of conduct which are declared good constantly change, one cannot deduce from them any idea of the permanence of the good. It is exactly the same with the content of morality as with its name! if I say *"thob"* to a man who is ignorant of Hebrew, that word will evoke nothing— no image, no reaction. I shall perpetrate the same nonsense if I suppose that in saying "good" to a Japanese or to a South

American Indian, the same image will be aroused in the one as in the other.

There is a final link between morality and necessity which I would like to indicate briefly, though it is of an altogether different order from the relation studied so far and is to be examined more extensively later on. Morality is necessary. There must be a morality. Man cannot avoid that. It is part of the condition of the fall. Now endowed with the power to define good and evil, to elaborate it, to know it and to pretend to obey it, man can no longer renounce this power which he has purchased so dearly. He must exercise it. He cannot live without morality. There can be no society or group or individual life without morality. For one thing, the individual inescapably experiences the necessity of living in a universe where things are divided into good and evil. That is part of his psychological makeup. His security depends upon a value's being assigned to certain things and withheld from others. As a second step, he needs a line of conduct to follow. He cannot live from moment to moment. He cannot give rein to pure impulse. He cannot always be the man of *hic et nunc*. And even if he decides that it should be that way, he does so in consequence of a moral debate and a moral conclusion. It is because he has come to the conclusion that since instinct is better than . . . and the *hic et nunc* has taken on the value of eternity . . . he has reconstructed a morality. But that is the exceptional case.

Normally, man wants a line of conduct to guide him. He needs something steady. He cannot do without it in deciding what he will do tomorrow, and no matter whether it is a matter of industrial planning or of a moral program, it all amounts to the same thing: there is a choice of action to be made on the ground that it is an action which is considered good. This decision is on the individual level, and morality can also be individual. Each person has the power to distinguish the good. But most often society will intervene with its collective affirmation. This rests upon an economy of individual energy, and upon a collective need. The economy of individual energy is important, for if each person tries to start from zero there is an enormous waste of energy in ignoring all value judgments made in the past and all those around one in the present in order to reconstruct one's own judgment after taking everything into account. Since experience shows that such an enterprise rarely results in an original or singular decision, but that it usually brings the hardy explorer of the spirit back to well-worn paths and proved values, it is obvious that this waste of energy is not profitable. Collective wisdom does everything to avoid it, going in the direction of individual laziness. The individual's enterprise is massive and very risky (for a man's whole life could be consumed in it), and for such a predictably slight result. This is the more true if society distrusts the result which fails to conform.

Society can only exist when there is a sufficient loyalty of individual behavior, when all call the same things "good" and the same things "evil," also when a person can expect, or hope, that others will act in such and such a way. No social relationship is possible if there is no valid prediction of the other person's behavior. Now it is precisely the collective morality, the common scale of values which makes possible an identical judgment of things, and this prediction of the other person's behavior. Social life is literally impossible if it is not paired with a morality which is social in its origins and implications but individual in its application. That is why the greatest scandal against which a society defends itself with the most complete energy is the attack against its common values which, like its language, makes all mutual understanding and cooperation possible. Providing a morality for the average individual, who is satisfied with this strong and practical equipment, society can expect obedience from him. Individual as well as social necessity is satisfied. No society, any more than any man, can do without morality. The latter is itself a necessity.

The Double Morality[1]

From everything we have just said, we can conclude that morality is not derived from a knowledge of the will of God. The good which morality acquaints us with is not the same thing as God's will.[2] An escape has been sought from this difficulty by supposing a veritable division within the will of God. On the one hand there is thought to be the redemptive will manifested in Jesus Christ, the God of love who wills to save men. On the other hand is the creating will, God the Creator who manifests himself in the creation. The first will would be known only through revelation. The second could be known naturally, in the contemplation of nature.

Rather than address ourselves to the theological problem, we refer to the study, among others, of the persons of the Trinity by Karl Barth. There is no division among them. There are not several degrees, either in God's person, or work, or will. He is one in all, and he cannot be known except through and in his revelation. There is no knowledge of the original creation refracted through fallen nature, and still less of the will of love which presided over it. This knowledge of the creation and of the original nature can only be had in Jesus Christ, in whom all things were made. The unity of God's creative and redemptive will appears in an especially obvious way in the promise of the resurrection and of the new creation.

Let us leave that, and let us now observe that the assertion of a natural knowledge of the creative will still does not resolve the problem which has been proposed. In effect, an attempt has been made to show that man cannot have knowledge of the good according to God, because that good merges with the redemptive will and with the person of Jesus Christ. But at a secondary level it could be said that the good which man knows, and which he expresses in his morality, comes from God, that it is a creation of God. It is not the sovereign and supreme good, but a divine good even so, and created as, for example, the sense of justice, of human love, are created.[3] That would mean, then, that there is an ideal world halfway between the divine and the human—the world of values, to be exact. We are in full Platonism. We absolutely do not deny the grandeur and value of the Platonic ideal and of its philosophy. We say only that it is in no way Christian, and that it is in no way compatible with Christianity. All efforts at conciliation have only ended by diluting the substance of Christianity. It is possible to speak of moral values as Christian, and we shall see in what sense; but in any case it must be recognized that they are definitely in the domain of the human. They in no way participate in God. In the last analysis they are a creation of man, not a manifestation of the "divine" in him.

Moral values depend upon matters such as environment, economic factors, education, religious ideals. There is nothing closed, nothing stable, nothing universal; yes, nothing objective about them. If they exist it is sporadically, ephemerally, fluidly; and in no sense are they shared by all. How can they be seen as a sign of God's creation? It should be a question of much more than vestiges, since these moral values created by God *in* the world of the fall (before the fall there was no need for them) must have kept in this world their full significance and vigor. Moreover, the argument from authority would seem to us to be quite a sufficient reason for asserting that these moral values are not creations of God. Nowhere does the Bible mention these values or their creation. So if we consider scripture to be the rule of Christian faith, that is enough. But there is an additional conclusion to be drawn from acknowledging the purely human character of the good formulated by man, and of moral values; namely, that this good cannot be used as a common standard between Christians and non-Christians. For one thing Christians cannot, strictly speaking, point to an implicit Christianity in non-Christians ("Since you behave like Christians, that means that you are Christians without knowing it"; and that was the great temptation of Christians with regard to Gandhi, as it is the temptation of some with regard to Communists today).

What makes a Christian out of a man is his confession that Christ is his Savior. Pagans can behave very well. That is never more than an accord with the human rule of the good; and the objective quality of their works can never be taken as evidence that they are acting in accordance with the very will of God, for, as we shall see, only God can discern what is good in our works. That is not our business and we are not capable of it. On the other hand, we cannot agree to any judgment of Christianity in the name of what men call the good. The latter can neither be a verification of Christianity nor a proof against it. "People do good without being Christians; hence Christianity serves no purpose." Obviously, people do *their* good without Christianity! This only demonstrates that their good is not the will of God! I know that those who read that sentence will protest that it is only the unbearable arrogance of Christians which speaks thus, of Christians who think they are the only ones who know God himself! I shall only reply: this good according to which you claim to judge everything, where do you get it from? If it is of God, how and in virtue of what? If it is of yourself, how can you claim to impose your standard on the revelation of God? You would first have to demonstrate that God is not revealed in Jesus Christ. It is, in very fact, a question of reducing God to a human standard.

The pretention of the first temptation always reappears, and that is to be expected because it is precisely in the formulation of the good that man asserts his equality with God. Thus it is natural that man should wish to judge the revelation in accordance with the norm of the good. But that is sin itself. And here, too, in the same line of thinking, we encounter the uneasiness and scrupulosity of Christians. What men call good today does not correspond to Christianity. Social justice, the desire to be effective, national self-respect, class loyalties, the understanding of the meaning of history, everything which assures the man of today that he is on the right path and can take himself seriously—of all that, Christianity has very little to say. Of course, by feats of interpretation one can find it in the Bible. The prophets speak to us of "social justice." The claim has been made in every age. In the Middle Ages honor, loyalty, service to the lady, fealty to the lord, military courage, were the chief criteria of the good, and men tried to line up Christianity under that banner. But the blessing of weapons and the killing of infidels in the name of the faith scandalizes us today. What is truly scandalous is simply the operation whereby Christianity is adapted to the temporary and temporal notion of the good in a given society, under the pretext that at the time when something is good it must be Christian.

The same operation performed today, in terms of the liberation of the proletariat and of the underdeveloped nations, or the raising of the standard of living, or the development of educational methods (what man calls good today), is equally destructive of Christianity, and will probably be judged absurd and inconsistent a few centuries hence. I am not at all saying, of course, that these works have no value and that we should leave the proletariat enslaved and illiterate. I am only saying that in spite of outward appearances, and even of biblical texts (for example, liberate the captives), those things are no more Christian than twelfth-century honor, or the good use of feudal weapons, or the individualistic Stoic despising of riches. All those things can be based on biblical texts, and yet today all that appears valueless, outmoded; that is the exact word, outmoded, for it is a matter of mode and not of truth. That is why it is inadmissable that Christians should want to modernize Christianity by adapting it to the moral mode of their own times.[4]

This morality, strictly human, relative, temporary, and temporal, which is not the will of God no matter what form it takes, is nevertheless necessary. The Christian who is aware of its limits has absolutely no right on that account to treat it as false or useless. Morality is definitely not to be neglected, and as Christians we should persevere in taking it seriously. It is well to recall that Christian though we be we have not completely attained to the perfect stature of Jesus Christ and we are not yet in the kingdom of God. We are living on this earth at a given time in a given place. We are human beings like everyone else. By reason of that fact (and it must be thus, for Christianity is not a school for inhumanity) we share the errors and perceptions, the hopes and beliefs, the values and judgments, the virtues and limitations of the people of this time and place. It is to be expected that, at the human level, we should judge to be good that which the people of this age call good. It is to be expected that we should feel judged when we disobey that good.

Paul exhorts us to give heed to this judgment in accordance with the world's morality: "For we aim at what is honorable not only in the Lord's sight but also in the sight of men" (2 Cor. 8:21); and Peter tells us that we should be prepared to make a defense to anyone who calls us to account for the hope that is in us (1 Peter 3:15). The judgment brought to bear on us in the name of morality must put us seriously on our guard, must make us question the significance of the value of our actions, must make us inquire whether our disobedience to morality is obedience to

God or to our own sin. We should have a very powerful motive before rejecting human morality, and we should be quite clear about that motive. We have no right to dismiss this morality with a wave of the hand because it is human. Doubtless the judgment imposed upon us is not God's judgment, but it is very important as a sign of the value or lack of value of our lives, and still more of the quality of the testimony which we bear to Jesus Christ.

The two texts cited remind us that obedience to the current morality, doing what those around us call "good," is one of the elements of the Christian life itself. Hence, this morality built by man has value in the sight of God. Even though it is in the realm of the fall, even though it is not commensurate with the will of God, it is indispensable if and because it is relative. The fact that Paul adds the qualification "in the sight of men" shows that it is a matter of a relative good. But we are called to bear witness in the sight of men to another commandment and we must not make the rejection of their morality a prerequisite for this testimony. To the contrary, we should take care lest the rejection of human morality create a useless stumbling block, for that stumbling block can be Satanic even when it is produced in the name of God. If we do reject human morality in the name of the gospel, we should be careful not to polarize the entire act of witness and the whole dialogue solely around the problem of the content of morality. If that happens, all the gospel message is dissipated and the testimony of grace becomes impossible. That is the oft repeated failure of the churches when they have gone into non-Christian countries and required a *prior* transformation of behavior, concerning themselves with polygamy, with nudity, with homosexuality, and fighting against customs not in conformity with Christian morality. Under that procedure the preaching of the gospel becomes impossible because the center of the struggle has been misplaced. That is why Paul reminds us: "To those outside the law I became as one outside the law, . . . that I might by all means save some" (1 Cor. 9:21–22) .[5]

Scandal in the face of human morality may sometimes be
necessary for the sake of Jesus Christ, we shall see within
what limits, but always in the frame of reference of the
preaching of the gospel and never as a combat between two
moralities. You can obey the morality of man. Normally,
you should do so. Note that the Bible nowhere condemns
that morality. It is quite remarkable that the word of God
should be so inflexible toward religions, toward magic, toward idolatry, that it condemns relentlessly and without
forbearance the slightest spiritual deviation, but that it
scarcely concerns itself with differences in morality. It only
makes a point of that when such moral conduct is in consequence of a spiritual attitude, of a heresy, of an idolatry.
Only as a sign of these does morality become important.
This type of tolerance, of moderation toward moral decision, is astonishing. Yet it can be understood if we reflect
that, at bottom, morality is so closely bound up with man
that to deny morality, to reject it, is purely and simply to
deny man himself, is to abolish his state of life.[6]

Since the fall, and because of it, man is in a moral universe from which he cannot be dissociated. The circumstance of his break with God has become his reason for
existence and his very life. To tear him loose from that universe could not possibly reconcile him with God! To under-
take to repudiate man-made morality is to act either demonically or angelically: demonically in that it throws man
back into the situation of the demons, who have no moral
life but only an opposition to God; angelically in that the
Christian who would do such a thing claims that he has escaped the human situation and has returned to Adam's
state before the fall. To claim to repudiate this morality is,
when all is said and done, to fail to accept man for what he
is and to fail to accept oneself as a man. That certainly will
not help the Christian better to prepare his hearer whom he
has destroyed to be a hearer of the gospel. To the contrary,
it would be to cut himself off from his hearer decisively and
to withdraw his hearer from his own reality, because he
continues to be what he is in spite of our repudiation of his

morality. In addition, we should realize that if this man-established morality, the place of sin's decision, is nevertheless tolerated by God, that is also in the degree of its usefulness for man. We have frequently pointed out that man needs this morality in order to live, that every social group which emerges expresses itself therein. Life is possible within an ethical system. Apart from that it would be a constant warfare, and interpersonal relationships would be unthinkable. Therefore, we must respect this morality for its utility, since it is useful to man.[7]

Here we are at the level of a useful morality which man can both construct and obey—useful but not necessarily debased to a utilitarian status. It is in this sense, though with reservations concerning the term used, that we accept Bonhoeffer's idea of the natural disposition.[8] This natural disposition is, physically speaking, the shape of human life with a view to its preservation. To that, ethics corresponds, and the use of the reason to express it is indispensable and just. Evil, from that point of view, is always a form of the destruction of life. Definitively, this natural disposition is determined by God's will of preservation. The nonnatural is that which tends to oppose that will, granted always that the will of God also can sometimes be one of destruction, at which times it makes use of the nonnatural (compare, for example, the plagues of Egypt, the Assyrians). This implies that the categories of good and evil established according to the natural disposition, the useful and pragmatic, surely are not imposed upon God!

We cannot wish to see man placed in a more inhuman life situation. The existence of this morality does not bring man closer to God, and it is not with that in mind that the Christian should respect it. But it does allow man to subsist; and that is important if we assume that God does not want us to begin the harvest prematurely, but to the contrary that it is essential to keep alive, in order, and viable the world in which we are placed. Even though it is radically bad, it still must be livable. Air fit to breathe, sufficient nourishment, a harmonious order, the possibility of mutual relationships—these are humble but essential needs. We have to take them seriously if we are not to vanish into thin air. The Christian, because he is a man, should lend a hand in making the world livable. Morality is part of that task, the common morality, the morality of the group, interpersonal morality. We must respect it, build it, and strengthen it in company with our fellows. This is the more true since in all this complexity there are values to which the Christian cannot remain indifferent.

We said that after the fall man knows that there is a good. He does not know what it is. Yet each time man constructs a morality, or proceeds to an ethical choice, or makes a decision, there is a hope, an expectation, a call. In the absence of God's good, man concludes that this is good because he cannot do without it, but also because he, in fact, expects and hopes for the sovereign good without knowing it, without even thinking, perhaps, that it might exist. But it is this man who comes into being whenever he determines the good because he is bringing his hope to light, the end toward which he is striving in that way. Every time man is convinced that the system will be the perfect fulfillment of his desire he is disappointed, because only perfection will satisfy him. Thus, this expectation, this call of man, is expressed in the endlessly fresh starts toward the elaboration of morality (but not only there, of course), and for this reason whoever receives the revelation of God should give heed to men's hope, not in order to tell them that they are deluded in their attempt to answer the hope themselves, not in order to take up a position of superiority, but to help them give birth to their hope, and to formulate what they now call good, to obey it in keeping it as a necessity, in never letting it become encased in a dead order, in ceaselessly bringing it back to what it is: a cry of man into the night, to which man himself responds.

If we are led to a positive acceptance of the existence of this human morality, this means that for the Christian there are two moralities (insofar as we can speak of a Christian

morality, a question which we shall study later on). On the
one hand there is the revelation of the good according to
God, and all that is entailed by that. On the other hand
there is the elaboration of a morality by man in the given
circumstances in which he finds himself.[9] These two phenomena are in contrast with one another in all fields of action.[10] As far as their origins are concerned, we have spoken
on the one hand of the revelation, of the attitude adopted
by man toward God, then toward his neighbor, as a function of the word of God. On the other hand, we have spoken
of the creation by man, individually or collectively, of the
rule of conduct or of judgment, through quite diverse procedures and with the content also subject to change.[11] What
one calls "good" in the two cases is different. We have no
need to return to that. But it can be said that the moral
procedure itself is in contrast in the two cases. If one ex-
cepts the completely unreal vision of Sartre, one can say
that concretely the moral procedure always unfolds in two
moments, the settling of a good to be accomplished, and the
accomplishment (or nonaccomplishment) of this good in
consequence of a choice or a decision.

One might speak of a general ethic and a particular ethic.
The determination of the good can be collective or individual, determined entirely beforehand or in process of elaboration on the basis of experience; in any case the good appears as an end to be attained, or as a value to be put into
effect, or as a principle from which consequences are to be
drawn, or as a commandment to be embodied—in any event,
a predetermined abstract principle that man is to act out
or apply. Man's responsibility is located at the level of this
application, of this action. Whatever may be the refine-
ments of phenomenological thought it, too, comes back to
this, for example, with the concept of the "aim of values."
Now precisely this procedure of moral action has nothing
to do with Christianity; or rather, when one describes
Christianity in this manner (which happens very often),
that has nothing to do with the revelation of God. To say

that there is a law of God to be carried out, that there is a Christian morality (described in the letters of Paul, for example, or in the Sermon on the Mount) the requirements of which are to be fulfilled, that there is a sovereign good which we can contemplate mystically and then apply afterward: all that is to import into Christianity the experiments, judgments, and interpretations of the world's morality.

In the faith the moral procedure is entirely different.[12] There is not, in fact, any presupposition or determination of an objective good. We shall see that the law of God itself is not this objective good. There is only a personal relation with God for each person, in which the good is revealed in its character as the will of God. Now, that good is not an end to be attained, and which one approaches step by step through asceticism. We learn, for one thing, that it is fulfilled in Jesus Christ. For another thing, we have to determine our behavior in the present circumstance, not as part of a distant end but as an expression of the love and glory of God. One can say (from the ethical point of view, and not in the soteriological sense of Philippians or Colossians: "Not that I have already obtained this") that the Christian acts in virtue of a personal drive which he has received to witness to a truth which is not ethical, and which he must make actual, present, living. He does not act by progressive approximations to a fixed perfection, but in a decision which is total and new at each moment. He is not on a path marked by successive stages in which morality is fulfilled better and better. The path and growth which are encountered in the Bible are those of faith, not of morality.

The moral work of the Christian is whole and entire in each instant. It is undivided. He expresses in it what he *is* at that moment. There is no adding yesterday's work to today's. There is only the renewal of one's being by the increase of faith through the power of the Holy Spirit who works in us. And this renewal of one's being is expressed in works which are always indeed new. I judge these works myself today in relation to the will of God which has been revealed to me; and I learn, in fact, that they are not the worthy and just expression of that will. In a certain sense this means that there really is no Christian morality. And that brings us to the underlining of another difference: all morality rests on the supposition that man is free, since in the last analysis the final verdict depends on the choice between good and evil which man puts into effect. If man were not free that would have no meaning. Hence freedom is truly a condition of morality.[13]

Now Christianity, on the contrary, speaks of a man bound by a personal will, of a man whose first principle of life is obedience. It teaches us that obedience is the prior condition of liberty. In human eyes this is quite incomprehensible. The idea that the moral life, righteous conduct, should result from the fact that we belong to someone is an impossibility, a veritable scandal, for all independent morality. The latter always tends in the direction of a greater mastery of self, of individual autonomy, while the Christian life is an ever deeper belonging to God. From the humanist point of view the belonging is an alienation; but in truth, and we shall study this in Part II, it is the very fulfillment of the only perfect freedom.

Finally, another contrast between the two moralities derives from the fact that God's commands will never aim at bringing a man to realize an ideal, which all moralities of the world tend to do. God's commands always relate to an action connected with the establishment and proclamation of his covenant, with his promised kingdom which is close upon us. Therefore, in Christian ethics it will never be a matter of doing some good or other, but of carrying out a certain task relating to the kingdom of God and to the witness which God calls upon us to bear.

In the Christian revelation there is no moral ideal, no typology of the good, still less a symbolism of the good! There is a revelation of the Word, who calls man to obedience because God is bringing to pass his salvation. From then on the Christian is not obliged to create his behavior at each moment, still less to create his own being, as in existentialism. He receives his being whole from his encounter with Jesus Christ (not with his neighbor!).

These principles make it possible for us, in any event, to understand the essential divergence which can exist between the two "moralities" that we recognize. The usual attitude consists in acknowledging a certain difference between Christian morality and the other moralities, a difference in content, for example, or a difference of expression. One analyzes in turn the moral systems of Confucius, of Socrates, of Kant, and of Christianity. To the natural man Christianity can, in fact, appear as one religion among other religions, as one anthropology among other anthropologies, as one philosophy among other philosophies, and as one morality among other moralities. Very frequently, moreover, Christian intellectuals by their philosophical preoccupations and the clergy through their concern with religion and morals have laid themselves open to this interpretation, have allowed these comparisons. And it is true that Christianity could look like a religion in its psychological and sociological expressions, and like a morality in its will to improve human life.

Now just as there is an irreducible contrast between Christianity and religion, as Barth has shown, so likewise there is an irreducible contrast between Christianity and morality. In a certain sense which we shall outline later on, one can say that Christianity is an anti-morality. Whenever it gives rise to phenomena which could be classified analytically as moral phenomena, that in no way justifies its being likened to the moralities. The difference is not merely one of language or of content. One can say that what might be called Christian ethics is the opposite to everything which constitutes morality in the general sense of the word.

All the moralities have characteristics in common, which is why we can refer to the general phenomenon of *morality*. Now it is precisely these common characteristics which we do not find in the conduct of the Christian life. The latter stands off from every morality by an irreducible specific character.[14] Thus it is not a matter of a few differences of detail or of content. It is a contrast at the very root of the phenomenon. One can say that on one side you have the ensemble of the moralities with their common characteristics and on the other side Christianity having nothing commensurate with any morality. It is the essence itself of revelation that rules out all ethical systematizing and all similarity with a morality. The Christian life is not a life conformed to a morality, but one conformed to a word revealed, present, and living.[15]

The specific character of the Christian ethical phenomenon will become clearer as we proceed, but it is necessary at this point to set forth this important fact in propositional form. To be sure, it leads to great difficulties. There is an ever-recurring temptation for Christians to bridge the gap between the Christian life and the moralities of the world, whether because it is hard to see how otherwise to state the Christian rule of life, or because the divorce from the world is a painful thing to accept, or because it seems wrong from the point of view of charity and humility to exclude whatever is not Christian from the realm of the truth, or whether, finally, because the spirit of the world has crept into the church; and for yet many other reasons the process of assimilation and identification between Christianity and morality, or a particular morality, endlessly repeats itself.[16] Now we must always remember that the biblical ethic can be confused with the others. Alongside the commandment of God there are other prescriptions originating with society, with nature, or with history which one can also take for ordinances of God. This is the more true since God in revealing his will does not act in his overwhelming omnipotence, but he sets forth this will as an ordinary requirement, just as in Jesus he presents himself as an ordinary man. Karl Barth emphasizes that what finally differentiates this commandment of God is that it is not an obligation but a permission.

The commandment rests on the fact of man's liberation by Jesus Christ, on the fact that man becomes free through grace received in faith. The commandment itself appears as a sort of guarantee of that liberty. The commandment authorizes man finally to live as he was meant to live in the creation. In that character it is strictly different from all the other moralities.

And yet Christian ethics can be close to non-Christian ethics,[17] and Christian behavior to non-Christian behavior, in both good and evil. It is well known, for example, that one of the points of rapprochement between Christians and Muslims at the time of the Crusades was asceticism. Muslim asceticism admired Christian asceticism, and vice versa. Likewise today it is commonplace to say that Communist partisans show a greater sense of justice and a greater spirit of love than Christians. The question of Celsus, "What distinguishes Christians in the domain of virtue?" is repeated over and over again.

We need to remember, as a matter of fact, that what distinguishes Christians is neither a better behavior nor a greater intelligence. To compare asceticism with asceticism, and to find there an area of agreement, or to compare faith with faith or religion with religion, is to enter into an analogy, into a correlation of things human.

The asceticism that goes by the name Christian is the same thing as Muslim asceticism; and Christian social love is the same thing as Communist love. What does that show? That Muslims and Communists are Christians? Absolutely not! These things resemble one another from the point of view of the "natural" man, of the son of Adam; that is to say, of him who lives in his self-decision, or indeed in his self-determination and independence. Whenever a Christian finds Muslim asceticism similar to Christian asceticism, he is right to the extent that the latter is not Christian. In that case it is a matter of mixing the religious spirit of the world with the faith. In order to judge by himself what is good, the Christian ceases to depend upon his Lord; that is, he repeats Adam's decision. Whenever a Christian considers Communist love to be similar to charity, he is right to the degree in which charity has been altered into a humanist love of society, importing the same admixture of the spirit of the times into the revelation. There again, the Christian has decided for himself what love is, and it is he who has ceased to be what he was called to be. We should emphasize, of course, that in that case it is not because of Communist influence that the change has taken place! No outside influence was necessary. The change comes from within. It is because the Christian has ceased to know what charity is, through following the sociological trend of the community which says to him, "There is true love, there is the true humanism." Because he listens to this social voice instead of to that of his Lord he sees in this or that human movement, or human type, a love which he humbly, and rightly, recognizes to be superior to his own.

Well then? Well then, that which constitutes Christianity is the person of Jesus Christ. Everything derives from the fact that Jesus is God, that Jesus Christ is Lord and Savior. Apart from that there is only talk. But then one perceives that the problem is above all a problem of truth, and that it is only in this truth, recognized and assumed, that ethics can take shape. (We shall see the link between heresy and bad conduct.) For Christian ethics is going to be the relation between the person of Jesus Christ and a person who takes him as his Savior and Lord. Here, we are restored in the good which God says and does. Now that good is strictly impenetrable, incomprehensible, beyond our grasp from the standpoint of what man calls good. There is no comparison possible. The person who does not accept Jesus Christ can only pass judgment on the good from his own point of view, starting with what he calls justice or love at a given stage in a civilization. To him, Christian behavior will usually seem incomprehensible, absurd, sometimes bad. It can only bear the judgment which Paul referred to as "a stumbling block to Jews and folly to Gentiles" (1 Cor. 1:23). It is always a stumbling block to the humanists, the prudent, the virtuous, and the religious. It is always a piece of stupidity to philosophers, scientists, and technicians.

Within the faith, then, it is a matter of expressing this oddness of Christian conduct by starting with the person of Jesus Christ. But be very sure that this does not mean a striving after originality at all costs, or an ipso facto rejection of all modes of human behavior. There can be an occasional and accidental overlapping at the behavior level. Still, this overlapping will often seem odd once again whenever such conduct in which a man takes his bearings is found to be in an unexpected context, and whenever the separation takes place in a very short time. It is often a cause for scandal to non-Christians, who think that they are on common moral ground, when they discover that the Christians are interested in something quite different. It is at the moment of association and at the beginning of the road which both might travel together that the misunderstandings should be cleared up.

How often have Christians fallen short, rather than disappoint and shock their fellows, bestowing the name of "love and charity" on what is nothing but cowardice, a lack of clear-sightedness, and a betrayal of the truth. It is especially on the basis of these equivocations that Christianities are forever reconstituted. It is easy, then, to formulate an intellectually perfect orthodox theology; but the moment one is called upon to put into practice the lived and concrete expression of Christianity, one discovers that the most orthodox theology is of little use, that it is very poor at becoming flesh. Faced with the necessity of an incarnation of the faith, one feels the need to state Christian truth in such a way that it can be lived. From that moment on we witness a theological effort which ends in heresy. Barthian theology at the present time finds itself faced with that difficulty. Attempts are reappearing at reconciliation with the moralities of the world. Sometimes it is through Barthians adopting positions that are extremely indecisive and conformed to the sociological trend (for example, in politics with regard to socialism) . Sometimes it is through efforts already under way to arrive at a moral system. In the one case as in the other, the process cannot lead to a new theological education in the truth.

The problem of Christian conduct is one of the insoluble problems which people are always trying to solve by theological modification, and which it is important not to solve. Let us once again recall with emphasis that what constitutes the Christian life is not morality but faith, and the center of faith is not the good, but Jesus Christ. At this point Christian ethics breaks off all *possible* relations with every morality whatsoever.

If we have been forced to recognize the existence for the Christian of a double morality, what consequence does that entail? Obviously it sets up a relationship between the two, but what relationship? [18]

In an exceptional way, there can be agreement between the two in the immediate action. A given attitude, decision, or judgment on the part of the socialist morality or the Platonist morality could be entirely acceptable to the Christian; and we have seen, conversely, that a given work of the faith can be adopted by the non-Christian and considered good from his own point of view. But this agreement can only take place at the level of concrete and piecemeal operations. As Niebuhr emphasizes (*Nature and Destiny*) , the search for justice, resistance to tyranny, the demand for peace, are indications of moral judgments which are valid, but which are always intermingled with principles of violence and hate. The converse is also true. The exercise of power, always a violence, is also mixed with a certain quest for law and order. Those who speak from this standpoint of a "short stretch of road" which Communists and Christians might travel together are not wrong if it be understood that no adherence to the overall politics and doctrine of communism is implied, but that one is only saying that the requirement of the faith and the Communist strategy have come together on a particular point.[19] For Christians to have given their support to a particular commandment of Roman law (good faith, for example), or of Stoic morality, was perfectly right; but that support could not be extended to Roman law or to Stoic morality as a whole.

The mistake is made whenever one moves on from the concrete work to the system. When the non-Christian pretends to assimilate Christianity to this or that other moral system, that is not a matter of great importance. It is a misunderstanding which is inevitable. The natural man absolutely cannot understand, of himself, the irreducible novelty of Christian truth. He can have no idea of the double morality. Within his outlook Christianity can only be one religion and one morality among others. He has no way of judging otherwise. The mistake is only serious when it is made by Christians, when they confuse the results of the faith with this or that human virtue or ideal. At that moment they give up the strict relation established by Jesus Christ between "the words that I say" and putting them into practice.

Specifically, Christians attempt the following two types of conciliation. For one of these the morality of the world is a minimum which is not opposed to Christianity. Christian morality simply includes the world's morality but goes still further. Thus Christianity is an additional requirement. Aside from that, it recognizes whatever exists as natural morality. This could only have been maintained in strongly Christianized societies, where the "lay" morality was *in fact* a Christian morality secularized. That becomes absurd in speaking of the Marquesans or the Chippewas. Moreover, we have seen how impossible it is to establish a continuity between natural morality and Christian morality.[20] Another attempt at conciliation consists in saying: "Fulfill Christian morality, and you will find that society will accept you." [21] (Be Christian and you will be rich, you will be successful.) This is a very serious misappropriation of Christian truth, and all that one can say is that in that case there is no Christian life left *at all*. No system of values, no human conduct, no moral mythology, can be identified with Christianity in its essence. There can only be accidental and temporary conjunctions.

In the event that there is agreement, it does not mean that Christian morality is an extension of natural morality, nor that it completes it, but only that the life of faith does not annihilate nature and that God does not abandon humanity, even in its most rebellious state and at the focal point of its sin.[22] But this in no way confirms the interpretation: *primus usus legis* (or *usus civilis*), whereby the law, or Christian morality, has a restraining and inspiring function for all.[23] We have already indicated the sense in which that seemed impossible. Let us remember that there is a theological error in that interpretation; for in it morality is depicted as coming from God understood as the supreme Being, and it could be accepted with that status by many. But, on the part of the Christian, that implies that he does not base his morality on Christ, which is the worst of all betrayals. Now the moment he establishes this foundation in Christ he can no longer be understood by non-Christians. No further agreement is possible.

Finally, one may consider a morality of the world that is humble. When Karl Barth supposes it possible to agree with an ethic which stops giving absolute weight to its own wisdom, which does not claim to be the "last word," nor to be dignified by a myth, nor to define a "good," he is quite right, but it seems to us an illusory idea because hypothetical and without a concrete instance! For let us not forget that any ethic which emphasizes, for example, the limits of the human situation, the precarious quality of moral judgments, *always* carries this relativism and skepticism to the ultimate!

In the majority of instances, moreover, there will be a conflict between the two moralities, or again, ignorance and indifference on the part of the world's morality toward Christian morality. This last would be the case of secular-ism. The Christian cannot ignore the morality of secular society. He should take it into account, as we have said, just as he should take into account every other morality of the society in which he finds himself. But secular morality, for its part, can ignore, and purposely so, the existence of an independent Christian morality. It is under no obligation to hold its requirements as of any value. Yet, in principle, it does not have to oppose them either. It respects . . . Thus there is indifference, and secularity henceforth can assert that there is no conflict, and that there cannot be any since the supreme value is tolerance. If a conflict breaks out, it will be the fault of the Christian who will have shown his intolerance and so will have transgressed the secular moral law—which is true.

The secular person obviously cannot perceive the motives which keep tolerance from being the final value for the Christian, and which produce an intolerant behavior out of certain concrete consequences of faith. In this case the conflict is provoked by the Christian's application of Christian morality. Conversely, it can happen that the morality of the world is openly contradictory to Christian morality. So it is with Communist morality (for example, the idea that there is no personal virtue); belonging to a class makes a man good or bad, no matter what his personal behavior might be; or again, anything is good that works to the benefit of the proletariat (including lying, betrayal, murder). It is the same with the Nazi morality, or the technician's morality (of which the scale of values is entirely contradictory to Christianity).

In these different instances, from the non-Christian point of view, the conflict may be resolved in two ways. One may forbid Christians to display their allegiance to Jesus Christ by any action. Of course one leaves the inward man free, his beliefs and his spiritual life, but it is important that this interior life should not express itself in outward conduct. What seriously embarrasses the unity of action of a society is divergence of action, not divergence of belief. Already in the Roman Empire it was not the Christians' belief which was held against them, but their refusal to participate in the imperial ceremonies and their refusal to tolerate other religions, other socio-moral attitudes. As long as the Christian conforms to the common action in practice he is perfectly acceptable. If his faith does not express itself in any peculiar act, if in a Communist regime he obeys the party's orders, if he works to build up socialism, if he never witnesses publicly to his faith, if he does not criticize the government even for its anti-religious policies, all will be well. In other words, all will be well if he does not live as a Christian, if he does not obey a Christian ethic. Hence the first solution is the total elimination of Christian morality. The other solution consists in subordinating Christian morality to the other; that is to say, to use Christian morality in support of the conduct demanded by the non-Christian morality. When in the Communist society the Orthodox Church in 1943 appealed to Christian charity to develop a sense of fellowship and to make special donations to the state, when the churches in Hungary and Czechoslovakia develop the theme of obedience to the state, as a duty of conscience based on Romans 13, that serves the Communist morality, and the latter is quite happy with this appeal to Christian behavior in that case and in the interest of that particular cooperation.

In a much more general way one finds the same attitude, for example, among the bourgeoisie and with the morality of the technical world: the value of work, consecration in everything that one does, sacrificing to the common life, the spirit of service rather than of enjoyment — those are virtues eminently useful to technical development. With that starting point technical morality gives broad recognition to Christian morality just as long as it collaborates in this development (while rejecting everything that is contradictory in that same morality). The poor man's conspicuous dignity, the subordination willed by God of the servant to his master, the sacrifice of the temporal to the spiritual—all that, as we well know, was widely used by the bourgeoisie in its morality to maintain the working class. So here one picked up certain features of Christian morality to the extent that they were useful in building up the bourgeois world, and these were integrated into a general system which was alien to them. Everything in this same Christian morality which was contrary to involvement in the bourgeois world was not forbidden, to be sure, but it was gradually eliminated, passed over in silence, thrown into the shade. Now by the very fact of this amputation, what had been an authentic Christian virtue ceased to be that when it was integrated into another moral system and turned aside from its source and from its end. That is why the bourgeois morality, since it is not used for the glory of God but for the development of a certain type of society, is really a caricature of the Christian life and at bottom its worst deformation—this in spite of the fact that in its concrete works it exhibits many points of identity with Christian morality (for example, family virtues, the dignity of the individual, charity).

Obviously, if Christians accept one or the other of these two solutions, the conflict is resolved. If the church in the socialist world yields to the Communist order in all its manifestations, the problem is resolved by an external compulsion. If the church is in the hands of the bourgeoisie, if its priests and pastors are recruited exclusively from that class, the tension is appeased by the church's conforming to society. Now for a Christian neither of these two solutions is acceptable. In the one case, he cannot agree that his faith should have no tangible consequence and should remain purely inward; in the other case, he cannot agree that the Christian virtues should be turned aside from their source and from their end. But it must be understood that if the Christian maintains this double requirement (that on the one hand, his faith should be expressed in specific attitudes and that the whole problem is one of incarnating the truth; that on the other hand, the Christian life is whole and indivisible, that it has no utilitarian purpose, that its only meaning is the glory of God), if he refuses to put this Christian life to the service of the state, or to the efficiency of technology, then here again it is he who is responsible for the conflict. We must be very clear on this point. Whenever there is a conflict, or at least a tension between Christian morality and some other morality, it is the Christian, and he alone, who provokes the tension. The non-Christian is in no way responsible, since he has no reason to see faith's requirement as a higher value. But then that also means that there is no tension between the two systems except for and in the Christian.

For the Christian: there is no tension for the others. We have seen how society, the group, and also the non-Christian individual, seeks to eliminate a tension which is unbearable and which there seems to be no reason to maintain. The Christian, to the contrary, finds himself in a tension between the morality of the society in which he lives, which he must carry out, and the will of God.[24] Whether one opposes a morality of distress to a morality of values (Ricoeur) or a morality of responsibility to a morality of conscience (Weber), the first being a morality which judges acts by their consequences and not by their intentions, the second a morality with an absolute regard for certain values regardless of consequences, in both cases (and one could find other qualifying functions) one is implying that the Christian is caught in an opposition of moralities which he can neither reject nor bring to an end. *In the Christian:* this tension exists only in the very person of the Christian. It is not a conflict in itself. It is not an opposition of doctrines, nor an objective difference in the scale of values. It is not a theoretical, nor an intellectual divergence. If it were that, the conflict obviously could be resolved.

When the commandment of God is known in truth, in the revelation and in grace, then it *unmasks* the lie of our commandments and of our morality. It *opposes* the human high-handedness that chooses its own good and comes to terms with the permissions and the marks of "satisfactory." It *rules out* the reservation whereby man wants to reassure himself by obeying God conditionally. It *strips* man of his power to judge good and evil by himself.[25] As a result, it devalues all human morality. But that is not to say that it eliminates it and destroys it.

In any case, whatever might be the similarity of content of a commandment of God, or of the values of God's law, and human moralities, there is a radical difference of meaning and purpose: "The divine requirement is distinct from all others in that it makes us the property of Jesus Christ in order to put us at his disposal. . . . It is at this point that the question is settled whether our power and our duty are those of God's command, whether we have to do with *that* command or with some other." The command of God, as distinct from every other morality, has only one meaning and purpose: to bind us to Jesus Christ.[26]

There is not, on the one side a system of Christian morality and on the other side some other system to which it is in theoretical opposition. We shall see that it is impossible to formulate Christian morality as a system. It is never a matter of anything but a Christian life which is a consequence of God's will. This life is lived, or it is not lived. If it is lived, there is a Christian conduct (hence morality). If it is not lived, there is nothing. Therefore the conflict takes place at the level of life, of the incarnation of the truth and of a requirement. It comes into being on the occasion of a decision which has to be made. There is not, in that, any problem which might be solved intellectually. Of course, from a theoretical point of view it is very easy to find answers, solutions, and accommodations; but at that level there simply no longer exists any significant Christian ethic at all. Hence, to talk about this tension is not an intellectual game. It is the very reality of the Christian life, and it has to remain such. Properly speaking, that tension is what constitutes the person of the Christian involved in the world. It cannot be stated in abstract terms because it only manifests itself at the occurrence of concrete situations in which decisions are called for. And each time the decision is made, the conflict abated, there has been a response but not a solution. The conflict renews itself immediately, at a different level, in the new situation which is created.

Thus the entire life of the Christian is lived out in this tension between the two moralities. It can never arrive at an equilibrium or at a "satisfying" solution. It is never finished. We are not in the presence of a clever dialectical game in which the combinations are always changed; because when all is said and done one of the principles in conflict, the will of God, strictly does not lend itself to any synthesis and can never become an object in our hands. On the other hand, just as this tension manifests itself solely in concrete situations, so it is also renewed with each individual person. The temporary solution to a contradiction which is found by a given individual will not do for his neighbor or his son. The experience of the contradiction has to be fresh for each one. What one of them has done can only be a testimony and in the last resort an example for his neighbor. But this tension which is inseparable from the Christian life does not produce neuroses since it is an element in the circuit of faith and hope. These two forces which bind us to Jesus Christ reduce the tension to the modest dimensions of our earthly life and keep it from overrunning our person, the key to our psychology, and from becoming the despairing negation of all response.

Over and above the tension in which he finds himself, the Christian knows that there is a response already given, incomparably more vast than the conflict which he is faced with. And that is not external, alien to his contradiction. It is not a compensating conviction. It is not a response incommensurate with the anguish which may be born of the conflict. As a matter of fact, if the conflict exists, it is precisely because of this faith and this hope. They are antecedent to the tension. It is because Christian faith and hope are manifesting themselves in a life that that life is henceforth plunged into contradiction. Hence, there is not first of all a conflict between the will of God and the world's morality, then afterward a hope which would come and abate the conflict. There is first of all the hearing of the word of God, who in manifesting his will produces faith and hope in us; then afterward appears the conflict into which we enter whenever we wish to obey God's will.

This conflict is necessarily produced whenever the decision of God calls in question the order of values established by the world. It is well-known that Kierkegaard especially emphasized that the call which God addresses personally to a man suspends the ethical order in which he normally lives. The vocation which God formulates for that individual cannot enter into any moral frame. This does not mean that there is an objective and collective abolition of the order of values. That order continues to subsist in the group for those individuals who have not heard the requirement of God; and he who has heard the call cannot speak of the suppression of that hierarchy with its behavior patterns. But for him the break has been brought about by the intervention of God with respect to every morality, even if it be Christian. There is truly for him no longer any good but that expressed for him in this command of God, since the encounter with God which entails moral consequences does not begin by creating an ethic. It begins as an encounter of the one who lives in sin with the one who brings grace, of the one who is destined for death with the one who raises him from the dead, of the one who is predetermined with the one who liberates him; and from this very fact there is a negation of every morality, of every order, of every hierarchy of values.[27]

The morality of the world constitutes part of the next-to-last things. Bonhoeffer has shown that they were neither condemned by the finality of revelation nor validated by a complement of grace: "The Christian life does not destroy these next-to-last things, but neither does it sanction them."[28] The good defined by the moralities of the world has nothing to do with the good or with our salvation, but it is still useful for the possibilities of life on earth. Niebuhr says also that every moral obligation has as its purpose to promote harmony and overcome chaos, and on this account it contains an element of validity for faith, but not the final validity or even a validity *integrated into* Christian truth, or assumed.[29] Moreover it is necessary at this point to make a distinction among the next-to-last works; that which is the work of man,[30] technological work, economic and political works, can be seen, as Bonhoeffer does, as a necessary step toward the last things. For these next-to-last things do not exist "in themselves." They only exist in relation to the last things, but neither are they a road which leads to the last things directly—the judgment has to take place. On the other side, the morality of the world, insofar as it reveals the knowledge of good and evil, is of a different order. It fulfills the practical function of preserving the world. It is not in any way a preparation for the last things. It is of a *lower* validity and excellence than all the other works of man. But because of its modest usefulness to man, the Christian cannot claim to treat it as nothing. So also Christians in a situation of tension with respect to morality have to set forth the law of love in the face of these ethical relativisms, and precisely as the limit, the barrier, the opposition to that relativism which is legitimate from the natural point of view but which needs to be brought into relation to the affirmation of the love of God with all which that entails.

Under these conditions the Christian should not try to resolve the conflict by denying in one way or another this morality of the world. Here we come upon another aspect of the lie which we have already denounced, whether in the form of a synthesis of the two moralities, or as a more or less camouflaged negation of the specific character of the Christian life when it aligns itself with one of the world's ethical systems. How might this elimination of non-Christian morality take place? Historically it has taken place in two forms. First of all, within Christianity there has always been a great temptation to transform Christian morality into a universal morality and to impose Christian conduct on everybody. For Christians, Christian conduct is so obvious, so superior, so valuable *in itself* that they cannot understand its not being obeyed. In a so-called Christian society, where the church enjoys official recognition, where the state protects the Christian religion, there is only one morality, that promulgated by the church, which everyone belonging to that society must obey.[31] This brings about a dreadful situation; as we shall never tire of repeating, the Christian life can only be the expression of the faith. Whenever you make Christian morality a universal requirement you cut that morality off from its own root, and you ask those who do not have the faith to live as though they had it, which means in the last analysis condemning them to hypocrisy.

The problem has, of course, been perceived, if it has not been stated as bluntly as we are stating it here. There have been two different answers to it. In the Middle Ages the answer was found in the theory of implicit faith (this man who lacks a personal faith belongs, nevertheless, to the church. Thus he participates in the church's faith and one can expect Christian behavior of him). The seventeenth century offers an example of the other answer, in which Christian morality is treated as natural morality. It is not necessary to live by faith in order to obey it. One need only follow his nature. In both cases, the heresy resulted from considering morality in and of itself, instead of as the personal will of the God of Jesus Christ. It was supposed that Christian conduct was the most important thing, rather than the relation with Jesus Christ. The Christian's action and the church's action can never consist in setting up, externally, elaborate moral obligations which are supposed to have value in some universal and undifferentiated way. God's commandment should remain a commandment—that is to say, a personal word—and it should come after the evidence of grace.

In fact, it is not enough that God's law be known intellectually so that man might be convinced of its excellence. It has to be received within the work which God wrought in Jesus Christ, and that cannot be received except in and through faith. That is why teaching the law to children and making them practice "Christian behavior" does not mean much in any event, and it will certainly be called into question when a true grasp is had of the preaching of the gospel. But obviously there is the constant temptation to replace that preaching by a moral education, called religious, for the children as well as for the masses. It is a temptation which rests upon the need for security and ease of operation. It is easier to have someone live according to the precepts of a morality. The results are more assured, more apparent, and one can count on them in a pinch. For the organization of a Christian society one must obviously depend upon a morality, since that alone can be a common standard for everyone and can be imposed from without. One is not obliged to take inward differentiations into account. The preaching of the gospel, to the contrary, exposes one to all the risks because it is open to God's freedom to intervene (or not to intervene). No society can be organized from that starting point because God's intervention cannot be counted on, and it does not take place massively and collectively. We now come upon a third aspect of the same temptation.

One of the great temptations for French Christians and theologians of the present day is to draw a false ethical conclusion from the great theological rediscovery that Christ is the Lord of the world. That comes out in two errors.

1. Many hold the conviction that since the world's man-made morality is *also* within the realm over which Jesus Christ is Lord it is by that fact legitimized. But it is forgotten that that lordship is affirmed over a world in revolt, whence the rebel forces have not been eliminated. The fact of the lordship of Christ in no way justifies all the world's projects. It only means that (a) those forces are potentially overcome; (b) whatever man's enterprises may be, they

will all come finally before God to be judged; and (c) the end of history is determined, known, and inevitable. It is the reintegration of the whole in Christ.

2. The second error stems from the idea that since the lordship of Christ is exercised in the church *and* in the world (according to the well-known symbol of the two circles), the difference between the two domains is thus only relative. It is then supposed that morality made by man *to meet the problems of the world* also comes from God, as long as the Christian faith has nothing in particular to say in that area. So, granted that Christianity has nothing specific to say about economic and political problems, one must depend upon those human solutions which are the most valid. But here again one is forgetting that the criterion "valid—not valid" can never consist in superimposing Christian morality (or the requirements of faith) on the world's morality in order to find points of agreement; for to do that is to suppose that human morality and God's will are two dimensions of the same nature, which is not only contrary to biblical revelation but also empties the incarnation of all meaning.

Obviously, the fact that the lordship of Christ applies to the whole world and to all mankind means that the command of God is valid for all. But that command cannot be heard, *recognized* as such, and obeyed except through and in faith. Hence, the proclamation of God's commandment as such has no meaning for pagans. Now in this sense there are certain passages in Karl Barth which could lead to confusion. We must at this point get rid of an ambiguity. When, for example, Barth says that the Christian ethic is affirmed as valid for all,[32] this is based on the notion of responsibility: "The covenant of grace is the beginning of all the ways and works of God and thus the human existence which it determines is that of every man. Hence every man is a responsible being"—that is obvious. But this absolutely does not mean that the Christian ethic as such is enforceable and rightly recognized as the only true ethic for a pagan. It can only be discerned as true within the received revelation, and it can only be recognized as enforceable from the starting point of a known grace. So every man is in truth responsible as he is in truth under the lordship of Jesus Christ, but the ethic which flows from faith cannot be set before him as valid par excellence.

That God's requirement should be set before men at the same time that the gospel is proclaimed to them, that they cannot take flight into irresponsibility, and hence that the law and the commandment should be affirmed as valid also for them even if they are not Christians but because they belong to Christ (whether they know it or not)—all that is true. But it is no less true that the life in Christ which constitutes the reality of that ethic is also, and at the same time, impossible, incomprehensible, literally meaningless, and unlivable for them.

Thus, one of the essential rules of the Christian life is never to ask a non-Christian to conduct himself like a Christian. If grace really renews a person, if the Christian life is already evidence of the life of someone who is in Christ, if obedience to the Christian ethic is the loving response of a recipient of grace to him who has shown his love by bestowing grace, then how can one ask a man who has not received, or who did not know that he was under grace, to act as though . . . as though his person were renewed, as though he had experienced grace bestowed upon him, as though he knew that he was the object of God's love? The obligation placed upon him is nothing but restraint. The morality to which he submits can only be based upon the fear of punishment, and God becomes then the great condemner. In fact, that is what regularly happens in so-called Christian societies. The other aspect, in a secular or non-Christian society, derives from the same conviction that Christian morality is basically superior; and thus it carries within itself the implication that the non-Christian should obey it. But since in this society the Christians do not possess the means of constraint, they confine themselves to judging (including Christians who are solidly attached to secularity and who are "open to the world").

It is enough to reflect on the way Christians are scandalized when they come up against modes of conduct which are really inspired by another morality. If the worst comes to the worst, they will often be understanding toward an individual but uncompromising toward the state, for example. Christians never tire of demanding that the non-Christian state revoke the death penalty because human life is sacred before God, that the state enact a special statute for conscientious objectors because God said, "You shall not kill." These are the same Christians who rightly demand that the state be secular, but why do they not see the complete inconsistency? Why would the secular state recognize the will of God? Christians, likewise, are scandalized whenever the state puts a realistic policy into effect, puts expediency first, violates principles that are proclaimed as Christian. But how can one hold it against a state which is not Christian—and which cannot be—for not acting as a Christian state? [33] This state is subject to necessity. It usually obeys the necessity. Christians, alas, are in a splendid position to criticize the state, but only because they themselves are not faced with that necessity. Whenever they enter upon public functions they generally engage in similar politics because politics is always an art of the possible, which takes for granted that one acts with an eye to the necessities.

To be sure, it is not here a matter of justifying the excesses, the illegalities, the dishonesties of the state. It is not a question of saying, then, that "anything goes"—certainly not. But on the one hand the state is faced with necessities, and when Christians refuse to take that into account they are hypocrites. On the other hand the state is called upon to apply a morality which is not the Christian morality. It applies the morality of the world, but still a morality; and it is from within that morality and in relation to it that the Christian is called upon to judge whatever the state does. To protest to the state against torture in the name of

Jesus Christ is absurd. To protest in the name of the declaration of rights, a moral principle that the state itself has
established, is legitimate. So the Christian, recognizing the
relative validity of that morality, should recall it to non-
Christians, for it is an element of the preservation of society, a principle of life; and he should, in a way, act as a
guardian of it. The Christian and the church should take
absolutely seriously the declarations, principles, formulas,
values in which the moralists, the politicians, the jurists,
and even public opinion express their convictions; and taking them seriously they should assume them, recall them,
and confront men's actions with the principles which they
have prescribed for themselves.

Thus the Christian is not to judge this morality as such.
He is not to place the two moralities in competition and
assert the superiority of one over the other, because they
are not in competition in society. Christian morality is not
something to proclaim objectively as a requirement applicable to all. In what name would this objective superiority
be recognized? In the name of Jesus Christ? But in this society Jesus Christ is not recognized as the Son of God. In
the name of the content of the morality? But who is to
judge the superiority of the content of one over the other?
In the name of the conduct of Chrisitans? But in point of
fact the Christians do not behave "better" than the others.
And then, too, better with respect to what?

We are in the same dilemma in the scene of public action
as in private action. Why should we ask an alcoholic to
give up his vice for the sake of Jesus Christ if he does not
believe in Jesus Christ? When you broach this question you
realize that there are only two answers: either you appeal
to the current morality which is accepted by all—with its
extreme weaknesses and tendencies to change—or indeed
you witness to Jesus Christ, and you pray for this man's
conversion which would be translated into a new way of
life. It is in the same sense that we should pray for the
authorities, who are human beings. But beyond that, we

should maintain dialogue with the non-Christian and with the secular state on another level. That is, recognizing the validity of the morality which they are following, it is *also* fitting to proclaim the will of God in terms of witnessing, and of declaring that will as coming from the God who is not recognized as such. It would not be set forth as à morality to be obeyed without recognizing God. "The Lord of heaven and earth says . . ."

Christians and the church generally do not dare to talk that way. They are afraid of being ridiculed. They are careful to denature God's will. They do not act like the ambassadors of that Lord. Instead of admitting as natural the obedience of man to his human morality, instead of telling him about the Lord's will which calls him to something else, Christians commit a double error. They present as natural a morality which is supposed to represent the will of God. They act in the same way toward the state and toward community groups. That is why their judgments and opinions in these domains are so often nonexistent. Either they mistake for God's will a moral attitude which is purely sociological, or they are scandalized by conduct born of necessity. But when, on the contrary, a Christian declares God's will in the presence of the state, then he introduces his own personal tension into society.[34] He himself becomes a source of contradiction. But this is remarkably fruitful. By it he keeps society "open," prevents it from crystallizing and developing sclerosis.

When the Christian does not condemn, when instead of trying to do away with the world's morality he declares the consequences of the lordship of God, then he plays the most fruitful, the most positive, the most original role possible: putting the tension into society and thus keeping it alive. He restores society's ability to develop. He offers a truly revolutionary interpretation of life. And it is precisely he alone who can play this role. He causes positive, living, and fruitful contradiction to gush forth in the heart of a society which prefers to be simplex and which pretends to deny and resolve the contradictions. Does the state employ violence? So be it—but in so doing let it not claim to be good, just, and human. Does human justice depend for its existence upon constraint, based on punishment and the threat of punishment? Of course! It would be childish idealism to hope for anything else. But then let it not be called justice and good. Are law and order indispensable? Is authority's requirement of obedience and respect legitimate? Should the mobilization of people's wealth, hearts, and bodies be set forth as a moral duty? Perhaps. But then let no one call it freedom.

Now justice, love, freedom, are not human inventions. They are not platonic values. They are decisions of God. They cannot be broken. But they are in critical contradiction with the pretentions of man, of society, of the state. This contradiction is not something to avoid.[35] It needs rather to be brought out as strongly as possible, not for opposition's sake, but in order that this man, this society, this state, even if one is opposed to them, should *live;* for without this contradiction they would die. The excess of law and order, of mobilization, of duties and restraints, cannot be curbed from inside by a self-discipline, nor by a juridical organization. They only come to a halt before an external obstruction. The latter is the No of the Christian requirement, formulated simultaneously with the Yes to this social moral order. Ricoeur rightly says that the Christian must constantly make the choice: whether to obey the will of God—that is, to love—in sacrificing human justice, or to exercise human justice (accept the moral duty of belonging to society) in sacrificing love. This choice can never be final. It has constantly to be repeated. It can never be satisfying. One can never "set his conscience at rest" when he has opted in this manner. It is too simple to say that "as a Christian I should obey God rather than man." That is true of course, but it cannot be done in strict justice. If in obeying God I disobey the state (which God ordains that I obey) I disassociate myself from my neighbor (whom

God ordains that I love). In judging the unbelievers I cast them far from me (and I shall no longer be able to witness in their presence). I am not so surely "on the right path" as all that. So the only possibility is to go from decision to decision, from choice to choice, to maintain the tension between the two requirements, in such a way that the breach continues in the hearts of those around us and in the society in which we live.

In the wall of morality which man wants to build for himself, behind which he hopes to find shelter from God, there must be a breach for God's will to pass through. It is the tension lived by the Christian between the two moralities in this society which is, of itself, the breach of God, the breach through which God passes, whenever his word causes his requirement to reecho in a life within which the Christian has born witness, in a society in which the Christian has lived, in which he has participated. And when the word is presented so alive that God's requirement is beyond dispute, then the tension can disappear, for the word carries its decisive contradiction to the moral order which can only explode. The choice becomes radical and necessary. There is no longer any obedience which holds to the order of the world. There is a judgment of that order by holiness. The explosion of the revelation destroys the ethic of the world. Whether it is a question of the morality of the individual, his decisions and his choices, or whether it is a question of the moral order of society with its imperatives, ideals, and structures, the tension would be still another compromise and a betrayal if it were the lasting solution to the contradiction. But now this tension is itself called continually into question by the requirement of absolute obedience, of undivided loyalty, which the word of God causes to reecho in our lives.

He who lives in the tension between the two moralities should not think himself more righteous than he who chooses the one while sacrificing the other, for precisely to him living in this tension the question of the prophet is ceaselessly directed, "How long will you go limping with two different opinions?" (1 Kings 18:21).[36]

Let us recall once again that all of man's ethical effort, all his seeking, all his constructions, are not just simply denied and rejected by God. All of this is still a matter of a work of man, and although it issues from sin it is a work which God saves *with* man, with the works of this man, but which God saves in taking it upon himself in the death of his Son, which he saves by the passage through judgment— and not because that work would be good of itself!

Niebuhr is undoubtedly right in saying that this ethic will be judged by Christ and not by the Father, hence judged on its possibilities and its sin, not on its finitude. But we need to go farther. Insofar as this ethic is a product of disobedience, God only maintains it in destroying the evil which it represents. But he only destroys the evil in taking its consequences upon himself in the expiation. At that moment, in the heavenly Jerusalem, that which man has called good throughout the course of his history, and under various disguises, will become an integral part of that which God himself calls good. Hence we can say that man participates in this way, by grace, in God's very will for the heavenly Jerusalem. But we have no right to draw any conclusion from that concerning the present validity in and of itself of this human morality—and still less can we assume a continuity between this morality and the declaration of the good in the kingdom of God.

II

Morality of the World

Without getting into an exhaustive study of morality and of the various moralities,[1] let us state at the outset that precisely within the perspective of the recognition of a double morality it seems indispensable to stake out certain points of reference with respect to it and to the moralities which exist in the world. We must do so with realism. Much later on we shall have to examine the fact that realism is one of the very characteristics of Christian behavior in the world. But here, by the very nature of our project, we are already prepared to accept a realistic analysis of the ethical phenomenon. Indeed, this is not a matter of formulating an ideal morality valid for all mankind, and of giving reasons why it should be obeyed. Neither is this a question of searching for the "if" and the "why" of the authority of an eventual morality.

We have said that, in accordance with revelation and as a consequence of faith, that which ought to be done, that which ought to be obeyed, is the will of God. From then on we have no reason to give voice to a wish concerning ethics, nor to embellish it with a justification, nor to construct a new system. One needs, quite simply, to consider what is the reality of the ethical phenomenon, under all its aspects if possible, and in its contemporary manifestation and presence. We cannot go along with any glorification which would tend to make of morality more than it is, which is what nearly all do who live a completely worthy life or construct a satisfying ethical system. We cannot transpose into an ideal and an absolute a morality that, in its wording as well as in its practice and authority, is a real fact. Morality does not transcend man. It is of man.[2]

The rejection of idealism requires that we consider ethics at the level of man, and nowhere else. Nothing either in observation or reflection would lead us to make of morality an event from heaven. Such a result could only be produced by metaphysics, and the standpoint which we adopted in advance prohibits that free play. Morality is of man. It is created by him. That was the teaching of Genesis. It is also an observation that anyone can make for himself, if he is not dominated by sentimentalism, the concern for justification, or the idealist philosophy of the moment. To be sure, this formula of a morality created by man should not be taken in a simplistic or one-sided sense. It is manifold and ambiguous; for example, the product of the group or of a moral requirement, an expression of intellectual rigor or of an act of conscience. We shall have to consider these various aspects of morality. But in every case the origin of morality, of its authority and of its structure, lies with man himself. It is neither a divine gift nor a product of higher nature over and above man.[3] It is not universal. It is tied to the power which man has taken upon himself of "knowing good and evil" and of deciding concerning them. By that decision man does indeed relate himself to the gods. But the process is not, as it has too often been described, that the gods (and, what difference does it make—transcendent reason?) formulate a morality which they communicate to men. Then the latter, by observing that morality, raise themselves above the human status.

The reality is quite other than that. Man, importuned to be like the gods—and of course it is just the same when man denies the existence of God, the obsession to be like God being characteristic of Sartre, whose entire work is explained by this resentment—decides concerning good and evil. Thereby he becomes indeed like the gods; and then follows the frustration of application, practice, and judgment. That is when man really finds out that he is not a god. Realism in the examination of this phenomenon is the only attitude that allows us to grasp, in its entirety and without confusion, what it is.[4]

Without giving way to an academic failing, it is useful to recall that the moral phenomenon is made up of a great number of diverse elements.[5] When all is said and done, whatever the frame of reference adopted—for example, aspiration, tradition, virtues, the final end—the object of the moral life is *always* the fulfillment of what man in a given time and place calls the good. That is why we cannot entirely agree with Gurvitch when, in the course of his analysis, he takes pains to eliminate the term good itself. To say that "the moral enterprise is a struggle against the obstacles to human effort (collective or individual) regarded as a showing worthy of disinterested approbation" is undoubtedly right, but one is obliged to add that this approbation will take place because there is a general agreement on the temporal idea of the good! It is erroneous to reject this from the sociological investigation for fear of entering upon a philosophic debate concerning the good!

First of all, there is an "objective" morality, which is a system of values or of imperatives, whether formulated or not, which are set forth as possessed of an objectivity indispensable. to all members of the group. This set of moral principles affirms the superiority of a certain conduct, and presents certain ideal objectives to be achieved. In the last analysis, its authority always depends on an assertion of practicality. There is always a matter of success in some domain or other which provides the foundation for the authority of objective morality. The promise can have to do with happiness, or with the development of a higher type of man, or with reward, or with the favor of the gods, or with stability and security, or with the achievement of progress—in any case it is the declaration that in carrying out the rule of morality one will find himself in a better situation than the one in which he now is.

In this objective morality, we can discern at least three constituent elements quite different from one another: first of all, theoretical morality. As a system it is drawn up in an imperative manner, whether by a religious authority or by a philosopher. It can represent a moral ideal, but it is generally a work of individuals, of outstanding persons. It contains a strong intellectual element, and its authority is the more firmly established and affirmed for being less immediately felt by its contemporaries.

Next, we come upon sociological morality, that which springs from a collective necessity, whether that necessity derives from religious or magical beliefs, or from a political imperative, or from an economic need. In any case, this morality is not the expression of an individual conscience, but of a collective conviction based on individual convictions, yet at the same time constraining them. It is not generally set forth in a systematic and structural manner, but it stands for a very broad assemblage of values and imperatives, more or less consistent, more or less inconsistent. It is related either to the necessity for preserving the group as such, or to the ideal image which the group has of itself and of humanity. In any event, this morality is coupled with a requirement and with an authority.

Last of all comes moral custom. In the ethical domain the group follows certain customs, which are no longer requirements (in that, they differ from the preceding case) but conformities. These moral customs are derived from the past. They are not a striving for the future. Their authority rests on their antiquity, on tradition (and not, as in the case of sociological morality, on a currently valued ideal image). They are not just manners; for these moral customs are also, for their part, imperatives. They have a content of regulation which is not to be departed from. A definite judgment falls on whoever disobeys. Yet there is, to be sure, a close connection between manners and these customs. Well-established manners become custom, and a custom which is attacked, demoted, and contradicted by the moral ideal of the moment will be treated as manners. Similarly, custom has only a social (collectively decreed) sanction, and to a certain degree it can be the same for manners. In any case, the latter stand for a purely factual aspect. At that level, there is no conflict between what is and what ought to be.

Manners are purely and simply the actual comportment of the members of a group in some sphere or other. They can be completely out of accord with the theoretical morality. They can be relatively and hardly so with the sociological morality. In that case, the conflict may lead in the long run to the formulation of a new sociological morality, but the latter puts up a resistance. It brings down judgment on the new manners which call it into question, and which now become "bad manners." The struggle takes place on the collective level and on the individual level at the same time. Sociological morality and manners can never be identified with each other. The former, in reality, always formulates an imperative ideal principle, sets forth patterns to be adhered to: but it does so precisely because one does not adhere to them naturally, does not live that way spontaneously. Sociological morality tends to teach manners. Moral custom, on the contrary, may very well have no quarrel with manners.

As a counterpart to this objective morality, there is a subjective morality. It is made up of at least two elements. We have first to take into account what might, in a pinch, be called "the imperative of conscience." The individual feels imperatively within himself that a given act is good, and that he must obey it. The "voice of conscience" indicates good and evil to him. It is a purely individual phenomenon. There appears to be an intuitive knowledge of a transcendent reality. The good, known directly, imposes itself authoritatively. If one disobeys it, one feels discomfort and judgment. If one obeys it, one experiences satisfaction and happiness. Whether the origin of this imperative is biological or sociological, whether it is the personalized product of education or of economic status, or indeed the expression of deep-seated impulses, complexes, resentments, uncovered by psychology, we have no need to go into that here. Up to the present time no explanation seems absolutely conclusive.

The other facet of this subjective morality is choice or

decision. The individual, confronted with objective moral-ity in one of its various forms, or, again, having felt the command of conscience, is placed, knowingly or unknow-ingly, in the presence of a choice: to obey, or not to obey. He must make his own decision, for it is he who is going to act. At that moment (and only at that moment) there is properly speaking an ethical "situation." The individual is going to decide of himself concerning his action. He is going to risk the judgment, to make himself carry out the good. He is going to choose. This choice may be radical and creative of being, to use a currently popular concept, or it may merely be a matter of a succession of fragmentary, modest choices which together will make up the practice of this ethical life. One can say that in this way man succes-sively chooses himself. The choice is what transforms the individual into an ethical subject. From then on he will be led eventually to formulate systematically the reason for his decision. In that event, he constructs a theoretical ob-jective morality.

These data are very summary and lacking in philosophic refinement, but as truisms they are useful. We should espe-cially be careful not to leave out any one of them, or to bring only one of them into consideration. The moral phe-nomenon is the *ensemble* of these constituent parts. Moral-ity is not *only* the ethical system of Aristotle or Kant. It is the usual temptation of philosophers to consider that alone. Even more, it does not consist exclusively of the sociologi-cal imperative and the scale of values or the manners of a society. That is the preoccupation of sociologists, who make light of all the rest. But neither is it simply a personal choice and decision. A frequent mistake of Christians, exis-tentialists, and phenomenologists is to reject objective mo-rality and to treat only the worth of the choice as essential to morality. These various partial views are errors. The basic elements to which we have called attention are mutu-ally complementary.

The Diversity of Moralities

6 The imperatives, the values, the virtues, the ethical systems, whether highly developed or not, differ greatly according to places and times.[1] That obvious fact bears repeating because, even among enlightened intellectuals, the medieval presupposition persists that Western morality is really a universal morality. There is a morality everywhere and in every society, but not necessarily the same morality. Morality has no permanent content.[2] Murder is generally reproved, but that is not always true. Without mentioning our own societies, where in time of war [3] murder is enjoined (but this is a collective decision, and one can say that it is a question of a hierarchy of values, in which one's country is valued above human life), it has to be observed that individual murder in time of peace has been set forth as a requirement of a moral kind (sometimes closely linked with magic or with religious rites). Such was the case with the Assassins, the Sicarii, the Thugs. The foundation in religion or magic absolutely did not annul the ethical quality of the decision which the member of the sect had to make, nor the ethical character of the requirement which the group laid upon that individual. The murder was not merely a magic act. It belonged truly in the category of a virtue. Nor can one argue that this was true only of restricted groups. The moment there is a group with its moral requirement, there is a morality.

Among the Incas, for example, there is *no* respect for life, and yet we are dealing with highly civilized social groups. Therefore, we cannot say that respect for life is a universal commandment, the foundation for a natural morality. It must not be argued, finally, that these examples are aberrant, exceptional, abnormal, and therefore of no importance, for most of the "associations of men" in historically resistant societies exhibit requirements of the same type. Moreover, since Freud, we know that the "abnormal" is very important, and that it can be the key to all the rest. Murder, presented as a moral requirement and a value, introduces us to a more or less universal moral phenomenon, that of vengeance.

In most societies, vengeance is a moral duty, dictated by the tribal and family solidarity of the human group. It has played an immense role, and certain moralities have been developed out of that principal concept. The Bible knows it in stating the principle of an eye for an eye, likewise the Greek and Roman societies, in the nineteenth century the Corsican society with its vendetta, or today the "underworld" of pimps and gangsters. Set forth by the group as a duty, felt in the moral conscience as an obligation, coupled with the concepts of good and evil (he who gets revenge does good, according to the common judgment; biblically, the *go'el* is he who gets revenge, so is the savior, the redeemer!), vengeance is one of the deep roots of moral duty. It is from the standpoint of vengeance that values are elaborated which are useful for justification or validation: honor, group solidarity, loyalty.

This moral notion is commonly reproved today. As soon as the state becomes organized it suppresses the exercise of vengeance, which then gradually ceases to be a moral duty and is turned over to a third organization which regulates the problem juridically. When the mechanisms of police and law courts are strong enough, at the same time that the loyalties of the smaller groups weaken, this moral duty dies out, to become in our day the object of moral reprobation. For different reasons, vengeance is considered an evil in the pseudo-Christian society of the West and in the anti-Christian Communist society.

This observation concerning vengeance can be extended to the central values of the moral systems of any given moment. We believe it can be said that a morality in a society regulates itself in relation to a value which is declared or felt to be essential. Thus there is a sort of moral axis. One can speak in this way of an ethic of the *sippe* among the Germans: all being coordinated with a view to the essential relation of the individual to the *sippe,* the good being, in fact, defined as that which is useful to the *sippe.* One can also speak of an ethic of loyalty in groups constituted around a chief, for example among the Gasindi. Later on, in the feudal group, the good is summed up in loyalty to the lord of the manor and everything is to be judged in relation to that imperative and pledge.

Such a morality can produce moral obligations which we today consider scandalous. We have called attention to vengeance, which is not individual (it can only become that when an ethic of man is developed) but relates to those bound to a group or to a lord. One curious fact is the system of cojurors. Whenever a member of the *sippe,* or whenever the lord is brought to trial, it is a *moral duty* for other members of the group to come to the trial and swear that he is right, that what happened was what their brother or their lord said happened, and they must do that even if they know nothing and have seen nothing. Their oath brings the decision of justice upon him alone. From then on, justice can be based on a lie or on assertions unrelated to reality. To lie is an ethical imperative, as it is an ethical imperative to affirm anything at all under oath. Lying and false swearing are, in this situation, moral duties—let us not forget it. It is not evil, it is good to act thus in the interest of a brother of the clan or of the family. But then where is the respect for the truth which we look upon as one of the most universal axioms of morality?

Let us recall the summary judgments passed upon the Old Testament in the nineteenth century, based on the notion that the moment the biblical authors recorded events which they knew were inexact they were no longer worthy of credence in any sphere. As a matter of fact, the concept of intangible truth and its moral value is tied to a very narrow and definite type of society and mentality. Sociologists today speak with a certain condescension of the notion of a prelogical mentality, put forth by Lévy-Bruhl, and yet it is still true in the degree in which it reminds us that our values, and our modes of thinking these values, are neither universal nor constant. We have just seen some examples in which values that we consider beyond dispute (respect for life, truth, and so on) are unknown, and that an ethic can be created "in the interest of . . ." The supreme value can be the chief, the group, and every moral system (including, of course, individual virtue and the moral conscience) plays a role "in the interest of." This is not at all confined to a primitive stage of humanity.

In the modern era we encounter at least three moralities "in the interest of": nationalism, acts are judged as they relate to the supreme value which is the nation (or one's country), racism, communism. There we are confronted with true moralities, subjective and objective, a hierarchy of values and a distinction between good and evil, virtues and judgments. But the moral criterion is extremely simple in the three cases. It is a criterion of interest. Everything done in the interest of one's country, one's race, or the proletariat is good. Everything which goes against that is bad. This rule, sometimes implied, sometimes expressed, justifies behaviors and provides the individual with a clear vision of moral duty. Is the vision simplistic? Indeed it is, by comparison with the philosophers' meditations on ethics, but man needs these simple hierarchies. That is what he lives, and not phenomenological or existentialist elaborations. Moreover, these moralities "in the interest of" are not so much more superficial than, for example, the bourgeois mo-

rality of the nineteenth century. But they call in question
the moral values labeled universal.

We are always shocked when Lenin talks about the physical liquidation of the bourgeoisie, or of lying as a good.
We can cite still another example, a very significant one,
that of Sparta. Education there necessarily led the child in
the direction of stealing and homosexuality. These two
deeds were looked upon as pedagogical values. Theft was
a proof and demonstration of cleverness, of trickery, and
of the capacity for action. Homosexuality was the means of
creating an indestructible and complete fellowship between
two comrades. These two pedagogical means were intended
to prepare young people for war. Theft and homosexuality
were not glorified as the good, but the precept not to steal
and the prohibition of pederasty (at that same period in
Israel this was punished by death) were not formulated.
The whole Lacedaemonian ethic, since it was exclusively
social, ended in considering as good everything which,
through danger and the braving of the group morality itself, might prepare a young man for his role as a warrior.
Of course one can counter all that with an overall denial:
these are not moralities.[4]

Thus Augustine, in judging pagan manners, demonstrates
that there is no such thing as pagan morality. But one has
to decree in advance that only Christian morality is morality.
But on what grounds? In virtue of the concept of a good
which is universal and always exactly like itself, and which
is expressed by Christian morality alone? We have seen
that that is untenable. In reality, for the people of a given
society this is good and that is bad. We have to see it from
their point of view and not from our own in order to agree
that they have there a morality in all its aspects. One has
to adopt the relative point of view of human understanding and not the absolute point of view of metaphysics.
This is so very true that one must remember that morality
as lived does not aim at principles, values, and abstract
statements. It promulgates particular modes of conduct. It

formulates imperatives and prohibitions in relation to concrete situations. It is always about the relations between people who live in a given place at a given moment.

No living morality enjoins searching abstractly for "the good," or "the true," but it specifies acts, feelings, objectives, which it characterizes as good or as true. It gives strict contents. It is the theorists who have been happy with abstract terms, or who have wanted to endow these terms with a universal content. But in the very degree in which living morality is precise, it is necessarily tied to a moment of history and must change with the circumstances. Again, if one wishes to deny that what we have here is a morality, one can say that to the extent to which these duties, obligations and imperatives are aimed at a target, have a purpose (for example, pedagogical), they do not constitute a morality, for the latter is characterized by an unconditional regard for certain values and by the unmotivated quality of virtue. This position seems to us untenable. All morality has a goal, even if it be to bring to pass the good. The unconditional, the unmotivated, belongs to the subjective level, and not to the level of objective morality. Now only of the latter were we able to say that it was a "morality with a view to, . . ." "in the interest of . . ."

In fascism [5] and in communism, individual virtue is quite as unconditional, quite as unmotivated, as in Stoicism or Confucianism. The situation is truly ethical for the individual, who must respect such and such a value and choose such and such a behavior. Let us not object that in these systems disrespect is punished; that whoever does not accept the racist or the proletarian morality is purged from the social group, and those who accept it are rewarded. Let us remember that it was exactly the same with the people of Israel, in medieval Christianity, in Calvin's Geneva, and in puritan America. Are we to say that since there was explicit social coercion in all these cases there was no morality?

In point of fact, if we base ourselves not on a preconceived idea but on what people live and treat as morality, we see that the latter varies extraordinarily with times and places.[6]

This diversity of moralities is even more accentuated when, for example, Simone de Beauvoir concludes that there is no answer to the question "What action is good?" [7] "You don't ask a physicist which hypotheses are true." "Morality does not give recipes. One can only propose methods." "Whenever the content of an action belies the meaning, one should not change the meaning but the content." In the last analysis this leads to a pure morality of efficacy, since there will never be any external criteria by which to identify the good action. No value can be said to be universal.[8] No opinion of the good is common to all. There is no imperative which could serve as a base for the construction of one single morality. Therefore one cannot say that there is a natural morality inhering in the nature of man or of things. If that were the case, then morality would exhibit a certain unity and consistency in spite of geographical and historical points of view. That it does not do.

I am well aware that to this report on the diversity of morality one can protest:

> You are staying on the surface of the question. You confuse the content (which is indeed quite variable), and the applications which are manifold, with the moral function in and of itself (regulative, ordering, prompting) and with its underlying principle. All men experience analogous inward urges, similar goals. They have a moral experience in common. The objectivity and the universality of morality are to be found at the point of departure, in a sort of common vocation of the humanity in man. The divergent developments beyond this original similitude are only historical accidents, superstructures, which precisely because they are superstructures presuppose a fundamental, human moral unity. You think the whole ocean is rough because you see the waves, but these are

only on top of the quiet mass of the depths, and the reality is in those quiet depths.[9]

This abstraction of a moral phenomenon considered in and of itself, without content, without tangible reality, without a defined rule, seems to me simply unimaginable. It is a purely intellectual operation, completely gratuitous and at the same time dreadfully facile.

Morality only exists in particular species. To try to consider it outside these species for the sake of asserting their mutual identity is merely to say: a morality exists everywhere. Let us suppose: man is a moral animal. But we have absolutely no right in intellectual honesty to go further and to draw the portrait of this universal, fundamental morality [10]; to supply it with a content and a function. It was precisely for each particular morality that one had begun by saying that the specific traits of this portrait, this content, this function, were only accidents, effects of history, whose divergences were to be rejected because superficial. Now the portrait, the function, the content, which we are going to determine for our universal morality will be, by the same token as the others, accidents, superstructures. How can they be otherwise? And what is more, they will be abstract and theoretical. On what authority, from the standpoint of what truth, am I to ascribe unity and universality to the content, to the function of a morality, or of morality in general, when none of the facts allow me to do so? [11]

We return to the situation expressed by the Bible. For all mankind there is a good and an evil. There is a moral life. There is the *necessity* to formulate a morality. But man is burdened with formulating it himself. There is no content given in advance. Nothing outside himself has determined: "This is the good." He is now the one who has to say it, and since he finds himself in unbelievably changeable situations his ethical decisions are subject to endless change. In order to challenge that, one would have to take the road followed by a great many moralists. On that road, one does not bother with what, in reality, is acknowledged as morality in a given place and time. One formulates a morality, whether by pilfering from all the moralities, or by assuming a revelation or a metaphysical principle, or by entering into a phenomenological analysis of the individual, and one decrees that this morality alone is just, eternal, and universal, the point of reference for placing all the others. This brings us directly to the theoretical moralities. Unfortunately, there is no more agreement among the theoretical moralities than among the lived moralities, which destroys the moralist's claim to universality.[12]

The Theoretical Moralities

7 It would, of course, be absolutely impossible to describe, however sketchily, the innumerable theoretical moralities developed in the course of time by philosophers, founders of religions, etc., the moralities of Moses, Confucius, Aristotle, Plato, the Stoics, Saint Thomas, Erasmus, Kant, Nietzsche—moralities based on the order and harmony of the world of ideas in Plato, on the rational nature of man in Aristotle, on the divine substance in Spinoza, on the objective mind in Hegel, on the collective conscience in Durkheim, all of which recognize a highest good. It would also be impossible to describe the moralities billeted entirely in man, linked to his exploiter-exploited situation in Marx, the morality of the libertines formulated by Bussy-Rabutin, the morality of eroticism expressed by Sade, the morality of violence in Sorel, phenomenological moralities in Husserl and Scheler, the morality of ambiguity in Sartre and Simone de Beauvoir, the "concrete" morality of Hesnard, the "biological" morality of Chauchard, and many others. It is futile to attempt to describe and analyze them. We shall rather try to understand this phenomenon of theoretical morality as a whole.

We must note that, with one or two exceptions (at least one outstanding one: Confucius), the occurrence of theoretical moralities, of reflection upon morality, of the intellectual elaboration of an ethic, is essentially a Mediterranean phenomenon. This abstract and general, cohesive and systematic questioning of human conduct is closely connected with the Judeo-Greek civilization. Moreover, it is this fact which has led the West to suppose that since there was no intentionally ordered system of ethics in the other civilizations there was no morality there. One should, on the contrary, reverse the point of view and observe that, among all the various civilizations which have had moralities, only (or almost only) the Mediterranean civilization has created theoretical morality. In short, theoretical morality is a phenomenon limited in time and space.

Let us recall, first of all, that theoretical morality is never "pure," that is, unaffected by its milieu.[1] It is always, to a greater or less extent, an expression of the environment in which it is elaborated. For example, the idea would never have occurred to Saint Thomas to construct a morality outside the basic principles of Christianity. The intellectual, philosophical, religious, scientific trends of the moment very strongly (but not totally) determine the moralist in his creation of a new system of ethics. Yet this moralist strives for an exact product. He wants to settle that which *should be* with the maximum of impartiality, to put a group of precepts together logically, to provide a rational justification for the requirements of the moral conscience of the moment, and in pursuing this ambition he goes far beyond the working morality of the group in which he finds himself. He generally goes beyond it along three paths [2]: either he pushes the moral precepts to the realm of the absolute by transforming them into an ideal, or he introduces rationality into ethics, or he systematizes that which, left alone, would remain somewhat incoherent. In any event, a certain discord is introduced between the existing morality and theoretical morality—a distance, a divergence, which can keep increasing, and which can even end in opposition even though the two share an identical point of departure and an identical context.

All of this brings us to a consideration of the great weakness of theoretical moralities; namely, their lack of application. Whether applicable or not, they usually are scarcely applied in fact. The inhabitants of a city, the members of a group, the citizens of a nation, give very little heed to the morality developed by one of their number. Who, apart from the specialists, is interested in Kant's ethics? [3] It is a matter for the philosophers, and the philosophers have no influence over morals. Even when there is a deep community of interests between the group and the moralist, the latter is still a stranger and his morality is not applied. In spite of the close relations between Sorel and the unions, his ethical works have remained a dead issue. Practically no one feels directly involved in the ethics of Aristotle, and still less today in the ethics of Husserl. A few intellectuals know them, but one can say that by the very fact that it is a matter for intellectuals the dialogue remains at that level, rather than at the level of practical behavior. And no one thinks to govern his life according to the outcome of the quarrels among the specialists in philosophical ethics.

Thus there could be a real temptation to deny any importance to theoretical morality. In fact, of what use is an ethic which is supposed to lay down rules for attaining the good when no one puts it into practice? [4] On the supposition that its only purpose is practical application, one can say that the enterprise makes no sense. We shall see that this extreme judgment is not entirely fair. At the same time it has to be admitted that these theoretical moralities, for all the impression they make on intellectuals by their expression, their inner logic and their cleverness, are of minor importance in the ethical phenomenon as a whole. Moreover, we have to distinguish two principal tendencies among the moral theorists. There are those who, on the basis of certain principles, attempt to set forth that which *ought to be*—the rule of the ideal life, the procedure for attaining perfection, holiness. That was the preoccupation of the ancients. They then create a morality out of whole cloth.

In our day, a more discreet trend tries rather to account for what is. The philosopher analyzes the moral procedures actually in effect. He does not begin with principles, but with observations of fact. He is not so much seeking to formulate an ideal morality as to interpret the lived morality. He is trying to be guided by the paths in which morality takes form. Psychologists and sociologists confine themselves to reporting what is, and they supply a minimum of explanation. One cannot speak of moralists here, except in the sense of the morality of technology, to which we shall return later. But with the given facts as a point of departure, there is a great temptation to elaborate a morality which, while setting forth ethical rules and bringing values to light, would proceed not from principles but from established facts.[5]

Such was Durkheim's ethical enterprise. Beginning with sociological investigation, he claimed to "produce a morality"—a theoretical morality with a sociological foundation, a morality which would be an interpretation of social reality and of man's group behavior, yet which would be imperative. M. Gurvitch has thoroughly demonstrated how the effort really led to a semimetaphysical morality. It was necessary to determine an absolute good to be embodied in society. An external criterion of morality had to be established, namely, community of interests. "The social being is the highest good, and there is a moral value in bringing conduct into conformity with that being." Thus, even though based on factual observation, sociological morality does not avoid the presuppositions of all theoretical moralities, in particular, that of the permanence of social nature and of human nature.[6]

Such also is Hesnard's investigation. With psychic and sociological analyses as a point of departure, he sought to define a "socialized morality of action favorable to man," which has the possibility of being a morality without constraint, tending to activity, and without reference to the interior life. To us of the twentieth century these attempts seem much more valid than all that went before, but perhaps that is merely our attachment to what is being done in our own times. The scientifically based moralities claim to be universal. They aim, finally, at bringing to pass the old dream of all moralists, that of laying down a uniform rule of conduct valid for all mankind. That stems from the presupposition of the universal character of all scientific inquiry.

In Hesnard's eyes, a concrete social morality should meet with everyone's approval because it would be based solidly on psychological analysis. On the assumption that the moral imperative would coincide with man's psychic tendencies and psychological needs, there should be no trouble adopting it, since man would go in that direction of his own accord. But first it would be necessary to rid morality of the notions of sin, restraint, and of the mechanisms of guilt feelings and defense. Moral concerns which inhibit action would have to be replaced by an accent on action achieved. There would have to be a transition from the negative to the positive, from the egocentric stance to the "act on behalf of man." Furthermore, since this morality would correspond to tendencies already in the individual, there would be no difficulty putting it into practice. In fact, once the psyche is released from the paralyzing vestiges of Christian morality, a moral choice would no longer be required. The individual would move instinctively in the direction of concrete social morality.

To a slight degree, Dr. Chauchard exhibits some of the same concern, when he tries to show that morality and biology are harmonious, and that it should be possible to find biological foundations for a common morality. It is not a question of extracting a morality from biology, but our present knowledge of the brain allows us to assert that the principles of traditional and spiritualistic morality are in accord with the biological activity of the brain. According to the biologist, man need only bring into effective play all the potentialities which are contained physically in the

lobes of the brain in order to discover the full application
of the great principles of morality. These moral activities
would be the expression of the activity of the frontal lobe
of the brain. There again, we see that one is led to dissipate
moral choice into thin air. The individual has no choice
to make in such conduct. He need only develop the biological components of his person, and that will lead automatically to a moral life.

Unfortunately, the moralities of Hesnard and Chauchard,
drawn from different but equally scientific disciplines, are
not at all identical! Yet their effort is interesting because
it exhibits a conscientious concern for practical application.
It is easy to formulate theoretically a magnificent moral system. The only real problem is to know who will put it into
effect and how. Hesnard and Chauchard, among others, try
to solve the problem by giving morality a foundation in the
instincts. But when we look more closely we discover that
there is no greater possibility of applying these systems than
others! The required conditions emphasized by Hesnard
are unspeakably difficult to fulfill, and will they ever be
fulfilled? With regard to the activating of the frontal lobe,
who is to persuade people to do this? It would seem just as
complicated as getting them purely and simply to live up
to precepts.

We classify the ethical attempts of existentialism among
the theoretical moralities. For in spite of the claims of existentialism to make the tangible, contingent world the object
of philosophy, and to take into account only the whole man
as he really exists, this philosophy ends in theorizing to the
extreme, and in considering (without meaning to) only
concepts unrelated to people. Sartre's plays and novels only
confirm the distance which separates man as he really is
from the existentialist concept of man. We shall take this
up again as part of the discussion of the morality of values.
Here we shall simply make two observations.

1. Existentialism's ethical inquiry is based on factual reporting which is undoubtedly correct (anguish, the absurd,

and the decisive importance of the presence of the other person). But it runs up against a criticism which in our view is conclusive, namely, that it rests on assumptions which it refuses to question, or even to see. We give two examples: first of all, the construct concerning the presence of the other person. The other person represents the requirement of an alienation from myself, so that it is encounter, or the impossibility of encounter, with the other person which constitutes moral existence. But we need to ask ourselves how it is known that I must give myself up to the other person. Whence comes this importance of the other person? Whence this obligation imposed upon me to consider the other person *in this way?* I do not find in existentialism any explanation of what, in the last analysis, is a presupposition; neither factual observation nor prior assumption (for this is ruled out) are there to justify what remains in a state of pure affirmation.

The second example has to do with the terminology employed. There is constant implied reference to values and virtues even though their preexistence is denied. Sartre says, for example, that justification can only come in solidarity with the dispossessed, and that to be free is to feel oneself guilty of all the world's injustice. But what does the word "injustice" mean if there is no standard by which to determine it, if justice is completely unknown and something to be *created?* What does "dispossessed" mean? at what level? Merely those who have not had the necessary material goods? But are we not reduced here to complete subjectivity? Or other criteria could be applied according to the anthropology adopted, and by that fact no justification is to be drawn from them. Why should it be "good" to identify oneself with the dispossessed? Likewise, when Simone de Beauvoir speaks of "responsibility," it is never specified to what question man should respond, before whom he is responsible, and with reference to what. When she speaks of "defeats" and "victories," once again, by what standards are these determined? "Certain acts can be regarded as good," she says, but who regards them, and on what grounds are they called good? One never comes out of it. The terminology cannot be emptied of its preconceived ethical content, yet one acts "as though" it had none.

2. The second thing to be observed is the close relation between this existentialist ethic and the sociological structure of the world in which it has flourished: first Germany in times of defeat and misery (1918–29), then France in its period of defeats and troubles (1936–60). Ethics denies preexistent values in a society in which there no longer are any community values. It destroys the objectivity of morality in a society in which, to all intents and purposes, there no longer is an established morality. It rejects moral idealism in a society which is driven to materialism by the sheer pressure of events, and it rejects individualistic ethics in a society which is being sociologically collectivized. It declares the world absurd because the society in which it is blossoming is disintegrating and the nations are declining. Finally, it shows that the mission of ethics is to provide man with justification, precisely in a society in which he nowhere finds a simple and sure justification. Hence we can say that this existentialist ethic is purely and simply an interpretation of local and temporal circumstances, a mirror of events. This ethic is indispensable in the United States and in the Soviet Union. The only role of Sartre, Simone de Beauvoir, and others is to raise to the level of doctrine, of metaphysics, of what ought to be, that which is simply the product of circumstances. By that very role, they supply the people of a moment with a sufficiently splendid justification for staying the way they are and being proud of it.

The majority of the ethical theories rest on an idealism. It would be impossible to exaggerate the extent of the damage which idealism has done to ethical inquiry, as well as to Christianity. For one thing, idealism establishes the good as an absolute, and from that fact, the superiority of morality over religion.[7] For another thing, it exploits numerous a prioris which completely falsify the problem. For example, the conscience is an absolute, individual, and universal category, having a defined content and in relation with the Absolute. Similarly: man is good by nature; Christianity is applicable in the political and economic spheres (which would avoid revolution), in the form of the law of love interpreted as cooperation (on that subject consider the "Buchman Movement" and social Christianity); man can follow his reason, etc. The question is not that of optimism with regard to man but that of an idealism which misrepresents reality and (what for us is more serious) revelation. The doctrine of the Holy Spirit should eliminate all idealism from Christian thought.

Let it be said, just the same, that these moralities are not without interest, even though not put into practice. The theoretical moralities bring with them three lessons. First of all, they are always a picture of mankind, drawn by one man at a given moment.[8] And that has its value. If one man's deep experience is a common heritage, if it in some way expresses what is general, then the formulation by Socrates or Kant of the vision of the just man, of the good man, is an image capable of speaking to the heart of each person, even if it is not to be realized, even if that good man does not exist. It can have a personal appeal. The man who becomes aware of himself cannot feel truly a stranger to Confucius' wise man or to Nietzsche's free man. This image created by the will of one man will not henceforth leave other men indifferent and unaffected. The heart of humanity cannot remain closed to what has thus been deposited in it.

We can no longer speak of the moral phenomenon today in the same manner in which it was spoken of fifty years ago, because of the fact that Husserl, Jaspers, and Scheler have passed this way, and that is true even if we have not read them—which is extraordinary, as though a certain osmosis were going on within the body of civilization. But we must be careful to note that this is true only for a small number of people, the intellectuals. Just the same, if this theoretical morality is sufficiently well known and widespread, it becomes not only an image of man but the image which a society has of itself. Marx is mistaken when he sees in morality nothing but an ideological superstructure which is a cover-up for reality. If a society proclaims virtues and values, that is not in order hypocritically to conceal the deficiencies (granted that can *also* be the case) but in order to set forth a goal and an ideal. That is the role of the theoretical moralities, which in a certain way are always telling us how society looks upon itself, what standards it judges itself by, how it asks to be seen by others. Even when the ideal is not fulfilled, it is none the less stated *in* that society, and is a part of its life.

Second, we shall say that theoretical morality is never detached from its social context. In reality, it is frequently closely related to the philosophic or religious trends. But more than that, at a given moment it can crystallize diffuse beliefs and subconscious aspirations. The moralist then plays the role of recorder and catalytic agent. He brings about the stock-taking, the formulation, the externalizing of that which had been latent in the group to which he belongs. We are rightly reminded of Kant's origin and puritan milieu, yet also Kant powerfully expresses the tendencies of that milieu, earnestly Christianized, but keeping only the morality of Christianity and concerned with the grounds of that morality and of the good apart from Jesus Christ. This crystallization can be one of the most legitimate functions of theoretical morality. It does not, in that case, merely innovate but it provides serious foundations, nor is it purely hypothetical. Therefore Lévy-Bruhl's analysis is correct when he treats theoretical morality, "metamorality," as an interpretation in intellectual terms of lived morality. It gives the latter a rationale, a foundation, a justification. But that is not always true. It is not true of all the metamoralities! One cannot place all the theoretical moralities on an equal footing in this respect. Some are really expressions of the diffuse tendencies of their times. Others are not so at all.

Finally, we cannot brush aside the fact that in some cases theoretical morality can, in the long run, exercise a psychological influence, can in the long run disseminate certain commandments, encourage the exaltation of certain virtues, and contribute to the formation of a new morality.

Theoretical morality can also, from time to time, provide a true answer to concrete tragic situations. A society can find itself in such confusion that the lived morality is no longer relevant and tends to fade out. The collective beliefs are shaken, whether openly or at the subconscious level. The group, the society, is incapable of meeting the challenge which events or institutions face it with. The moralist can try to respond, can attempt to formulate new values, new combinations of values, to propose possible and effective modes of conduct whereby society through its members might find a way out of the impasse. Then this theoretical morality may eventually be accepted, if people find, feel, and believe that it offers a solution. But such a thing can only happen in a crisis and during the course of successive adjustments with a great deal of hesitation. The assumption is very general that theoretical morality can be put into practice in the long run. That is why such moralities are taken so seriously. In reality it is nothing of the sort. Only *rarely*, after being integrated into the body politic with a great deal of toning down or dilution, can theoretical morality contribute to lived morality. This brings us to an investigation of the theoretical moralities which are applied.

In certain instances, quite rare it is true, theoretical moralities have actually been applied.[9] So the morality of Confucius, that of Moses, that of Paul, the Stoic morality, and the Marxist morality. It is a serious and difficult problem to know why some moralities have been adopted and not others. One would have to analyze each case separately, since each exhibits, in fact, its own specific character. Nevertheless, certain general observations are possible. All these moralities have been applied not in their purity, their integrity, their high point, but in adaptations in the form of a practical code, in their results and not in their sources of inspiration, and after many a corruption. The transition from the formulation of a requirement to its practical application brings about a very profound change in the very structure and in the significance of the morality. That was the "crisis" of second-generation Christianity, likewise of the second Marxist generation and of the "rediscovery" of the law of Moses. To the degree in which the doctrine remains absolutely pure it is not applied. It can be said that the morality of Confucius was applied to the extent to which he was betrayed by his followers. There is a great deal of truth in that. Perhaps a morality is more susceptible of application when it is susceptible to corruptions and to modifying interpretations. A system which is too strict remains foreign to man, who turns aside from its rigidity.

In addition, these moralities are for the most part adopted by a group or society not as morality, but as accessory to something else. It happens as a consequence of a religion, of a political movement, or of a social transformation. We must not forget that the morality of Confucius was not given general application until Confucian orthodoxy was proclaimed by the Han dynasty. So it was for Christian morality and for Marxist morality. It can even be said that the adoption of a theoretical morality by the state is a fairly general historical phenomenon. The state needs a covering moral affirmation whenever it claims to give true leadership to society. Now it is much easier for it to adopt a theoretical morality, because the latter is well-formulated, clear, precise, and systematic. Moral orthodoxy useful to the state only obtains when there is a "doxy." It is even possible that this decision on the part of the state is one of the principal determinants differentiating moralities destined to be applied from the others! After all, even Stoicism gained wide acceptance in the Roman Empire by way of the ruling classes.[10]

The objection may be made that we are misplacing the moral problem by making it a mass problem; that morality remains what it is within itself, even if applied by *only one* person (if it is theoretical, by its founder, for example); that the collective application is not what counts. Yet it is that application in common which does count. Morality presupposes relationships among the members of a group, and these members obey a morality of mutuality. Robinson Crusoe really did not know morality, and the solitary moralist who obeys his own ethic in a society does so in *pro* and *contra* relationship with his group. Indeed, the problem of collective application is decisive, not by reason of numbers, but because of the very nature of morality.

In addition, apart from the intervention of the state, the application may also come out of a social mutation. It is well known, for example, that Christian morality was inapplicable among the peoples of Africa and of the South Pacific, except in the degree in which social structures collapsed under the attacks of Western conquerors.

Finally also, it is when the theoretical moralities are a crystallization of surrounding moral conditions that they have the best chance of being applied. Application supposes a sort of prior agreement. When an ethical system is the fruit of collective aspirations it is quite understandable that it could be put into practice. It is easy to point out that just those moralities which have been applied, even though they were theoretical, were deeply rooted in social customs, aspirations, and judgments. That was frequently demonstrated for Christianity, Confucianism, etc. For this reason one can say in our day, for example, that among the various systems of morality proposed by the theorists, only the normal morality, of which we shall speak later on, has some chance of being applied. Others—existentialist, phenomenological, etc.—much more intelligent, more lofty, more true perhaps, have no chance at all of escaping the category of play.

Values

8 Exactly at this point it is impossible to avoid a discussion of values. The philosophy of values brings out clearly the metaphysical character of phenomenology and existentialism. As a morality, it is a theoretical morality, and even more a metaphysical morality. Hence it is subject to the analysis of the preceding paragraph. On the other hand, however, this philosophy of values emphatically repudiates this metaphysical character. It casts the ought-to-be out of the domain of morality. It claims to take reality into account and to base itself on experience. It pretends to say and to describe only that which is. Hence it should serve as an introduction to what we call "lived morality."

The essential question which we shall attempt to answer is, obviously, Does this morality of values fulfill its claims? Does it really take into account that which is? Here, then, one is justified in hesitating between a philosophy of values and a sociology of values—the first having principally to do with the justification, the validity and the authority of values; the second with studying their objective reality, their variations as functions of social settings. The leaders of this philosophy customarily repudiate the second aspect, considering it to be superficial and secondary. By way of concession, they will acknowledge that value is tied to sociological realities, and especially to culture. The latter, in fact, is in the background of the communication of values. It is the means whereby people conceive and share the same values. Cultures condition values. Yet they quickly come back to the fact that all culture is human, and that, when all is said and done, it is the person alone who counts. Often it will even be thought that it is value which determines culture, and that economic and political conflicts are in reality conflicts of values. Thus the sociological reality becomes secondary. From our standpoint, we would be tempted to put value back into its social setting, and only to treat as real the sociological analysis of values. But first, a few words are in order as to what it is we are dealing with.

This is not an easy matter, since the moment the question is raised of defining value, many phenomenologists and existentialists beg off. Value is not to be defined. It is felt. It is sensed. One leans on it for support and as a guide, but it is too atmospheric for any precise grasp. At the same time, there is an abundance of slanted definitions.[1]

Value is defined by the personal experience of the life of a man as that which permits him to endow the world with contrasting features, and which is only to be known in activity. There is no prior perception nor intuition of value. It does not appear to man except in his presence to the world. One can never deduce value from being. It is not a mode of conduct conformed to being. It is the opposite of a moral principle. It is often compared to a magnet, or to a magnetic pole, but again, it is not predetermined. It is in man's relation to the concrete that value can appear. It constantly calls for movement on man's part and can never be institutionalized nor objectified. Man chooses his values in acting, and he makes them currently real in his action. When he chooses values which cause him to act, then he carries out a moral act par excellence. It is evident that this philosophy presupposes the freedom of the man who chooses his values and who is free in his choice. The value is a motif in the decision of a personal freedom. Man in freedom runs up against the value, which sets a limit for him. The ethical subject is necessarily free, since it is his decision which is to promote the value and reject the antivalue. More than that, the freedom of the man is registered in the totality of choices which establishes a system of values peculiar to that man. It is also evident that this philosophy of values defines a "situation ethic." The value is not known in advance, but only by the man in a situation.

There is no prior good and no prior evil, in and of themselves, which a man might grasp. He is in an ethical beginning at every moment. One could say, in carrying this through to the end, that each man reconstitutes morality at each moment, for it is only when confronted with an obstacle that the individual invokes value and seizes upon it anew. This brief list of traits allows us to grasp certain difficulties and contradictions inherent in the philosophy of values. We must reflect, first of all, on the historical occasion of the appearance of this philosophy. Here is a philosophy which declares, on the one hand, that there is no metaphysical good, that there are no rules, no commandments, no self-contained imperatives; which sets up an ethic of ambiguity and compromise. On the other hand it promotes values, declares that the only ethical situation is that of choice, that value has an exclusively revolutionary function, and that man is free.

This philosophy developed in the period between 1930 and 1950. To locate this philosophy in its historical moment is immediately to bring out its double character as an "interpretation of the moment" and as a "compensation." At a time when Western civilized man finds himself plunged into all possible ambiguities, when there clearly is no longer a notion of good and evil, when the good is constantly contradicted, when there no longer is any sense of duty, when all action is the fruit of compromise, when a rule no longer has authority, then that philosophy triumphs which is the ideological translation of this state of affairs, and which puts individual choice above all prior moral certitude. But, also, at a time when human freedom is reduced on all sides, when external determinants are

more pressing, when "order" is everywhere triumphant and
a truly revolutionary movement seems no longer possible,
when values are in short supply and under attack, then
philosophy plays its compensating role in protesting the
existence of that which is about to disappear, and in affirming it the more loudly as its reality diminishes.

In addition, it is in the very interior of the philosophy
of values that the contradictions appear. We shall take two
examples. This philosophy claims to restore the concern
for the concrete in morality. One must take the fleshly man
as the point of departure. "I must begin with myself, with
my limited existence." These values are located strictly in
this world, as near as can be to what we are. They are an
object of experience, which is decisive (the moralities of
Kant and Durkheim are wrong in robbing man of his experience). The experience of value is an experience of the
individual person. The individual is at the point of departure. Now this project is indeed fulfilled in practice. Every
philosopher of value begins with his own experience and
his own person. That is quite fascinating, but it is a matter
of the experience of a philosopher who is a philosopher by
profession; that is, in this instance, a man of the West, in
the mid-twentieth century, specialized in a certain type of
reasoning and in a certain oracular language. And this man,
in describing his experience of value, claims to be convey-
ing to us a common experience, valid for any man at all,
and universal.[2] He claims that what he himself has experienced and recognized as value is real also for man as man.
A reading of these works makes obvious their lack of connection with man as he really is. No man, apart from these
philosophers, has experience of this type, acknowledges this
level of freedom or conducts his life within this perspective.
No man is the "ethical subject" who is being talked about.
The tangible, supposedly being restored for us, is the tangible of the philosopher himself.

Another contradiction involves the ethical concept of
situation.[3] This concept claims to restore freedom to the
individual by releasing him from prior determinations of

good and evil, to respect the complete subjectivity of the individual and to make him fully responsible morally. But if man be considered as he really is, to place him "in situation" is to place him in a concrete situation, defined by economic, social, and family factors. Now at that moment, the only moment of importance, the ethic of the situation becomes the most objective and objectifying imaginable. The individual in his private existence, in his intentions and feelings, does not count. What does count is the situation and his reaction to that situation. He is of a certain profession or trade. He belongs to a given class of society. He suffers from a given alienation. One will hardly take his virtues and vices into account, but only his situation. Whatever he might be within himself, he will never surmount that determining factor.

The operations carried out by the philosophers of value have to do, in fact, with a completely disembodied man. The choices, the freedom, the situation, all that is the fruit of an intellectual process. The man referred to by this ethic is a man of no time and no place. He belongs to no society. He has no sex and no work, and is a member of no group. He is solitary, under the influence of no thing or person. When society is mentioned, that is in order to say that it registers the desires and aspirations of the person. The reading of these studies, in spite of the continual reminders of concrete man, real man, historic situations, etc., submerges us again in the absolute of man in himself. It would seem that differences of profession or trade, of intellectual training, of the money one earns and the time one does not have, have no effect on the experience of value, on the person's ethical condition. This abstraction of man is, without doubt, the most serious inward contradiction of this philosophy.

Now we must come to the question essential to our purpose. Having considered this philosophy as such, we need to ask whether it gives a good account of reality. When it speaks of value, reducing ethics to this relationship with values, presenting value as decisive for human conduct, is what it shows us something real, or is it a construct of the philosophic mind? There is something we notice at the outset which should put us very much on our guard; namely, the extraordinary variety of theories concerning value, or the values, also a diversity of definitions, foundations, and functions. Value is treated as: the structure of reality inherent in our action, a way of qualifying the world, a motive for action, the perspective of commitment, the reason for our conduct, or indeed, the transcendental absolute which determines man from without. It can be the value of that which is worth seeking, or conversely, of that which is in fact sought. It can be the putting into operation of human reality, or an independent grandeur without antecedents. It can be a reality whereby a person becomes an authority for another person, that which gives meaning to event, that by which the world's meanings throw light on one another; or again, "the condition for my keeping my dignity as a person in the world . . . for my carrying out my projects for the good of the world." In the same vein, it can be "the reality which gives us authority sufficient to break through temporal determinism," or conversely, "Value is a relationship between the infinite source of all value, which should be called 'value' in the absolute sense, and the determined values that involve an eventual aspect of negativity."

The complete opposite of these diverse definitions would be that value is seen as the evaluation of a subject in harmony with an undefined feeling; also, the product of a relation between things and a collective ideal, or a collective affectivity. We could extend this list. The least that might be said is that the extreme diversity of these concepts is not reassuring. The problem is similar when we look for the foundation of this value and of its authority. It can be the existence of the social group, the transcendence of an absolute value, respect for the other person, an extension of the organic structure of being (satisfaction and lack of satisfaction), the collective social ideal, a structure of instincts, creation by God, etc.

Faced with these discordances, one can say that if value were a real object of common experience and easily knowable (as all the philosophers of value claim), there would be at least some common elements in these expressions, and certain identities. The uneasiness increases when we consider the arguments of each one separately (they are all convincing, and I have to say that I am just as convinced by the theses of M. Le Senne as by the contradictory theses of MM. Gusdorf and Mehl), and the fact that when we take a particular system, we notice that the development of the notion of value leads almost inevitably to profound contradictions within the system itself. Finally, we cannot escape the question: With reference to what does one define and determine values? All agree in saying that there are values and antivalues. There are givens which are values and other givens which are not, and who is to decide?

The answer is clear only with those who accept a transcendental, an absolute value which determines all the rest. Everywhere else we wander about in confusion. One person will give us a sample list of values which is not exhaustive: the unconditioned, the absolute, the good, the just, the holy, freedom, love—saying that poverty, weakness, sickness, are not values because they threaten loneliness, the turning of the person in on himself, that they are contrary to the expansiveness characteristic of the action of values. But this means that there is a prior determination, and that it is not true that values are freely chosen by man. There are values which preexist as derivatives of a preconceived idea of the author which he does not owe to values. Someone not sharing that idea would furnish a quite different set of values, and the two would disagree. Another person presents a picture of values from the standpoint of the instincts, but there is scarcely any necessary connection between the values chosen and a given instinct. The sex instinct, the maternal instinct, etc., give values of love, friendship, mutual communication, loyalty; perhaps, but one could just as well say that they create the values of eroticism, racism, lying, resentment, etc. In reality, the choice of values depends here also upon a presupposition (antecedent).

The question which is not asked is, nevertheless, On what grounds does each one decide what value is? and second, Where is the frontier of value? Where does it stop? What is it that makes it possible for it to become an antivalue? When all is said and done, the notion of value is so vague and uncertain (not with one author, but in the whole stream of the philosophy) that each one can insert just about anything he pleases. To be sure, that does not mean that there is no such thing, but perhaps we can conclude at this stage that value is, in any case, a notion created by the philosophers. It is not, as such, a real existent. But then, this brings us to a new question: This notion created by the philosophers, is it a general concept which, in spite of everything, does in an abstract way account for a number of realities gathered into one, or is it indeed an empty word alleged on behalf of a whole philosophical system? Is it a notion and nothing more, created to fill a place in the internal coherence of the system?

It is indeed certain, that when one gives up speaking of value, and refers instead to *values*, one observes that these do exist in fact, friendship, work, truth, etc. In every society, a given action, a given sentiment, a given aspiration, a given will, a given organization, a given idea, plays the role which the philosopher ascribes to value. Moreover, it is necessary to go far beyond enumerations linked to nineteenth-century Western civilization and admit that racism, violence, nihilism, prostitution, cannibalism, etc., are values, or derive from value. Thus man has an experience of the just and the unjust, of the true and the false, of the pure and the impure, but there is no experience of value. In other words, it appears to us that in society and in the life of man there exist extremely diverse realities, fulfilling diverse functions, stemming from diverse and very changeable beginnings, which the philosophers lump together and call values. In this way they set up a common denominator in order to avoid complete relativism and nominalism. The trouble is, they combine precisely such diverse elements that they do not succeed in establishing a true common denominator, nor in furnishing us with a concept of valid synthesis. Hence we shall say that we are concerned with these realities, but not with the fugitive and blurred concept of value.

We are well aware that this attitude will be attacked by saying that we are taking the content of the notion of value and ignoring its function, that we are keeping the outward appearance and rejecting the profound reality. But the disparity between the experienced phenomenon and what the philosopher calls the profound reality is too great to allow us to retain the latter. Thus we shall speak of those realities which are in society, and for a man, liberty, equality, the nation, power, group loyalty, the beautiful, wealth, etc., without forcing them into a unified whole. And whenever we shall be using the word value for convenience of language it will be without reference to the philosophy of values.

Finally, let us observe that most of the functions which this philosophy attributes to values, most of the effects of the presence of values, can be explained without recourse to that concept. That which defines the meaning of our presence to the world, that which instigates my commitment in the world, the goal which I pursue in being present to the world—in no sense is all of that the fruit of value. It is also explained by my education, my work, the newspaper I read, the conversation I engage in, the order which I receive from the state or from a superior, my most material interests. Someone will say, of course it is my relationship with the group or groups to which I belong, but all that is also a value—then everything is a value and value means nothing. To say that it is value which constitutes the subjectivity of the subject, which gives him authority and maintains his existence—that the value of the subject cannot be eliminated, without by the same token eliminating him as existence, is to attribute to value what amounts to being God. To consider that the divisions among men are the fruit of ruptures in the sphere of values is to underrate the objective reality of economics and politics. To suppose that a commitment to develop and grow with each renewable moment is made possible to man through value is to make an abstraction of the concrete reality of the registration of man's life in a duration of time which has meaning for him because it is his life, and for no other reason.

The meaning of history can be given by something quite other than value. Marxism, for example, strove completely to empty history of moral values, and in the form set forth by Marx, succeeded. Likewise, it cannot be said that a society without value-references would be unable to commit itself, or to commit individuals, by pacts and treaties; nor that all human ritualism is a reference to values. Common beliefs suffice for that, as would collective sociological prejudices and presuppositions, similarities of education, etc. Now the fact of believing and of having a given presupposition prevails by a long way over the reality of that in which one believes, or over whatever is in fact the basis for the presupposition. To believe in the same thing effectively unites men, makes them act together, gives them a reason for acting that way, even if what they believe in is absolutely without existence.

Hence we reach an important point in the discussion. The philosophy of values speaks of value as existing, active, objective, even though there is no other basis for it than certain schematic images, prejudices, beliefs, which have a certain effect. It is no mere quibble over words that we are raising here. To deny, on the one hand, the existence of value as an embracing reality, yet on the other hand to retain justice, freedom, love, means two things. The first is that these drives, these ideals, are constituent parts of a given society, of a particular civilization. They are embraced within it and are defined by man. They depend upon the cultural, intellectual, social, and economic context and vary with this context. If value is an objective thing "in itself," however, it embraces the culture and the civilization, determines them, and orients them; it attains to something of the eternal, to an inexhaustible richness, and stirs man to action. The second is that these drives, these ideals, have no other "value," no other power, no other reality than that which man attributes to them. They depend for their very being on human belief. They have no decisive or exclusive quality, while if one gives value its own specific greatness, it becomes a driving force which is really exclusive of all others—for everything that can be invoked in the economic and political spheres is in that case integrated into the order of values—and decisive in and of itself. The existence of the value suffices as the reason for acting.

These two consequences seem to us important, and (if one is to maintain a realistic attitude) determinative in our direction. Therefore, if we retain the word value, we shall use it for convenience to refer to one of the constituent elements of morality. We shall mean three things by it. First of all, we shall mean belief, man's conviction that there are values which provide a controlling reason for acting and judging. Next, we shall mean man's attribution of a value to certain facts, to certain powers. Man desires equality, for example, and he endows it with a value: or again, the nation and work are facts to which man ascribes a value, which he transforms into value; that is, into an object of belief, etc. Finally, we shall mean certain definitely existing realities, desirable, desired by people, possessed of a grandeur, in function of which man acts and judges, but which are independent of all synthesis, of all reference to a coherent objective system, possessed of no meaning in and of themselves.

If we consider values only in this way, we can make the same observation concerning them as concerning morality as a whole; to wit, that there is for man an amazing variety in the attribution of values and in beliefs. When one reads the philosophers of value it is certainly with great surprise that one finds them declaring that values are uniform, universal, that the differences are only secondary, that from one society to another there are only differences of detail, that the dissimilarities are on the surface, that a desire for the same things is everywhere manifest. In a similar vein, it is also said, that whatever the intellectual or moral level people always know what they are talking about when they refer to this or that value, that every value can be understood and recognized by man (irrespective of the civilization), that value is permanent over and above fleeting time (and therefore is a constant throughout history). All this means that *values* are always and everywhere similar, although it is never said so bluntly. Now this rests upon two presuppositions: that value exists in itself independently of circumstances (even if one says that it is tied to history and is not an absolute), and that there is a human nature which is always the same. Indeed it looks as though one has paid altogether too little attention to the realities. To say, without further ado, that if there were no common value shared by the different historic civilizations, the past would be incomprehensible to us, is to suppose that past societies are in fact comprehensible to us.

Modern historians know very well that, in reality, they are not at all sure of understanding past societies. They know very well that they do not see them as they were in themselves, but through twentieth-century glasses. To say that behind the differences in detail of sexual and family regulations there is among all societies a uniformity of social style, of sex and family relationships, is to believe in an essence of marriage and of family. In reality, if we take away the legal forms, the taboos, the beliefs, the moral prescriptions which are amazingly variable, what is left? The simple fact that there is everywhere a regulation of sex and family relationships as an object of morality—that is a bit thin! Only an abuse of words and of unembodied abstractions can permit one to say that there is a kind of unity of values in the human race and in history, a universe of values. We observe, to the contrary, an enormous variety. It is true not only that societies have not all had the same concept of the true, the just, the beautiful, freedom, etc., but even more, it is true that societies have not all treated these as values. Love is not considered a value in China, or among the Pygmies. To Athens and Rome belongs the credit for having made justice a value in and of itself. And Malraux has shown that the beautiful did not become a value until the nineteenth century. Economics has been a value only since the nineteenth century. In the Egypt of the Ptolemies incest was probably the highest value characterizing the king!

On what grounds do our philosophers refuse that title to race in racism, to violence, to prostitution, since in given social groups these things played exactly the role which they attribute to value? It is not merely the appearance which varies. It is not a matter of the exceptional case. It is not simply a different way of looking at things. There is an unbridgeable gap between systems of values. There is an impossibility of a relatedness of values among diverse societies. These values are linked with a given society and are interior to that society. They vary in content. We can, to be sure, acknowledge a certain continuity between the thirteenth and the nineteenth centuries in France, but the value of freedom is radically other, depending upon whether one looks at the thirteenth century, the sixteenth century, or the nineteenth century. Values perish with the societies to which they are bound.

In the last analysis, everything depends on man's decision with respect to what is called value. We can only speak of value in a given historical situation. But the history of a society, the decision of man, do not confine themselves to bringing to light a value which had been lurking in the shadows. They call out of nothing that which did not exist and make it exist. That is why, when the decision changes, when the situation is modified, the value disappears. And the relation between the content of a value and a given social condition becomes tragically apparent whenever two societies confront each other using the same words to cover fundamentally opposite values: so the Communist world and the Western world. What makes mutual understanding possible among men is not their dependence upon the same values, or upon an objective value, but the identity of their schematic images, of their prejudices, of their beliefs, of their presuppositions. It is that which supplies the content of the value of which they speak, and it is because of that that they know what they are talking about. It comes to them out of the manifold structures of the society to which they belong—material, intellectual, and spiritual.

It is also said that, in the final analysis, value always has a revolutionary thrust, that it frees one from tradition, from prescriptions and imperatives, that it represents an individual's power to oppose the established order. It is a requirement from above, a drive to burst boundaries, a source of open-ended morality pushing man to the full realization of himself. Value is said to initiate scandalous actions, calling the prevailing morality into question, establishing the distance between value itself and the specific determinants. Finally, it is said to be a basis for the contingency in which man sees history, politics, and the social order, and whereby he refuses to confer upon these the character of absolutes. And, to be sure, value would be degraded were it to be integrated into the social order, were it universally recognized, and were it no longer to require a personal commitment. At that moment it would cease to be a value and would be no more than a thing. But this conception always assumes that value is recognized by a particular person and by a specific power.

If, to the contrary, we reflect upon the reality into which values are inserted, we shall see that there is as much validity in value integrated into the social order and duty as there is for the value of demand and conquest. Why be partial to one over the other? Why deny value to the social order, the institution, the organized, the traditional? These are not merely obstacles which allow value to stand out in contrast. They are a framework without which the value of opposition could in no way exist. The value of conquest or of self-affirmation can strictly exist only in the degree in which the value of the social order permits this affirmation and this demand. If we talk justice, there is as much value in the judiciary and in the democratic organization as in the demand for what is just on the part of philosophers and of the economic democracy of the Communists. And to say that the organized no longer assumes personal commitment, and hence is not a value, is an absurdity; for of what use are the most just institutions, for example, without people who enter into them precisely because they express the justice for which they were conceived?

On the contrary, everything called value strictly presents the complementary features of the stable and organized together with the over-and-above requirement. The two factors cannot be separated; that is true, but is value a mere thing in the first of the two? And why should it not be, if we have given up the mythology of value as a living quality? Value instigates both an order and a will to transgress that order, but one is no more a value than the other. Value is registered just as much in a closed morality, in the equilibrium which the social group would like to finalize, as in an open morality, as in personal aspiration which breaks down barriers and puts the equilibrium at stake. When personal aspiration becomes a social movement, when the social movement becomes a sociological pattern, when the sociological pattern gels into institutions, those are successive stages of expression. They are not a transition from value to nonvalue.

The proof is essentially that the people of a society precisely attribute value to a given institution, commit themselves to its defense, and judge in accordance with a scale of values which comes to them for the most part from the sociological structure into which they are integrated. If that is indeed the way it is, then we can say that there is not a distinct sphere of ethics and another one of value. In the philosophers of value, the relation between the two is complex. Ethics never has the values as its objects, we are told, but the values can inspire a certain ethical behavior. They set the boundaries to the field of the moral life. They orient it. "The domain of values supplies us with the soil of the moral life." All that is correct, but it would seem that one ought to go much farther and consider values as one of the constituent elements of ethics, in the various meanings of that word, in its diverse applications and throughout its range. In the one case as in the other, it is man in society and society through man who are the creators. They assign value, just as they define the imperatives and distinguish between good and evil.

A little later on, we shall say that these ethical determinations by man are not arbitrary. So it is for value. Man is not free to choose just any value he pleases. He is committed within certain precise limits. He is not free to decide: this is value. But granted the limits and urges which we shall study later on, it is still man, and only man, who brings it about that a word, a thing, or a person acquires value. Nowhere are there hidden goddesses for man to disclose, secrets of creation which he contents himself with embodying.

Now the polarity between revolution value and nonvalue order has led to another polarity, and that is the last point to which it seems necessary to call attention. The philosophers of value often set up an opposition between value and the sacred. The sociologists had already described the sacred as the instigator of traditional morality, taboos, while value would correspond to the occult power which makes possible the transgression of the sacred. The sacred establishes order in the social phenomena, and organizes relationships. Sociological religion, civilization, a society, find their security in the presence of a sacred which is the source of imperatives; while value, in order to manifest itself, requires people who are free and who express themselves spontaneously because they must be "subjects" in order to interpret value. This opposition would seem to us completely unacceptable. The bond between value and the sacred seems an unbreakable one. It has been established (Caillois), for example, that if there is a sacred of order, there is a balancing sacred of transgression which presents the same characteristics. In primitive society "value" is thus an integral part of the sacred, and in all societies value only exists through the belief that one brings to it.

To say that one only knows value in action is, in reality, to assume belief, for no one acts unless he believes in the action. Historically, each time man expresses or assigns a value it is always in conjunction either with the originating or the introducing of the sacred. Value does not validate except in the measure in which it makes sacred. It would not be itself if it did not commit, did not produce respect, if it could always be called into question, if it did not arbitrate, if it did not give meaning to life and a motive for action. Now all that is just exactly part of the sacred. The bond between value and the sacred is rigorous rather than occasional. It is said that "value partakes of the attributes of the sacred," but as a matter of fact without these attributes it would be nothing. Man would not treat it as value. Justice which is only an exact definition on the part of the philosophers or of the jurists is in no way a value in the eyes of men. It only becomes a value when, in its national, social, and metaphysical character, it has the power to attract, to win loyalty, to bring exaltation, to make a man commit himself on its behalf; when it contains the power of the sacred. Thus the relation between value and the sacred turns out in fact to be a reciprocal one.

To say that the sacred always evolves in the direction of becoming a thing, is to misconceive the nature of the sacred. It can be that, to be sure, but also it is always other than the thing in which it becomes crystallized. Moreover, that would not distinguish it from value, for we have seen that the normal process for the latter is also to change itself into things, and that it is at one and the same time creative of order and destructive of order, like the sacred.

Also, in this connection we need to make a final observation which reveals an oft neglected aspect of value. Whenever man develops a value out of a fact, whenever he transforms a simple fact, an institution, a relationship, into a value, this very generally has a disastrous effect. As long as the fact remains a fact, it has within it but little power to ravage man spiritually, or even physically. It is unarmed. It is to be feared only from that moment when man supplies it with value; that is, according to the best authors, reasons for existence and the regulation of life; the basis for the relations between man and the world; the creation of an effective structure for the world in which one lives; a clear purpose for the instincts, the goals which man sets for himself, and the justification of his acts; the significance of the meaning that one finds in his life—a way of being present to the world, of structuring and designating the real, the limits of freedom, etc.

If we take into account not the philosopher but the common man, the things in the modern world which fulfill the various functions we have enumerated include the nation, work, technology, the economy, the state, the party, progress. These are facts transformed into values. Now these facts can be perfectly legitimate and normal as facts, but the moment they become value they bear within themselves the power of a sacrifice offered or required, the reason for man's integration, a devouring drive for conquest, the demand for respect and adoration. The fact of being a citizen of a nation becomes nationalism, and the fact of the state produces the totalitarian claim. Let us not speak of antivalue, for it is in the nationalistic, statist, productivist, partisan, or technological vocation that the man of today finds the whole meaning of his life, the rationale for his commitment, the right to express himself, and to meet his neighbor who shares the same values. But this leads to the exclusion of the other, who because he does not have the same value is without value. Modern wars have become unatoneable wars because they are all wars of religion, through the fact that nations and states have values. Modern work and economic life are more crushing because they express a religious function which legitimizes all sacrifices, through the fact that work and production are values. The philosophers of values tell us that these are creative of intercommunion, of person-to-person relationship, a source of witnessing to and creating the individual personality. So be it, but let us never forget that a communion which creates itself requires the excommunication of those outside, and that this affirmation of being, in this fallen world whose prince we know, always pays by the sacrifice of this same being, or by the destruction of the other person.

The Lived Moralities

A lived morality is located at the sociological level, not only because, as we have said, there is no morality except in relationships among individuals, but also because the various elements of the moral phenomenon are directly or indirectly produced by the social group. In view of the facts, we cannot accept the principle of "the philosophers of essence" which refers all morality to "an action on the subject of the essence of the supreme good." But if it appears to us certain that man is the creator of ethics, that in no way implies agreement with "the philosophers of existence," who say that the subject himself creates his own values, for the subject scarcely has the freedom of decision and of interpretation. He is part of a social group without which he would not exist, and the entire creation of morality depends upon the dialectic between the subject and the group (or groups) to which he belongs.[1] However, this is true provided we are not considering morality as a decision of the individual, or as a protest against the social order. As we have said, these two factors are constituent elements of the whole of an ethic, but they are not the only ones, and they only have importance in relation to the others.

The connection between morality and society is certain. The relation between them takes three forms. First of all, no society can exist and develop without a morality. We have already indicated that morality is a necessity for any group whatsoever. Society must supply its members with a criterion of good and evil, a hierarchy of values, a list of imperatives, goals to be attained which are characterized as "good," a definition of the just and the unjust, and prohibitions setting the limits to freedom of action. Without these the society could not operate. Were it based exclusively on self-interest, or exclusively on restraint, it would meet with an insurmountable psychological obstacle or would dissolve into ceaseless conflict. For half a century now, we have been referring to the moral crisis of the Western world. One feels, one knows, one diagnoses the point at which this moral crisis becomes a threat to the entire society. The crisis is manifest precisely in the fact that society does not furnish the individual with imperatives and values. Each one searches on his own. Each person prescribes the moral law for himself, and each little group for itself. There is no longer a common base for action. No longer is there any ground for civic virtue and for loyalty freely given. This lack of a common morality not only vitiates individual conduct, but jams the political mechanisms and the economic organizations as well.[2] Everyone agrees that institutional reforms are powerless without the moral reform of the individual.

It is precisely in the area of moral reform that no one knows how to proceed, for such reform depends purely and simply on the existence or nonexistence of a morality, and it is not in the power of any individual person to bring that about. The experience of our time shows, and the humanities are helping us to understand better and better, that people can only live together and cooperate with one another on the ground of a shared moral structure. The latter is their reason for accepting one another and for agreeing on their common objectives. That is true of marriage (which has no ground for continuing if the moral unity of the couple does not enter in to take the place of first love), and of a nation as well. One of the obvious problems—for example, in international affairs—is that the absence of a collective morality prevents an international society from taking form. In the international order, on the one side the Soviet Union applies a very precise morality drawn from Lenin, while on the other side the West, more or less unconsciously, applies a traditional pseudo-Christian morality. There is no common ground between the two. Hence there can be no sufficient legal agreement which is able to continue. With opposing scales of values and moral objectives, there can be no lasting cooperation.

In order to fulfill its purpose, morality necessary to the life of the group should present a dual quality, which could appear, at first sight, to be inwardly contradictory.[3] First of all, this morality should be an "individual-psychic" morality. People need to be convinced that it does in fact define the good and the just. They must not be in doubt about that. They must feel it individually as a value in itself. Either the person must obey it instinctively as a discipline, not an outward discipline of arbitrary restraint but a discipline which is felt inwardly to be just and legitimate; or the individual must knowingly give it his adherence because he sees in it motivations for his conduct which are sufficient and just in his own eyes, and also the justification for his actions. Also, this morality must be "socio-political."[4]

The individual phenomenon which we have just indicated must be the individual phenomenon of all the members of the group. Thus this ethical system will be collective and common. Otherwise it will not fulfill its role of assemblage and cooperation. It must be the basis for a common order. It should *also* (not solely, nor at first, but *also*) provide the economic and political structures with a reason for existence. If one or the other of these two factors happens to be lacking, the society ceases to be tolerable for the individual, or to be enduring itself. Durkheim is surely right when he discerns three factual elements in morality: the spirit of discipline, an adherence to the social group, and the autonomy of the will through which the sociological factor is personalized, and thanks to which man proceeds to criticism and loyalty, which is the moral act.

The second order of relationship between morality and society has to do with the origin of morality. If we look at the facts, and assuming that we renounce any belief that morality is a gift of the gods or is registered in human nature from its inception, we are obliged to say that morality is a product of a social group to the degree in which it survives and develops. The group, by a sort of vital reflex, establishes morality as a working condition of its life. Each group develops the morality which is necessary to it, more or less extensive, more or less complex, more or less imperative. By social group we must understand not only the all-inclusive national society, but also restricted groups (associations, political parties, church, family, unions), voluntary or natural (social class, "milieu"). Each of these groups, in the measure in which it is alive, develops a morality which seems imperative to its members. In an all-inclusive society there can be several systems of morality more or less corollary, more or less contradictory. Their interrelationship is established in a fluid hierarchy which does not necessarily correspond to the importance of the group. It would seem that Durkheim's idea that the importance of the group determines the degree in which its morality is imperative and its place in the hierarchy does not hold true. It is not exact that domestic goals *must* give way to national goals solely for the reason that one's country is a higher social group. That is sometimes the case, but not necessarily.

In an all-inclusive society there can be a conflict between two moralities belonging to different groups. One of the most common of these conflicts will be that between a morality of order, of custom, of discipline, of imperative, and of obligation, and a morality of revolt against whatever is fixed and established. It is perfectly useless to pretend to choose between the two for the sake of saying that morality consists of the one or of the other. They are two complementary aspects of one and the same phenomenon, belonging to two trends of different groups, or again, to two successive stages in the evolution of one group. But in any event, neither is the morality of revolt a purely individual matter. A purely individual morality is illusory, since it always refers unintentionally to the collective morality. More than that, it is gratuitous because it can be arbitrarily modified by the lone individual who settled on his own private morality. He is not bound by what he himself has created. So the morality of revolt derives from the conviction of a group of people who feel bound by the imperative or desirable character of this new morality in opposition to the old. Finally, this collective quality is equally true of religious moralities. As moralities, these do not exist as direct translations of the religious imperative, but they come into being just to the extent that there is a religious group which feels the need of living its religious ideal in common.

The third category of relationship between morality and society stems from the fact that morality is never arbitrary, since it is a product of the social group. We cannot analyze here the process of formation of a morality. One scarcely believes any longer in the collective conscience so dear to Durkheim, a moral conscience of the group which transcends the individual and establishes the obligatory character of morality, society being the one and only moral power able to make law for man. If we retain in morality the "ought" element together with the "desirable" element, the imperative quality together with the value quality, then it is not merely a matter of explaining the moral obligation which would be imposed by society. The phenomenon is much more complex than that. A society recognizes "values" which the people who go to make up that society recognize together. These "values" seem to them respectable, desirable, nice, and in combination they apply with authority to people's mutual relationships. There can be norms, imperatives, which flow from this, and even sanctions in cases of resistance, but no single, systematic process.

It is probable that the recognition of values, with their quality of desirability and authority, and the formulation of norms, come not from a kind of homogeneous collective conscience, but from complex mechanisms of human interrelations within the group. And the general sociological characteristics of the group may to some extent explain the traits of its morality. Yet that is not enough, for the interrelations of individuals within the group are not indeterminate. They are not interrelations pure and simple, but interrelations occasioned by . . . So we need to insert two particulars. Every group is organized around what might be called a "principal motif." This is quite obvious in the case of simple and restricted groups—the family around the motif of the love of the couple or the education of the children, the church around the worship of God—but this is just as true for an all-inclusive society.

In every society there is an essential motif, a chief center of interest, an undisputed assumption, a goal recognized by all. It can be said, for example, that Christianity was this principal motif in the twelfth and thirteenth centuries, as was the proletarian revolution in Communist countries, the idea of the city-state in Greece of the fifth century before Christ, and technology today. This principal motif is always both ideological and material. It is bound up with a certain structure and it expresses itself in an aspiration. It is not a belief alone, nor is it a fact alone. It involves a combination of the two. It is in relation to this principal motif that the group's hierarchy of "values" is arranged, and that the striving toward the desirable and the imperatives of the obligatory are established. By a sort of tacit covenant, the members of the group undergo this moral organization around the principal motif which they approve of by consensus. But this principal motif is always bound up with the various group structures, and the morality takes shape out of these structures: economic, technological, religious, political, cultural, and demographic. The morality expresses the structures in terms of obligation and duty, with a view to preserving them, perpetuating them, and regulating man with respect to them.

At this level the Marxist analysis is partly correct. The structures appear essential to life, hence it is good to respect them and to crown them with the halo of value. The ethic based upon them will be respected in the very degree in which one feels this necessary character of the structures and in the degree in which the motivation of the society is itself recognized as desirable. If this analysis is correct, we can understand that morality cannot be created arbitrarily. It is not within the power of a man to create a morality (that is the weakness, as we have seen, of the theoretical moralities), nor is it within the power of the state nor of an authority. That is why the moral crisis cannot be resolved by a decision. Therein lies the weakness of the argument of those who pretend that man is not the initiator of morality and does not determine good and evil for himself. "If the existence of the true and the good depended on my choice of them, that choice would never come to pass because there would be no reason why it should not immediately destroy itself" (Mehl). That is true for Robinson Crusoe, but it is false for man involved in society and in collective action. The argument applies to the solitary, entirely abstract individual of the philosophers of value. It means nothing as applied to the assortment of people.

When a society no longer acknowledges a central motif, or when its structures are no longer felt to be necessary, no morality can remain valid: or the same is true when the morality which is affirmed is out of harmony with the principal motif. Hence the moral phenomenon is established both in connection with the concrete structures of society (and we recall that among these concrete structures we include cultural and religious structures) and also in connection with the principal motif of organization and signification which is recognized by all. That means that there is not *one* origin of morality. It is useless to debate whether the origin of morality is to be found in religion, or in magic,

or in economics. The thesis of the historic genesis of morality out of religion is strongly contested, but that of its historic genesis out of economics is contested just as vigorously.
There are certainly numerous sources for the historic emergence of morality, and similarly, for the formation of different moralities, the sources certainly vary according to epochs, structures, and circumstances. There is not just a single scheme of creation for morality which would be dupli-
cated in all societies.

In any case, it appears quite clearly that the moral process
is never a theoretical process of the prior knowledge of an
absolute good, an absolute justice, or an absolute truth,
which would then be put into practice. It is in relation with
the concrete and in action itself that the individual knows
what ought to be done. He acts, and he knows at that moment that his action conforms to a good, a true, or even
that it ends in creating them. In a certain sense we approach
Kant's *Critique of Practical Reason,* or a certain interpretation of value, but always provided that it is not a question
of man as such, but of man living in a society, in relation
with which both his action and his judgment are exercised.

Together with many others, we have said that there are
among the lived moralities quite a variety of proportions
between the imperative and the value, between the collective pressure and the individual choice. Moreover, one must
not identify the two polarities. The imperative is not solely
the result of collective pressure. It is felt as a duty through
the individual conscience which makes its own choice in
carrying out this duty; and conversely the desirable is not
only a matter of the individual. A communal society, a religious society, is entirely founded on "value." But then it
presents two difficulties. The first has to do with what is
called the "primitive totality." It is probable that in the
primitive clan the individual remains indistinct, is not dif-
ferentiated from the rest of the clan. If he acts, it is not for
personal motives and in consequence of a choice. It is in

the sense of a collective will, from which no individual will stands out. The primitive totality was in nowise a constraint of the individual. The latter did not yet exist and had no need to be constrained. The child in its mother's womb has no need of constraint, for nothing differentiates it from its mother. Only progressively through the course of history does a differentiation take place which causes the individual to stand out.

But can one speak of morality in this primitive totality? Surely yes, in spite of all. It is a morality in which there is no individual decision, no choice, no deliberation, no personal act of conscience deciding that this is a value, but a morality none the less, perfectly constituted, operative, and complex. It is a morality in which the social imperative is so complete that it is not felt as an imperative. It is not distinct from the collective will. It is beyond dispute, and incapable of harboring a spirit of refusal, of revolt and negation. This imperative is founded on the essentially religious structures and expresses itself in taboos, prohibitions, etc. We know how numerous these taboos are, and that they sometimes embrace the whole of individual activity. This is a truly ethical order which determines behavior. The taboos are furnished with a collective loyalty which entails the reprobation of the person who transgresses. Public blame clearly reveals the moral aspect of what might otherwise be looked upon as exclusively sacred.

This (decisive) reference to the sacred is a reminder that primitive morality contains another element. Alongside the imperative there is the desirable. In fact the entire sacred brings with it this concern of a projection into the future of that which is to be attained to, of that which is good, just, and holy. The mysticism which characterizes the behavior of the "primitives" implies this presence of value, but that in no way supposes the affirmation of the individual. This striving toward the desirable, this assertion of value, also is an affair of totality. It is the social body in its lack of differentiation which tends toward, which recognizes, a value.

Consequently, morality does indeed exist, even if it is in no way a personal affair and even if the individual is completely absorbed in the group. According to Gurvitch's theory, it is possible that magic may have been the means of the emergence of the individual personality. It is possible, in the face of a collective morality based on the religious sacred, that there might have been a consequent rebellion, an affirmation of the individual by means of a magic which would in that case express a personalized morality, a "morality of aspiration" opposed to the traditional morality. It could equally be true that the values are asserted with the greatest vigor in this use of magic. Mana (occult power) in archaic societies replaces what we call the world of values—perhaps. The important thing is simply to remember that, from before the time of the emergence of the individual person from the primitive totality, there is a morality, and that this gives way to a new type of morality of individualization, yet without the former morality's really disappearing.

This fact brings us to the second difficulty. It is now a habit to treat traditional morality as unworthy of consideration, with its imperative, its moral law, etc., and to limit morality to personal affirmation, to view morality only under the aspect of decision, of choice. There is only a moral situation where a person makes a choice between two possibilities. For some, even the choice in and of itself, regardless of what it bears upon, is of the essence of the moral attitude.[5] Wherever man decides for himself, there he performs an ethical act. Thus it is the commitment, the act of conscience, the control of one's destiny which constitutes morality, and not the objective and prior determination of a good, a just, and a true.

We have already encountered this assertion in our discussion of values, but we wish at this point to add two observations. The first is that this presupposes that man is free and that he decides, chooses for himself freely. Morality, then, is this exercise of freedom. If there is no freedom there is no longer any decision nor any morality in an act. In fact, when one examines the writings of these moralists, one perceives that it all rests actually on the presupposition of freedom. That should be a topic for reflection. At the very moment when sociology, biology, and psychology are drawing the deterministic circle more tightly around man, are emphasizing his conditioning, are picturing a still greater conditioning, at the moment when political regimes and economic planning are reducing at full speed even the apparent and outward sphere of liberty, at the moment when psychoanalysis is uncovering for us the extraordinary interconnectedness of our inmost impulses—it is at that moment that the philosophers tacitly adopt the metaphysics of Sartre and assert the possibility of a pure and simple negation of determinism! That is getting out of it cheaply. And the success of this philosophy can be explained on the principle of compensation for what actually is. If we do not adopt the presupposition of freedom then neither can we limit morality to decision and choice. These are present, to be sure, but at the level of the outward appearance of freedom, and resting on a base of determinism. They constitute only a part of the moral life.

And here is the second observation. To reduce all morality to an individual decision is to narrow ethics down to an extreme degree. How often does choice enter our lives? How many days go by without my having a real choice to make? How many of my actions and thoughts are the products of a thought-out voluntary decision? In most cases, for the average man, it is a matter of automatic, involuntary obedience to a moral order, resulting from education, environment, and social and psychological frames of reference. He practices the virtues. He is moved by the misfortune of his contemporaries. Normally he is honest. He does not commit murder and is ashamed when he is untrue to his wife: but all that is unquestionably morality, and it involves no decision or choice. Habits, reactions, imitations, those are the things which make up 99 percent of our moral behavior. To eliminate those things is to reduce the moral life to a very tiny domain. But more than that, by an amusing reversal one can say that it means presenting morality as an "ought-to-be" once again. Man must develop his conscience. He must build up his freedom. All that is an "ought-to-be," and yet it is just those philosophers who accuse morality of the "ought-to-be" who set forth this morality of choice. Thus they merely exchange one "ought-to-be" for another! Not only does the morality of choice reduce the moral life in each one of us, it reduces it also in the course of history, for it assumes a completely individualistic society, a society in which the individual is treated as a value, in which he stands out from the structures.

As a matter of fact, this morality of decision is a romantic idea adopted in the nineteenth century and formulated in philosophic currency in the twentieth. To be sure, choice and decision have an important place, are an important value, in lived morality; but they are only one aspect of the moral phenomenon and they are always related to the social framework. One could not write today as Durkheim wrote: "There is a common quality in all actions which are called moral, namely, that they all conform to preestablished rules. To conduct oneself morally is to act according to a norm which determines the behavior to be followed in given cases even before we are under the necessity of coming to a decision. This domain of morality is the domain of duty, and duty is an action which is prescribed." And yet it is true! If one looks at the facts, and not at some theory of man and of society, that is indeed what morality is—but not that alone.

In any case it is not possible to say that if morality confines itself to the determination of an ought-to-be, and separates this from being, it shuts itself off from humanity and has no common ground with it. That is true for the theoretical moralities, but in the real world morality does indeed fix upon imperatives and preestablished rules. There is indeed an objective "you ought" in lived morality. It is not merely a "doctrine of committed human activity which has the purpose, at the very beginning, of throwing light on the meaning and function of the values which orient the human adventure" (Gusdorf). Morality expressed in these terms is just as theoretical as that of Kant.

To link morality solely to the affirmation of man, to see it as the posting of signs for the ascent of man in the creation of self with ever higher prospects, the guide and companion of self-fulfillment and of the achieving of the equilibrium of self with self, is to make of it an extremely rare event having nothing to do with the man in the street, and to turn it into a mystery. To deny to morality everything that might be the intervention of an orthodoxy which judges man's action, is to deny the fact. The only argument advanced, moreover, is that that kind of morality would bring about man's alienation, and that the success of human life is not found in alienation. This supposes that morality is the success of man through his own efforts (which is already a fixed prejudice about what morality *ought to be*), and that man is free. We have said above that this latter is a pure belief. To be sure, one can insist that those who are content with a closed morality developed in the social group, with its imperatives and its cheerless duties, are lazy, weak, cowardly; and that the "moral man," the "authentically alive" person, rejects this mediocrity and sets up an open morality of decision, of aspiration, of conquest, and vows once and for all to fulfill himself. We heard that prior to the phenomenologists, especially in Nietzsche and even in Hitler. But it seems to us more responsible not to reject either the one or the other. Morality lived by the mediocre person and the coward is morality lived by man, just as much as, and even more than, the morality of heroes.

Man's Stance with Respect to Morality, Moralism, and Immoralism

10 Man adopts a certain stance toward morality, toward every morality, and toward that which exists in our own society (not the technological morality yet). That is to say, he never completely carries out the morality of his group.

1. There is always a certain distance bewteen morality and individual behavior. It is commonplace to make a distinction between morality and morals, between the ought-to-be and that which is. This is so obvious that we shall not enlarge upon it, but we are obliged to conclude that this opposition between morality and morals is becoming less and less exact for three reasons.

First, to the extent to which, at the present time, we do not conceive morality as an absolute, but as relative, thus exhibiting differences of content according to differences of time and place, no longer possessed either of religious or of natural permanence, to that extent morality no longer presents a completely rigid contrast to morals. It adapts more readily.

Second, to the extent to which morality is derived from the social group, it is obviously a product of *morals*. But in this area two elements of opposition between morality and morals still persist. One of these is the time lag. Morality necessarily lags behind morals. It evolves less rapidly. In reality, it is an expression of yesterday's morals. Yesterday's morals tend to become today's morality, and today's morals will instigate tomorrow's morality. The other remaining difference is a difference of rationale. Morals are a spontaneous phenomenon, while morality is always more or less structured and organized. It is a collective ideological construct. This construct can be more or less conscious and intentional, but it is always there. It is ambiguous with regard to morals, for it is always capable of two different objectives: either it can have as its purpose to conceal reality, to camouflage behavior and morals, to refuse to look at things as they are, in which case it is an ideological disguise; or it can express a genuine desire for the true, the good, the just, etc., as a judge of morals. All morality involves these two factors. It is never entirely the one or the other. It is usually a desire to reform morals in the direction of the good, and at the same time a desire to camouflage.[1]

A third factor in the rapprochement between morality and morals has to do with the progressive development of technological morality. The latter tends to educate behavior in such a way that it exactly expresses the technological good. Thus the contrast between what should be done and what is in fact done grows less and less; but just because it is a matter of "what should be done" in the technological order. Elsewhere, the development of certain techniques (sociological and psychological) tends to alter the relation between morality and morals. The outlook of social psychology and of depth psychology leads to the conclusion that duty, moral obligation, and the sense of sin are harmful to man. The idea of the moral is progressively being displaced by the concept of the normal. From the standpoint of socio-technological behavior, the good is expressed in that which is normal. To set up a conflict between the normal and the moral imperative is harmful both to the individual and to society. Consequently, a systematic effort is made to promote a morality of that behavior which corresponds to social utility (the sinless morality of Hesnard), and which expresses normalcy as determined by investigations, polls, etc. (the Kinsey Report, for example). At this point, practical conduct at the individual level is presented as morality, and then there is confusion between what is and what ought to be.

2. But in our society there still exists a morality with the appearance of being imperative. This morality confronts the individual. What, then, is man's conduct in the face of this morality? What attitude does he take? What does he make of this morality? For him it is, in fact, a matter of resolving the conflict between his life and morality. No man likes the conflict nor accepts it. Two courses, and only two, are open to him: moralism and immoralism.

MORALISM

On the whole, this is a matter of an operation by which man, in one way or another, takes possession of morality, turning it into an instrument for his own advantage, an object which he does not modify but which he makes use of. It is in the degree in which man takes morality seriously and faces up to it seriously that his attitude will be that of moralism, and that he will use morality to his own ends. But then what is it good for?

1. In the hands of a moralist, morality becomes essentially an instrument of justification. We shall not dwell on the importance and mechanism of justification. It need only be noted that there is a twofold process in justification. Either a person will construct morality in terms of his own behavior and will end by showing that the good is what he himself does. That is direct justification. Or he will modify his action, his attitude, his works, to conform to a moral commandment which he obeys *in order to be able to* declare himself just and to *affirm his own justice,* hence to affirm his superiority over the unjust. However harsh, or difficult, or pure it might be, this system of morality will never be other than a mechanism of justification, since it is never observed except for the sake of being able to say, "I am right." In both cases it is a veritable procedure for creating a good conscience.

Morality thus utilized by man is a means of distinguishing the good from the bad, assuming, of course, that I am on the side of the good, whether by direct or by indirect justification. Hence it is a way of avoiding being called into question. Since I am on the side of the good, I neither call into question what I myself am nor the society to which I belong. But conversely, it authorizes calling into question, and finally destroying, all those who are on the other side, those whom morality condemns. This was a frequent aspect of the drama of the Christian morality of puritanism. The puritan, declaring himself righteous, condemns everything not himself. That moralism has rightly been criticized in *The Witches of Salem,* or better by A. Chamson (*Le Crime des Justes*) and by a number of novelists since.

2. Next, moralism turns morality into an organization of convenience. Morality is then an instrument for facilitating human relations in the extreme. Taking that direction, moralism flourishes in the comfortable societies, the societies of ease (bourgeois society, for example) and of conformity (since conformity is the best guarantee of good social working relations, so in the United States and in the Soviet Union). But the convenience achieved in a society through morality can present itself under different aspects.

The first convenience consists in establishing a behavior type on which everyone can depend. There is a norm of average social behavior which makes it generally possible to know how my neighbor will behave. I can count on his not disturbing my automobile, not insulting me, etc. I look for a certain gesture from him, a certain word, because the common morality dictates these. I am going to behave toward him in terms of this legitimate expectation. I assume a given action on my neighbor's part and so I myself act in a certain way. I do not lock my car. I put out my hand. We can count on these relations as a result of morality. That is why, when my neighbor disappoints my expectation, does not behave as one had a right to expect, there is a moral scandal. That is, in fact, the source of moral scandal. It is easy to see that this common observance of one and the same morality offers an extreme facility of relationships, which can thus be calculated in advance and counted on without distrust.

The second convenience stems from the possibility that morality offers of classifying and judging. It is, in fact, impossible to live in society without passing judgments on people, without setting up a scale for the classification of individuals. It would be a superhuman task to approach each new individual with a completely fresh outlook, with a total absence of prejudice, a complete simplicity of heart. That would require a great love and a great availability of the self. For the convenience, the facilitating, and the expediting of relations, man prefers to cling to certain assured criteria which help him to know into which previously marked pigeonhole to place a given individual. Can one consort with him or not? Can one use him, and to what extent is he to be trusted? Morality permits a ready response to all that when it is transformed into moralism. The latter avoids having to enter into the complexities of people, their manner of life, their motives. If it were necessary to go into that for everyone there would be no end to it. The opposition between appearances labeled by morality's judgments and the profound reality of the person, which calls for a different judgment, has been shown by Faulkner and a number of other novelists, all based in this regard on Dostoevsky.

The third element of this organization of convenience is the transformation of morality into a screen by which to avoid personal human relations. Each person presents a moral facade to all, which allows him to remain hidden in social and personal relations. Only the moral facades confront each other, and in reality they make easy coexistence possible without collision or conflict. Morality permits us to avoid real and direct contact with our neighbors, for it must never be forgotten that person to person contact is, in reality, dreadfully painful. In this contact, the person who reveals himself to me in his reality becomes my neighbor, and this neighbor then obliges me to reveal myself, to reveal what I am in the depths of my being. Deprived of the protective armor of morality, one is only what one is. It is always painful to let oneself be seen *only* for what one is, to confess publicly that which one would like to keep to oneself. Now this manifestation, this revelation, this confession, is forced upon me solely by the relation with my neighbor. It is in my relationship with the other person that I am stripped cruelly naked. As long as I am with an organization, a crowd, an anonymous person, some visitor or other, I can take shelter behind a cluster of conventions and pretexts. The best mask is that provided by morality, which allows me to be seen at my best as the virtuous and just individual, which after all I would like to be. A little goodwill on both sides suffices to make the two parties believe in the game and to be satisfied with each other. But that is only a meeting between two masks and two accomplices. It is not at all a meeting with one's neighbor.

3. Finally, moralism turns morality into a procedure for self-determination. That is to say that morality becomes in man's hands a means of declaring himself autonomous and completely independent—autonomous with respect to society (which no longer determines me when I have monopolized its morality and can decorate myself with the badge of justice and virtue consistent with what society can say about me) and autonomous with respect to God whose will I have bound, thanks to moralism, and whose (favorable) judgment of me I know in advance.

In this aspect of moralism we can include not only the person who faithfully copies the collective morality, but also the person who overthrows the false gods and the prevailing good conscience and who sets up his own moral criteria and redefines the good for himself. That is to say that moralism is not only a sociological operation. It is a quite individualistic operation as well. The individual can claim to shut himself up in his own system whence he is about to destroy others, wearing all the while his own badge of justice. But in the degree in which he is self-determining, in the degree in which he asserts himself as knowing good and evil independently (which he defines in terms of his own experience, his own spiritual pilgrimage, etc.) and in which he sets himself up as the judge of all, in that degree the person thus creating a moralism, doubtless superior to the others, is performing in reality exactly the same operation. Though more discerning, more intelligent, less expedient, this systematization of morality by oneself is nothing other than the permanent assertion of the self-determination to which man always pretends, and it necessarily ends in the development in the person of a good conscience, which he had pretended to overthrow in eliminating the factors of traditional morality.

4. We can analyze, last and very summarily, the effects of moralism. For people generally, moralism is surely the greatest force in the destruction of the person. It is a destruction of the person of others through judgment, classification, the refusal of personal relations, and the refusal to consider individual determinations. But this also has its repercussions on the person who does the moralizing. In rejecting personal relations the latter rejects himself, for we are more and more aware that every person is, to a great extent, a product of his chain of relationships. Now the moralist shuts himself up in a system of explanations and justifications, then crystallizes. Finally, he transforms himself into a value (self-determination), and these two facts rob him henceforth of the ability to call himself into question and to be called into question. But if we put these three things together what do we see? What have we meant by this threefold indication?

Simply this, that in reality the moralist denies himself by denying his own future. For if he refuses being called into question, he refuses all possibility for serious development; and if he excludes his neighbor, if he denies him, he eliminates his own future by the same token, for we have no future except to the extent that we have a neighbor. The latter formulates for us the demands of life and truth, and to the extent to which he makes us reveal ourselves it is he who opens for us (for us in our reality and not in our seeming) all the available potentials which are excluded by an attitude of moralism. We can add still another effect of moralism with regard to Christians, that it is the force destructive of faith par excellence, for moralism leads the Christian to integrate God into himself. When this person declares himself *autonomous,* when he ascribes to himself the capacity to *judge,* when he *determines the good,* when he *justifies* himself, he is performing four operations which belong exclusively to God: for God alone is autonomous, judge, determiner of the good, justifier. The moralist strips God of his being and claims this for himself. This usurpation is the exact opposite of faith. Such, schematically described, are the effects of moralism.

Immoralism

If moralism is so catastrophic, must we conclude that immoralism is the answer? But as a matter of fact immoralism is no more right than moralism, and it usually turns out to be nothing more than a particular aspect of moralism, leading to the same results. When a person rejects the system of morality with which he is faced, he pretends to be an immoralist. What does he intend by that? What does that mean? It would seem that one can distinguish three forms of immoralism.

1. In some instances the immoralist is a person who follows his own passions and propensities. Often these passions and propensities are condemned by morality, mistreated, and repressed. Because he *cannot* repress them nor repress himself, the immoralist finds himself in opposition to the prevailing morality. He stands accused, but rather than accept that status, rather than submit to that condemnation (which is very distasteful) , he withdraws from the system and challenges the morality. In this way he turns the tables, and from the height of his propensities he poses as a judge of

morality. "I refuse to stand accused, so I refuse to be bad. I refuse to humble my instincts and passions, so the one who accuses me is bad, and I in my turn accuse whoever attacks me. I repudiate him and destroy him." It should be noted right away that this is an attitude of personal justification and a repudiation of the person who stripped me naked (*hence the very attitude of moralism*).

The person who thus repudiates the morality which has called him in question often claims to have performed an act of freedom and to have "liberated himself" from morality. But that is a fallacy. That person is in no wise free, for what he has henceforth "liberated" are only his passions, his instincts, his needs, which he shows by that very fact that he cannot master and to which, in reality, he is completely enslaved. The immoralist liberated from morality is a slave of his passions. The proof of this bondage, of this nonliberation, is the extraordinary need exhibited by this type of immoralist to explain and justify himself in the eyes of others. So it was with Gide or Lawrence, who spent their lives and dedicated their entire work in search of the public and social approbation of their immoralism (it is marvelous that this should have been blessed with the Nobel Prize; Gide had quite a success in his enterprise of justification), showing thereby that they were carrying out the same inward procedure as the moralist.

2. A second type of immoralist is the person, still more frequently met with, who is content to repudiate yesterday's morality (continuing in force today, but on the decline) in favor of contemporary morals, in favor of the present average behavior. This immoralist follows the sociological trend of the moment and of his milieu. He wants to be in fashion. He strives for the social middle. It is pure sociological conformism. Now the surviving morality is often out of harmony with these moral customs. Whenever this discord is latent or weak no one notices it, but when the discord becomes marked then the little immoralists spring up, preferring to follow the morals of their milieu rather than mo-

rality's imperative. Since it is in conflict with the group, morality is liquidated and the individual proclaims himself an "immoralist" (only, however, if this proclamation is looked upon favorably in the group, in which case all the members of the society call themselves immoralists in chorus) . Such is the exact situation of the Paris existentialists, who are content to follow a worthless sociological trend.

To be sure, in such a situation it takes more courage and independence to maintain morality! In the context of the French society of 1950, it is more difficult and more authentic, for example, to defend catholic morality with its rigidity than to attack it, but that is a backward-looking struggle and foredoomed to failure. What needs to be emphasized in considering this form of immoralism is that, at bottom, it is a concern for social facility, for ease of relations with other members of the same group. Morality would be a source of friction among them, so its negation is a way of having simple social relations. In other words, it is exactly the same operation as moralism. It answers to the same concern and to the same absence of personality. The only difference is that it is applied to different circles and different times. That is why, for example, René Bazin and his opposite Hervé Bazin are found united in the same project!

3. Finally, we bear in mind a third type of immoralist. In truth, it is more a question of the theoretical amoralist who rejects morality for fundamental reasons, for example scientific reasons. The two most celebrated are Freud and Marx. But in both these instances two observations are in order. The first is that these destroyers of morality deceive themselves when they think to destroy morality in and of itself, for in fact they are never attacking but *one* type of morality. For these two examples, Freud and Marx, it is a question only of the bourgeois morality of the nineteenth century. The other observation is that in point of fact as soon as these theoretical immoralists have destroyed a system of morality there issues from their own work another system of morality as a replacement. Their amoralism is only

a phase of transition between two moralities, and they themselves are the creators of the new morality. They cannot avoid it. After Freud there was born a pragmatic morality based on behavior and the normal.

The case of Karl Marx is even more striking. For one thing, the Marxist society of the Soviet Union is surely the most moralistic of modern societies. It resumes the good old bourgeois morality in its depths, as well as in those expressions of it which Marx thought he had liquidated. This is necessary if the socialist society is to live, and if it involves the morality of the nineteenth century that is because, in its economic phase, the Soviet Union is at about the same point as was Western society at the end of the nineteenth century. For another thing, and this is much more significant, we are viewing the creation of a systematic Marxist morality by Mao Tse-tung. His greatest contribution to Marxism is certainly the transformation of Marxism into a morality. The two facets of this theory are as follows: there is a predetermined mold of the ideal socialist man, and each person should be poured into this mold. Moreover, he should continually be passed through it so as to be ever better conformed to the ideal model, since no living person fully embodies the perfect virtue of socialist man (one would think he were reading the good old handbooks of morality of 1830).

In the second place, there are six criteria of the good, and one can classify people as good and bad by applying these criteria to their actions. The six criteria are: to unite the peoples, to further the building up of socialism, to consolidate the dictatorship of the proletariat, to consolidate democratic centralism, to reinforce the control of the Communist party, to further socialist solidarity. Upon analysis, these turn out to be criteria of behavior which have as their purpose to expedite a certain political and social technique. In other words, we are looking at a special form of the development of one part of the technological morality, which we shall examine later on. Thus the amoralism of Marx leads to the formation of a technological morality. Hence we can conclude that immoralism is always illusory. Either it is a justifying hypocrisy, or it is a hoax which serves to cover up a social conformism or a return to another morality. Amoralism has no value in itself, and is in no sense a resolution of the conflict between man and morality.

Man absolutely cannot escape taking one or the other of the two stances. Either he is a moralist, or he is an immoralist. He cannot be simply "moral." He cannot tolerate facing a wholly intangible morality which would be a veritable expression of the good and the true, and which for that reason would be a pure exaction for him. In that case morality would in fact be for him nothing but an accusation. It would entail a process of calling into question. Now man cannot submit to this accusation, this calling into question, and let it go at that. To be considered simply moral, a man would have to submit to this condemnation by a morality which he would recognize and accept as true. Having done the impossible to accomplish the good, this man would say: "All of that is nothing in the presence of the absolute truth and of the absolute good. This truth condemns me." Moreover, the man truly and simply immoral would be in the same situation. He would accept the same condemnation of a morality which he, too, recognized and which he, too, acknowledged as true, and would then say: "I acknowledge this good and this truth to be such, but I refuse to carry them out." In the one case as in the other, the situation is intolerable, unacceptable.

Man asks nothing more than to be justified and to be right. If he is moral, he is right thanks to morality (and he becomes a moralist). If he is immoral, he is right in opposition to morality (and he becomes an immoralist). Man cannot stand going on living and continuing in the situation of the accused. It is an absurd situation from which he necessarily seeks to escape. And what he will not accept from an absolute, religious morality, he will still less accept from a relative, contingent, and limited morality. He will throw out the latter the moment it resists him. This leads us to two incidental remarks. First of all, Christians should remember that when a so-called Christian morality is developed it brings man to this same impasse. Such a morality is in no way different from the others. In the second place, it can be said that in order to escape this impasse a third path would be open to man, namely, recourse to a court of higher appeal in morality. This is exact, but then it brings about the intervention of an outside power, and immediately we are out of the problem of autonomous and natural morality.

Technological Morality

11 A transformation in the lived morality is taking place under our own eyes. We are entering into a new form of morality which could be called technological morality,[1] since it tends to bring human behavior into harmony with the technological world, to set up a new scale of values in terms of technology, and to create new virtues.

Contemporary morality, such as it exists in our society, and which is currently called bourgeois morality, is made up of two quite different elements. One of these is what is left of the Christian morality developed in the Middle Ages and transformed in the sixteenth and seventeenth centuries. It emphasizes the individual virtues and is oriented toward charity. The other is a technological morality, emphasizing collective virtues and oriented toward work. We must remember, moreover, that these two elements are not contradictory. It is Christian morality, in the form which it took from the sixteenth century on, which has been preparing the way for the development of technological morality.

In fact, this "Christian" morality corresponded at that time to the development of the bourgeois world. It emphasized the protection of property (theft becomes an important theme in this morality). It makes work a virtue. It affirms individualism. It dwells on the fact that the world was entrusted by God to man for him to exploit. That justified man in committing himself to the course which the bourgeoisie opened up, that of work to the point of excess, productivity, the priority of economy, etc. For its part, the technological enterprise was the more justified through the emphasis on the ridding of the world of its religious taboos by Jesus Christ. This emphasis came in with the Reformation in the sixteenth century. The world is no longer a place inhabited by obscure powers, gods or demons, which need to be feared and respected. It is material, and man can do in it what he pleases.

Finally, the Reformation completes the picture by establishing a clear dichotomy between private life, with its personal virtues, salvation, on the one hand, and collective, economic, and political conduct on the other, which latter are free of the control of the church and are outside the "spiritual" domain. There is, then, a sort of spiritual indifferentism in socio-political questions (whereas the Catholic church had always attempted to subject socio-political activity to spiritual direction). Thus this Christian morality favored the spread of moral "values" belonging to technology. The entrance of these values into morality led to the formation of that particular morality, that bourgeois morality, which we shall not describe because it has already been described frequently. In addition, this morality was quite vigorous, for wherever Western society penetrated it tended to impose itself (African countries), and the Soviet Union, which had pretended to eliminate the morality of the bourgeoisie, came back to it even with an accentuation of its characteristics, with an entirely new rigor, at least in the interior of the Soviet Union, and with application to private life as well. Thus we know the severities reserved for adultery, and the fight waged against alcoholism, against youthful depravity, against theft, all according to very bourgeois ideas.

The fact is that this morality was perfectly adapted to the development of the technological society, let us say in its first phase, which we still experience in the West, which is at its height in the Soviet Union and which is just beginning in Africa and Asia. But in the West where we are entering the second phase of the technological society, this morality is no longer sufficient or adapted. That is why we are seeing the formation of a new morality, purely technological, with the progressive elimination of the Christian moral elements contained in the bourgeois morality. This technological morality does not yet exist in its entirety. It is in process of development, but it is certainly the morality of tomorrow.[2]

Technology supposes the creation of a new morality. It informs the whole of public, professional, and private life. One can no longer act except in relation to technical ensembles. Hence there is need to create new patterns of behavior, new ideas, new virtues. At the same time, new choices are set before man which he is in no way prepared to face. Now the more technology is precise, exacting, and efficient, the more it demands that the performer be efficient, precise, prepared. These are not merely questions of competence. They are matters requiring dedication. This man must know how to use the technique, but he must also know how to be its servant. His moral qualities must be at the level of the new world which technology is unveiling. Some moralists have already foreseen this problem, but the idealists have resolved it exactly in reverse, saying that technology puts man's life at stake, that a new morality must be founded which will permit man to give a meaning to his life once again, to recover the unity of his life, and which will restore the value of freedom.

The project is laudable but inadequate, desirable but inexact. It contradicts reality, for if such a morality were instituted it would make man rebellious toward technology, unavailable for full technological service, reticent in the face of progress, oriented toward a different center of interest from technology, placing the latter at the bottom of the scale of values, all of which is completely inadmissable in a technological society. Hence this project (once again, desirable) has no chance of success. The probability is that a new morality will be created which will put its blessing upon man's subjection to the technological values and will make him a good servant to this new master, in trustfulness and loyalty, in the spirit of a service freely rendered.

Technological morality exhibits two principal character-istics. It is above all a morality of behavior and second, it ex-cludes moral questioning. It is a morality of behavior. That is to say, it is solely interested in man's external conduct. The problems of intention, sentiment, ideals, perplexities of conscience, are none of its concern. Still, it ignores these only as long as they remain inward. If these interior movements were to lay claim to outward expression, then the techno-logical morality would enter into conflict with them, for con-duct must always be determined by external and objective motives if man's attitudes are to be consistent with the technological world in which he must live and act. The situation calls for a behavior on man's part which is exact, precise, in harmony with the working of all the categories of techniques which are proliferating in our society. And this behavior should be fixed, not on the basis of moral prin-ciples, but in terms of precise technological rules—psycho-logical and sociological. The external act alone has value, and this act should be determined for technological motives. This is one of the principal results of the sciences of man, which—in spite of their proclamations and declarations—are all and always sciences impregnated with morality aimed at adapting man to the technological world.

We well know that the optimum use of techniques of any kind depends upon the user's being psychologically adapted, upon his freedom from scruple and uneasiness (moral or physical), upon his being in tune with the ma-chine, upon his being in sympathy with the operation, upon his being sufficiently motivated, upon his having a scale of values which allows him to find satisfaction and dignity in his own eyes in the very exercise of these techniques. This behavior in harmony with the techniques, which is de-manded of man if the techniques are to have their maxi-mum efficiency, must be a behavior which is morally justi-fied. Hence it must not be a behavior which is externally imposed, mechanical, forced, but a behavior to which man gives his adherence for moral motives. Only, this behavior is not itself established for moral motives! It is determined by the organization, by efficiency planning. The more the organization—of work, of government, of family life, of living conditions, of traffic, of public health, of recreation, etc.—is perfected, and the more exactly the patterns of behavior are established, the more does efficiency planning tend to displace the moral imperative.

The former moral objective of duties and imperatives, the "closed morality," is progressively eliminated by the organization. It is the latter, now, which dictates the true duties, the true social imperatives, and which supplies them with moral value and in this way justifies them. But at the same time this leads to a questioning of the problem of choice between good and evil, a questioning of individual decision, of subjective morality, of open morality. There are fewer and fewer choices to be made (I mean *real* choices), because good behavior is that which is called for by the technique, is described by the technique, is made possible by the technique.

We have already seen that for contemporary moralists morality is the domain of ambiguity, but when they speak that way they are speaking out of their reflections, out of their wishes, out of traditional society. They are not at all talking about a morality which would be of use to a technological society. In such a society, technique excludes ambiguity. The good is clear. The behavior valid for a technical world is dreadfully uniform. It obviously imposes itself upon the individual. There are not a hundred ways of employing a given technique to achieve an end. The technique is itself a way of acting. The conduct demanded of the individual can scarcely be doubted or disputed.

Contemporary man is very generally convinced that the technique is the good, that it concurs in man's good and will bring about his happiness. Should man recoil before this prospect, the proof of the technical good is confirmed, reinforced, and assured by the various pressures at the disposal of the technological civilization: the testimony of its successes, the importance of the necessity for its development, the certainty of progress, the marvelous concordance of the techniques. How can all that fail to convince a man inwardly that he should participate with all his heart in the development of such a good? And if problems still remain, the techniques of psychology will be able to reach into this heart itself, to personalize the objective reasons for the behavior, to obtain through technical procedures loyalty and good will, joy itself in the carrying out of the "duty," which like everything else ceases to be painful and exhausting in the comfortable world of techniques.

On the one hand, in the eyes of contemporary man technical progress is a good in itself, and on the other hand the techniques insure the necessity of a behavior favorable to progress. Technology offers man a fulfillment of the good which is easy, effective, and justified in advance. Man's decision is obtained through adhering to technical progress. There can be no debate, no personal decision involved in the matter. The good is obvious. It goes along with power. There can be no question of escaping it. One will end with a perfected conformism never yet achieved in the moral sphere. In fact, never until now had morality been armed with an unassailable authority. Never before had the good been obvious and beyond dispute. Never had there been a factual identification between the good and happiness. Never had there been a coincidence between individual moral decision for the good and material social development. All this has been realized and achieved by technology. The technological good is irrefutable. It cannot be challenged. Man is moving toward a situation in which he will no longer be able to choose evil. In a certain sense, one can conceive this as putting an end to morality.

In this technological morality there is also set up a scale of values which are truly valid for man and which the individual accepts as such. Without doubt, one of the important facts in this sphere is the transformation of technology itself into a value. For the man of today technology is not only a fact. It is not merely an instrument, a means. It is a criterion of good and evil. It gives meaning to life. It brings promise. It is a reason for acting and it demands our commitment. "A way of dealing with the world and of characterizing it in terms of our continuing and of our momentary requirements." This definition . . . what is it a definition of? of technology? or of value? There could be no better demonstration of the fact that technology has become a value than by pointing out the ambiguity of this definition. Now it is word for word the definition of value given by one of the contemporary representatives of the philosophy of values (Gusdorf). But this is even more exact at the level of the average man. Doubtless for him, in various ways, technology is a value. In various ways, because the meaning which technology has given to his life can as well be comfort, the possession of an appliance, rather than the liberation of the proletariat thanks to technology, or humanity's newfound happiness. This is a criterion of good and evil, for without the slightest doubt everyone today treats technology as a good (a gift of God, etc.), and people cannot avoid talking that way.

Whenever anyone suggests that technology presents certain disadvantages people rush to its defense (it isn't technology, but the fault of man who misuses it . . . but if it is true that the evil here is man's doing, that then means implicitly that technology is the good). And this good is set forth as a thing not to be challenged (it is not possible to call technology into question). One can call everything in our society into question (including God), but not technology. It is seen, then, to be the decisive value. And as a value it is desirable. It indeed merits the dedication of all resources in its behalf. It indeed merits that man sacrifice himself to it—and one finds it normal that there should be martyrs of science, today in reality martyrs of technology. We could easily go on and show that each trait applied by the philosophers to value, in order to characterize it, would exactly apply to modern man's belief in technology, to his judgment of it, and to his behavior toward it.

But we must pass on to a second value of this technological morality, that of the normal. In this technological society the normal tends to replace the moral. Man is no longer asked to act well, but to act normally. The norm is no longer an imperative of the conscience. One gets at it through average behavior, whether this is determined statistically, or by psychological evaluation, or by whatever means. Everything concurs in confirming the predominance of the normal. Increasingly the criminal is treated as a sick, abnormal person, in need of care to help him return to average, normal behavior. Similarly, the highest virtue demanded of man today is adjustment. The worst judgment a man can suffer is to be called maladjusted. (Maladjusted to what? Very exactly, to the technological society. Sociologists and psychologists are agreed in acknowledging that technology is the most frequent cause of maladjustment.) The chief purpose of instruction and education today is to bring along a younger generation which is *adjusted* to this society.

The socially maladjusted exactly corresponds to the immoral of the earlier societies, and the normal exhibits the same characteristics as the older morality. For one thing, it functions as a definition of the good, as a norm, as a requirement to be met imperatively. For another thing, it is a value which makes it possible to judge, to estimate deeds, people, and events. It is a personal, individualized aspiration. Everyone strives today to be normal, and this normal repels the older notion of virtue, of good. Moral judgment is no longer tolerated over against the decision of normalcy. As long as conduct is normal there is no reason to reprove it in the name of morality. It is no longer legitimate to declare good or evil that which is accepted as normal. This is highly characteristic of the Kinsey Report, for example, which rejects traditional sexual morality, not in the name of objective science, but really in the name of the morality of the normal. Now this normal is not exactly the same thing as moral custom.

There is in the concept of the normal a concern for precise knowledge, for the rationale of behavior, for adjustment to the objective conditions of society, for confrontation with the psychological and sociological sciences, since in the final analysis it is the clinical technician who decides what is normal. We see, then, how this value depends upon technology, and is finally subordinated to technological value. It is partly because the normal is established in relation to behavior as registered in a very precise society, the technological society (and it is no mere chance that we see the substitution of the normal for the moral going hand in hand with the setting up of a technological society), and partly because the normal is discovered and developed by techniques, and in no other way.

Finally, we should bear in mind a third value characteristic of this morality; namely, success. In the last analysis, good and evil are synonyms for success and failure. According to the bourgeois formula, stemming from a particular interpretation of the Bible, virtue is always ratified by material success. But with the passage of time (and the temptation was too great for this to be avoided) the conclusion was drawn that success is the clear sign of virtue, since it is virtue's reward. Virtue is invisible. Success is visible. Hence success allows us to presuppose the existence of virtue. The next step is to say that success is, in itself, the good. One is an abbreviation for the other. With this orientation one then seeks to base morality on success, whence the demonstration that "crime doesn't pay." When all is said and done, the reason one should not be a criminal is that it isn't profitable. But if we proceed in this direction we are obliged to admit that strength is one of the essential factors of success, and then we very soon realize that the crucial polarity is not so much that of good and evil as that of strength and weakness—thence, also, the ethical importance of the champion.

The champion is necessarily a representative of the good. In another perspective, that of the Communists, the expression of this identity between success and the good is found in the necessity of adhering to the direction of history. The direction of history is only seen by hindsight at each stage, in the success of a given enterprise. If it did succeed, that *then* means that it was indeed in the direction of history. And since, in the last analysis, it is history which determines what is good, the direction of history manifests the good in the form of success.

As a matter of fact, underneath both the bourgeois and the communist ethical formulae there lies the conviction that one does not argue with results. A successful action is necessarily compelling and is not to be called in question. Now this is essentially linked up with technological operation, since the latter is just what insures effectiveness and results. To be sure, there can be various criteria of success. In the bourgeois society it is money, honors, titles, a higher rung of the social ladder. Under totalitarian regimes one of the essential signs will be membership in the Party. The latter is the content of the good in itself. It is also the guardian of the good. To be outside the Party is not to participate in the good. To be against it is evil. Now the Party is never anything but an instrument for political effectiveness, for the technique of propaganda and of government. Here we find the link between technical procedures and the determination of the good. And likewise, we again find virtue as applied to socio-political action taking precedence over every other virtue.

But we must not forget that the instrument of success in our society is always a technological instrument. Quite consciously it is demonstrated for our benefit that the ultimate goal of technology is not merely a material result, but the fulfillment of the good. Economic abundance will permit man to develop himself spiritually, morally, and culturally. The socialist regime paves the way for a new man, who, freed from alienation and from capitalistic contradictions, will be good. That will come to pass thanks to the technique. But if such is indeed the goal of technology, every technical success participates in the ultimate good, and to oppose this development is to be truly evil and demonic.

Technological morality demands of man a commitment. It calls for the practice of virtues. It cannot be said that it requires new virtues, for these virtues are old, but they are validated, placed in the foreground. Formerly treated as minor, they now become major and exclusive. To a certain extent one may also speak of new virtues—work, for example. Let us not forget that in the traditional societies, in *all* societies, work was looked down upon, treated as animal toil unworthy of man. Every moral, social, and spiritual elevation was translated into an abandonment of work. It was considered a necessity in a pinch, but a damnable necessity. And this is true not only of "primitive" peoples, shepherds, nomads, but of all civilizations—Incas as well as Chinese, Greeks as well as Hindus, Scandinavians as well as Egyptians. They all held work in contempt, and Christian society also. In spite of the two or three biblical texts counseling work, it must not be forgotten that the stream of theological opinion was that work was a mark of condemnation, a sign of our fallen nature, and consequently a necessity which had to be accepted, but in no wise a good or a virtue.

This opinion is changed with the theologians of the Reformation, who for the first time presented the positive aspects of work. But the latter will not become a virtue, and a cardinal virtue, the father of all the virtues, until the bourgeois society of the eighteenth and nineteenth centuries. That is the first time in the history of mankind that work becomes a good, and "worker" a title of nobility. Now let us not forget that that was the time when the power of the bourgeoisie, when its rise to power, was based on work. Having become the ruling class, the bourgeoisie promoted the source of its authority to the status of a value for the whole society. This was the more fitting since the lower classes all worked (as they had never worked before) and one had to grant them a moral satisfaction in exchange for the sacrifices one was demanding of them. "To work is to pray! This work which you are constrained to perform for the glory of the bourgeoisie is a value, both moral and spiritual. You are doing good thereby, and are working your own salvation." Now if all were expected to be mobilized for work in this way, this was, in the final analysis, because of the development of the technique. It was technique which both required and made possible this dedication of man to work. The work which has become the principal virtue in our society is technological work. And the virtues which are elaborated in this morality are all connected with work. Thus, while often of ancient vintage, these virtues now are attached to a new objective.

They are splendid disciplinary virtues: the virtues of self-control, of devotion, of trustworthiness in one's work, of responsibility in the performance of tasks, of loyalty, of sacrifice to one's occupation—all are fitted into the central cardinal virtue of "doing good." They all are linked to the employment of techniques. All the virtues by which we see man glorified (and justly glorified) are virtues of work. The performance of superior work is the gauge of these virtues, and sacrifice and devotion especially are functions of the creative achievement of technology. All these virtues really have as their aim to facilitate the working and utilization of techniques. This entails three consequences:

1. The gradual elimination of the other moral values: family virtues, good fellowship, humor, play, etc. All that is pushed into the background and counts for less and less. A man may act ignobly toward his comrades or his wife, but if he practices the virtues essential to work all is forgiven him. He is cited as an example. Most of the great heroes of our day, scientists, aviators, etc., are of this type. These virtues are eliminated simply because, in the eyes of modern man, they no longer count, inasmuch as they have nothing to do with the "central motif" of our society.

2. It is constantly being said that technology is nothing without man, that when all is said and done the decision rests with man, and that he is the master of the techniques. But one forgets that, in reality, man is the one who is put into shape to serve the techniques, that the virtues created

for him are virtues of work, that the important word is adaptation, and that man has to be "adapted," that consequently morality subordinates man to the techniques.

3. In the technological morality the standard of conduct is objective. A technically well-made combination must function. Whenever it fails to work, if the technical calculation was correct, then there is a human flaw: laziness, dishonesty, or ill will. The evil is of that kind, in a word, sabotage. To be sure, there may be sabotage, objectively considered, whatever might have been the intentions of the individual. What should work doesn't work. That is the fault of the man, whatever his motives might be. The evil is in the sphere of behavior, and like the good is objectively discoverable. In addition, it is also obvious that this behavior which affects the whole of society should be thoroughly punished. The moral sanction gradually ceases to be a matter of the inward domain of the conscience and becomes political or social.

But there is another very noteworthy virtue in this morality; namely, confidence in the future, an ability to face up to tomorrow, an assurance in hope which is astonishing in troubled times. It is the virtue of "all is possible," which of course expresses in large part the value of the normal. All is possible. Not only is there no predetermined moral or spiritual limit to action, but further, the only acknowledged barrier is that which is not possible today but which will be tomorrow. Nothing is surprising any more, atomic fission, sputnik: that all belings to the normal course of events. Tomorrow it will be done better. In fact, this virtue especially expresses a morality of the unbounded, of the limitless, to which modern man is perfectly adapted.

The boundlessness of means and of technical success produces a morality of the gigantic and the limitless. The colossal, the "world's biggest," are expressions of this morality. Man no longer recognizes any limits to his conquest. When man becomes involved in the process of technical development, at no time does he have occasion to stop and say No. In the conviction that technology leads to the good, and that in the final analysis morality is closely linked to technology, man cannot at any time come to a halt in this march forward (the problem of Oppenheimer and the atomic scientists). From then on, the "more" becomes a criterion in itself. The greater, the higher, the more powerful, that suffices. The new morality justifies automatically that which is "more." It is a close companion to technology in its development and justifies it as it goes along.

The good, then, appears as the surpassing of limits. What one cannot do today he will be able to do tomorrow, and that is good. From the fact that we have to do with a morality of the unlimited, we arrive at a rule of conduct for man which is perfectly adapted to the requirements of modern society, and which is coextensive with his professional activity. Through that aspect, we again see three characteristics of this morality, already indicated in the course of the discussion above. As a whole, it is a morality of occupation, of well-doing, which becomes a total, allembracing morality for the whole society. It is an essentially total, even totalitarian, collective morality. It is a morality which progressively atrophies the individual virtues of personal morality, and which ends in the disappearance of the individual moral sense in the degree in which it causes the moral problem to disappear.[3] Such are the characteristics of this technological morality in the course of its development. In the last analysis, it appears as a suppression of morality through the total absorption of the individual into the group.

Concerning all this we are obliged to conclude that an answer to the question of the good does not acquire validity through its being consistent with the social environment, or with the nature of man, nor through its intellectual rigor, nor through the gravity with which it treats man, but through its foundation. "It has no gravity, no depth of rigor, unless it be founded in such a way that man cannot escape it, either by pleading his freedom or his weakness, or again in thinking that he is himself the answer, which only resolves the problem by suppressing it."[4]

III

The Impossibility
and the Necessity
of a Christian Ethic

The Impossibility
of a Christian Ethic

12 It may seem paradoxical to assert the impossibility of a Christian ethic.[1] In the eyes of most of our contemporaries, Christianity is a morality first of all. And have not many epochs of Christian history been characterized by the church's insistence upon actions and conduct? Did not we ourselves speak, in chapter 1, of a double morality, thereby indicating that a Christian morality does exist?[2] Nevertheless every honest reflection must absolutely begin by acknowledging that such is impossible, that there cannot be a Christian ethic, that the whole of revelation is against it, and that every attempt to construct such a morality, no matter how faithful, is a betrayal of the revelation of God in Jesus Christ, and in the last analysis an imposture. We must keep this judgment constantly in our hearts and minds throughout our inquiry. Otherwise it will necessarily be false. In the knowledge that this search is by itself vicious, that the formulation of a Christian ethic is impossible, that every description of Christian behavior is at once vain and sterile, that the pretention expressed therein is prejudicial to the freedom of God—it is only with this judgment continually present to our intelligence and in our lives that we can proceed with this quest, staying within the grace of God, since we shall have remained under judgment.

The morality which may be formulated will itself be under judgment. It can never be a means of escaping God's free decision. It will never be a description of the good, of good conduct located outside the dialectic of judgment and grace. Only because we shall have accepted (not theoretically or in an a priori way, but in a living manner, checked and renewed at every instant) the fact that our enterprise is impossible and sinful—it, too, registered in Adam's attempt to know good and evil, and in the possibility of carrying it out given him by Satan—the grace of God can, if it be God's will, make it into something possible and truthful. For we must ever be conscious of the fact that our desire to define a Christian ethic is in no way different from that of all those in revolt against God who claim to establish the good and the evil.[3] The purity of our intention to serve God is in no sense a justification of our enterprise. There is no justification in good intentions, but only in Jesus Christ. The only thing, then, that can make this quest legitimate, and can render it possible, is God's decision, which we cannot prejudge, and which we can only await in prayer and submission.

The biblical concept of the good as the will of God immediately prohibits us from formulating an ethic.[4] An ethic is always, ultimately, the formulation of a good in itself. There can be no such thing as the construction of an ethic which does not pretend to determine what is good. Even Sartre, who claims not to determine anything beforehand, nevertheless presents us with a model for the only human conduct which is possible and legitimate, in the last analysis, a model of the good, when he shows the necessity for existing through the confrontation with nonbeing. That is the good! Every ethic *is a definition* of the good—that is to say, *a taking over*. It is man who defines the good even if he proclaims the transcendent. An ethic is likewise an assumption that the good is in some way *knowable* in itself (whether axiomatically, or solely through activity, through

the reason, through intuition, or through commitment),
and that it is a step taken by man which brings him to this
knowledge of the good. It is man who is the master, whether
for knowing or for misconceiving this good, which is always clothed in a sufficient objectivity. In this way it can
be known, even *analyzed* and *cataloged.*

The relation between the immediate situation and the
determination of the good necessarily entails the setting up
of types and norms, in the end a catalog. Finally, there is
always the question of permanence. Man would be living in
an insane world if he could not count on a permanence of
the good, on some consistency between yesterday and today, on a more or less enduring identification of value. So
true is this that man can never resist decreeing the universality of a morality, and the permanence of the same values
across all of history. No ethical construct can escape these
three characteristics. Now to say that the good is the will
itself of God is to deny the possibility of these three elements in any ethic which would attach itself to that will.[5]
As we have already said, there could not be a good superior
to the decision of God, in accordance with which that decision would be made, to which it would have to conform.
Rather it is the will of God which defines the good. It is
not man. The good cannot be something incorporated into
the construction of an ethic. It cannot even be its point of
departure; and if the ethic were concerned with making
the good into an existential value the problem, in the last
analysis, would be the same, for the good can neither be
known nor lived in a manner intrinsic to man, but only ex-
trinsic.[6]

At no time can man of himself grasp the good. He cannot introduce it into his way of life, nor into his social organization, nor into any system of any category whatsoever.
This will of God escapes him, and we have seen that he cannot discern it from within. He can only feel it as coming
from outside himself. If he were able, even in the slightest
degree, to live or to formulate an ethic of the will of God,

that would mean that he is superior to God, or what amounts to the same thing, that there is a good superior to God and that God is transformed into a thing. Now the good, the will of God, is not even knowable directly by man, but only through revelation.[7] And in the degree in which God is the living God, in the degree in which his will is living, in the degree in which his word is not a dust-covered record or a closed book, but only comes into existence when God himself speaks, in the degree in which "my ways are not your ways," in that degree the revelation is an act ever new which cannot be systematized,[8] nor analyzed, nor relegated to a past when it was alive but now that it has taken place it is delivered into our hands to do with what we will. In the latter case, it would be possible to turn this past, amortized revelation into one part of a system. Then one could construct all the theologies and ethical systems one wished.

Only when God delivers something into our hands we have clear examples of what happens. In Adam's hands the creation becomes a bramble patch. In Israel's hands the law becomes pharisaic casuistry. In our hands Jesus Christ becomes the crucified one. And when, in fact, man regards this revelation as a thing of the past which belongs to him, he falsifies it. Either the revelation is a living, present word and it cannot be systematized into a morality, or it is a dead letter which isn't worth using in preference to anything else in the building of an ethic.

The will of God remains perfectly free. It never becomes an abstract law of the presence of the one who puts it forth. It never becomes a philosophic or moral principle from which we would be free to draw conclusions, and which would remain as the origin of Christian reflection or conduct. There are no Christian principles.[9] Most of the heresies came into being as a result of transforming the word of God into principles.[10] That is also why the Bible never presents itself as a book of philosophy, but as a history. And when the will of God takes the form of a law, the latter always appears as a commandment. "Thou," it says to the hearer. It is not at all a question of a general rule promulgated by a legislator, but the start of a personal dialogue. In this commandment God addresses a particular person at that moment. The person either understands it as the present reality of God and will live in accordance with that word and in continued dialogue with God, or else he refuses to hear it as addressed to him personally, but in that case he can, strictly speaking, do nothing in the category which begins with "thou." He will have to substitute "one" in its place. And that is the falsehood. The ethic which is constructed from that standpoint is no longer Christian. It no longer has to do with God. Moreover, we shall be obliged later on to go more deeply into the significance of the presence of the law.

Thus the free will of God escapes us, and is of no use as the object of an intellectual construction, nor as a goal to be aimed at, nor as a reason for a manner of life. Kierkegaard is right when he alludes to the extreme case of God's demanding of Abraham the sacrifice of Isaac. There indeed we are faced with the exceeding character, without limit, unforeseeable, incomprehensible from the standpoint of prior principles, of this will of God. We are confronted with the leaving behind of all ethical norms. And yet it was the good which was at that moment affirmed, under appearances so contradictory to all that we call and feel to be the good that we cannot fail to be repelled by it. But such was the will of God. One can understand, under these conditions, the temptation of some truthful Christians to reject ethics altogether, and to fall back solely on obedience *hic et nunc* to the current word of God. However, that attitude is not entirely just. It is partial, and we shall see farther along that it is impossible to be satisfied with that.

For at the same time, let us always remember that "whenever the grace becomes event and revelation it ends in the institution of the law." [11]

However, we need to grasp the problem of the suspension

of ethics, not only in the specimen case of Abraham which Kierkegaard always went back to, but in a more general manner. Prunet can write: "John pushes to the extreme the paradox of the fulfillment of ethics through the suspension of ethics. Together with the other New Testament authors, he achieves the unprecedented revolution of denying to natural man the possibility of being an authentic moral subject." [12]

In order to show that the will of God can remove the ethical norms, or to show that the will of God is in itself the good in its entirety, one points traditionally to the special instance of the sacrifice of Abraham. But it is too easy to reply that this solitary example is not convincing because it is unique. It is an extreme case, to be borne in mind as such, but which is in no way conclusive. Now it seems to us, to the contrary, that one can adduce many other instances. There is the polygamy of the patriarchs, Abraham's attitude toward Sarah in Egypt, Tamar's seduction of her father-in-law, Judah, which is pronounced just. But, above all else, there is the dreadful requirement of the *herem,* the interdiction. We know that the interdiction is presented biblically as an explicit will of God. "The Lord said to Moses, . . . 'No devoted thing that a man devotes to the Lord . . . whether of man or beast . . . shall be sold or redeemed; every devoted thing is most holy to the Lord. No one devoted, who is to be utterly destroyed from among men, shall be ransomed; he shall be put to death'" (Lev. 27:1, 28–29). "Now this is the commandment. . . . Hear therefore, O Israel . . . when the Lord your God brings you into the land . . . and clears away many nations . . . and you defeat them; then you must utterly destroy them" (Deut. 6:1, 3; 7:1–2). God expressly ordains for his people the massacre of all the conquered inhabitants: men, women and children. All are to be destroyed, together with cattle, possessions, and houses. The crops are to be destroyed as well. It is not a matter of a theoretical commandment. It is applied, and we frequently see the approbation which God bestows on the carrying out of the interdiction. Arad and his people are given over to the *herem*. Israel vows to give them over if God will grant the victory; which is what took place (Numbers 21:1–3).

Again, there is Sihon, king of Heshbon: "And the Lord said to me, 'Behold, I have begun to give Sihon and his land over to you! . . . And we captured all his cities at that time and utterly destroyed every city, men, women, and children; we left none remaining" (Deut. 2:31, 34). The book of Joshua abounds in *herem* (6:21; 11:12; 11:20; etc.). It is frequently stated that this expresses God's will: "He gave them over by interdict, as Moses, the servant of the Lord, had ordained." "The Lord permits these peoples to persist in making war so that Israel can give them over by interdict without showing any mercy toward them, and so that Israel might destroy them, as the Lord had commanded Moses." And we know that Samuel, voicing God's will, orders Saul to give over the people of Amalek by interdict (1 Samuel 15:13).

Conversely, God vents his wrath upon Israel when the interdict is not fully carried out. We recall the story of Achan (Joshua 7), where it is recounted that the prescription of the interdict is part of the covenant, and that he who is caught taking anything interdicted shall be burned alive. But Saul also, when he spared not only the possessions but the person of Agag, saw his mercy severely rebuked (1 Samuel 15). Finally, Ahab allowed Ben-hadad to live because "the kings of the house of Israel are merciful kings" (1 Kings 20:31–34), but no mercy was to be observed! The prophet pronounces to Ahab the will of God: "Thus says the Lord, Because you have let go out of your hand the man whom I had devoted to destruction." [13]

We have to look this dreadful fact in the face. We must neither forget it (which is what is generally done in modern thought), nor push it aside by saying that this is a barbaric, primitive custom found among all peoples and having nothing to do with revelation. Let us note, first of all, that it is not historically accurate to say that the *herem* is a custom found to a certain degree among all peoples. The absolute interdiction which we come upon here is rarely *affirmed* elsewhere. Second, even if we are dealing with a barbaric custom, it is here taken up by God. A spiritual value is attributed to it which, in point of fact, makes it absolute. There is nothing we can do. It is all found in scripture, is a part of revelation, and nothing authorizes us to expurgate this or that text because it doesn't please us. It is true that it shocks our sensibilities, our concept of morality, and of the benevolent divinity, but it is dishonest to pretend for that reason that "it is not possible that God could have willed that." From that time on, complete capriciousness governs our attitude toward the Bible. We must take these texts seriously *as well.* Moreover, we will see their significance. First of all, it is sacrifice. It is a recognition by Israel that all belongs to God and comes from him, but also that the nation of Israel, the chosen nation, is holy. It is set apart and should remain so. It must avoid all contamination from the false gods which would alter the truth of which it is the bearer. Hence it must destroy everything pertaining to these false gods and everything which bears them witness.

There can be no halfway dealing between truth and false-hood. There can be no friendly relationship between the people of God and the world of sin. There is no mercy for the demons. And yet, the very attitude of the nation of Israel when it puts the *herem* into practice cuts it off very decisively from all those surrounding nations, which hence-forth will not seek to enter into contact with it. It is indeed, in that way also, a people set apart. But if we thus see quite clearly the meaning of the *herem,* it still remains just as unacceptable to our morality; and yet it is expressly de-creed as the good! What better illustration could one have that it is in point of fact the ordinance of God which *con-stitutes* the good, which brings it about that an act which the human conscience reproves is *nevertheless* the good be-cause God ordains it; and hence, that there is a truth about the good which far outstrips our judgment, and before which we can only bow in humility?

Now at the opposite pole from all we have just written there arises the obstacle of casuistry. Practically no morality escapes it, even that of the existentialists (Simone de Beauvoir constantly lapses into casuistry), even that of Haering, in spite of the fact that he condemns it. And yet casuistry is unacceptable from the point of view of faith. Soë [14] indicates two principal reasons. First, the Christian ethic is an ethic of life and life is dynamic. Each situation, like each person, is novel. Casuistry is necessarily static and never exhausts the ingredients of a situation. The command of God is not a general rule, or collection of rules. It is always particular for a person at this moment, in this situation. The command has no need to be interpreted. As Barth says,[15] the uncertainty concerning God's will in a given instance is always on man's part, not God's. That is to say, the question of clarification in each particular case does not relate to the content of the command, but rather to the situation of the person when faced with the command. In this way we are brought back to the level of real life, but that eliminates all casuistic ethics.

Second, casuistry presupposes the mediating role of the church, and it restores man's sovereignty before God by establishing just situations and decisions. The moralist takes the place of God, and makes use of the commandment of God as a possession. If one holds to scripture, ethics cannot regulate cases, nor give just decisions. It cannot promote its precepts to the status of laws. It often stops short of settling questions, but in that case one is tempted to ask: Is it still an ethic? of what use is it? It is indeed true that there are no ethical *problems* in the gospel.[16] Casuistry rests on analysis, on distinctions, on discriminations, in the last analysis on what Bonhoeffer calls "disunity." Now previously, as we have seen, that was a characteristic of the *ethics of the fall.* In the unity recovered through grace, in the union with God, we are in the presence of quite a different ethical orientation, exactly the reverse. But is it something we can *talk* about? Perhaps it can only be lived in Christ; for it is out of the question to interpret the law of God in terms of possibilities, of the circumstances of human action, etc. As Karl Barth quite rightly says,[17] there can be a casuistry of practice, in which a person faced with a case of conscience can encounter another person who helps him resolve that problem, but there cannot be a casuistic ethic, nor any technical method for applying the text to a multiplicity of cases, nor for drawing an inference of good and evil on the basis of the truth of the text.

When we were speaking of morality for mankind, we were saying that the Bible asserts man's inability to do the good. Natural man can know nothing of the true good. If he is capable of fulfilling what *he* calls good, he cannot in any event carry out what God requires. There is no just person, no not one. Now this situation is not very different for the pardoned man, for the person who has received the revelation of God. That is not grounds for saying that this person, a Christian let us say, is henceforth good. There again we meet with a frequent heresy in the churches: those outside are pagans, wicked.

The entire Bible constantly iterates that nothing has changed intrinsically or ontologically in this person who has been enlightened by the revelation. He is saved. He is justified. He is sanctified, but he is still himself. Called to the resurrection, he will die. Enlightened, he nevertheless walks in darkness. An instrument of the kingdom of heaven, he nevertheless is in the world. Knowing the good, he does evil. "Wretched man that I am!" cries Paul, noting this conflict between the law of the Spirit and the law of the flesh which is in his members. And because he has received the revelation of the will of God, disobedience and evil now take on a much more authentic form and vigor. Because he has received pardon for his sin, sin now assumes for him a seriousness which it could not have as long as he remained ignorant of the price which it cost God. *Simul peccator et justus.* The Christian has not become better able to do the good. We were observing above that he has not become more capable of developing an ethic knowing that the Bible bears the word of God, and now we have to observe that he has not become more capable of living this ethic, of carrying out by himself the necessary works. To the contrary, he now is aware of his inability to "work" his salvation, since there is nothing changed in his state of being a sinful man. That is why the construction of an ethic becomes even more impossible for him. That is also why the Bible is especially severe on those chosen of God who construct an ethic. It directly judges every morality made by a servant of God as a means set up by man to insure his own salvation.

When all is said and done, morality becomes a way of protecting ourselves against God's free decision toward us, against the fact that salvation depends on him, and on him alone. We establish norms (out of the Bible, to be sure) as a safeguard against God, against the unforeseeable wisdom which we call arbitrary. If only we could offer God an indisputable virtue, indisputable because derived from his own revelation, then we could put our minds at rest. God would not be able to condemn us. We would not be delivered into his hands, to his free decision. We still suffer Cain's anguish. Abel and Cain each presented an offering, and God chose one of them. Why? He rejected the other. Why? If we could prove to him that he has no right to reject that other offering, to reject us, and could prove it to him out of his own word, then we would have won.[18] We would have tied God up in his own system. We would know of a certainty what to expect and God would not be able to do anything we had not already known, that we were not expecting. Such is always the meaning of Christian (or Jewish) morality as seen in the Bible.

To be sure, this curse is not always clearly and con-

sciously in our hearts, but it is there. For we need to consider the significance of such an act. For one thing, it means
that we are turning God's word back against God himself,
which is a strictly satanic work. We see, in fact, that at the
time of the temptation of Jesus by Satan, the latter used the
word of God to seduce the Son of God. The same thing
happens when we make use of that word in order to bind
God, to protect ourselves against him. For another thing,
such a project means that we suspect God of injustice, of
wickedness, of tyranny. All morality erected over against
God is a refusal to submit to the free will of God, and
therefore is a defiance of his will (even, and especially,
when it claims to be an expression of that will), for at that
moment one denies to God his very divinity, from which
one expects nothing good. It is the proof that we do not
love God, and that our relationship with him is not one of
love, but of fear, of force, and of mutual compulsion.

The closer the morality put together by man is to the
will of God the more suspect it is, the more it is a proof of
the absence of love on the part of that man, the more
harshly it will be attacked by God.[19] That is why we witness
in the gospel the severe attack of Jesus Christ on the scribes
and Pharisees. We should never forget that they were not
"hypocrites" in the simplistic sense in which we employ
that word today. They were responsible men, concerned
with the knowledge and the application of the law, seeking
truly to carry out as well as possible that which had been
revealed to the fathers, and thereby to put themselves in
good standing with God. They were very genuinely good
men. Now in their intention and anxiety to live in accordance with the law, there was, to be sure, an aspect of truth;
but in their determination to be in good standing with God,
and so never to ask anything of him as beggars, and to owe
him nothing, therein lay the radical evil of their lives. For
that fact, *because* they fulfilled the law of God *in order* not
to owe God anything, Jesus Christ condemns them much
more severely, and conversely he welcomes those who did

not claim to fulfill the law, the heathen, the prostitutes
. . . precisely the immoral ones.

There is no Christian life without the action of the Holy
Spirit,[20] without his inspiration and guidance. Here again,
the necessity for God's intervening to guide our lives puts
an end to our pretending to erect a Christian morality. In
fact, we can bring to light the commandment of God as
much as we please, and if the Holy Spirit is not acting
within us our knowledge is in vain. We shall never be able
to carry it out. Now the Spirit blows where he wills. He is
unpredictable in his entrances as well as in his effects. He
cannot be bound. He cannot be possessed. He comes and he
goes. When we walk in his light we cannot be assured that
it will not suddenly disappear. When we think to seize
upon its reality we suddenly find ourselves confronted with
a void. As a result, we can put nothing together which is
consistent, continuous, predictable, neither in our work nor
in our conduct, nor in our strivings for an ascetic morality,
for a raising of the spiritual level, for a mystical progress,
because in the first place this intervention of the Holy
Spirit alone renders us apt for hearing and obeying the
commandment of God. It alone makes us hear the commandment as really addressed to us personally, and in so
doing it gives us the power, the capacity, for carrying it out.
Until the light of the Holy Spirit illumines for us a given
word of God, a given requirement, we have no intrinsic
power in ourselves, no prior aptitude for accomplishing it
which would go into action when the knowledge is given us.
The intervention of the Holy Spirit is not only a personaliz-
ing of the word. It also creates in us the faculty for accomplishing it immediately. And if we put off until tomorrow, if we store up in the secret places of the heart the
knowledge of the word which has been illumined for us,
perhaps we shall still understand it tomorrow, but in any
event we shall no longer have the power to fulfill it, for that
power is tied to the presence itself of the Holy Spirit. God

creates in us the will and the deed. But there is more. The intervention of the Holy Spirit can push us to action which is quite outside the rules and norms. It can incite us to novelty, to innovation. And on that occasion no moral judgment should enter in.

We do not have the right to erect a morality for the purpose of preventing the intervention of the Holy Spirit (and this, in a sense, is the significance of Dostoevsky's story of the Grand Inquisitor) , or of putting man in the middle of a conflict between Christian morality and the order of the Holy Spirit. What good is it, then, to formulate this ethic? [21] What good is it, since it is nothing without the Holy Spirit, and he can contradict it, and so turn us into enemies of God in spite of our good intentions? Then too, the Bible shows us that even if in our scruple and faithfulness we carry out the prescriptions of the law and the gospel in our own strength, by our own impulse, that is as nothing and worthless because not done under the guidance of the Holy Spirit.

What Paul says about our prayers goes even more for our works. If the Holy Spirit must be the interpreter of our poor prayers, our stammerings, before God, still more must he be the one to make worthy our unworthy works, to take them upon himself for God.[22] And the same acts, the same deliberations, the same decisions, which in factual objectivity are identical and ethically equivalent, do not have the same value nor the same meaning before God, according as they were or were not inspired by the Holy Spirit. This, then, accounts for the complete vanity of Christian ethics. What good is it to describe modes of conduct, to point out works to be done, virtues to be extolled, if after it is all done it is exactly as though nothing had been accomplished? And in fact, since all has been accomplished through Jesus Christ, nothing is accomplished through ourselves when we put our moral prescriptions into effect. Thus our morality never achieves the goal which it had set for itself.

Revelation tells us that to be in the covenant of God is much less a matter of doing something than of being someone, and in reality of living by the grace of God. Action, the bringing to pass of the good, the carrying out of some moral law (whether it be the moral law to realize oneself, to fulfill oneself, to behave as a knowing subject: all that belongs to exactly the same category as the execution of the moral imperative) has no value in itself. It is a matter of living, and of pursuing day after day a certain kind of life, filling a certain area of reality with the presence of truth. Of course, to the extent to which it is a matter of living, that life will express itself in a certain conduct, in an action. But the action only has value insofar as it is the expression of a certain life. That is also the meaning of the notion of responsibility. To the extent to which every Christian ethic can only be a sort of putting of the question: "Up to what point am I a partner of God?" it is obvious that it cannot exist as an ethical construct. Since man does not live in a void; since he necessarily—because of Jesus Christ—is confronted with God, is objectively judged by that destiny; since all that he is, does, wills, is constantly and objectively called in question by God; and since such is the content of Christian ethics; then the latter can neither be a code nor a collection of objective principles.[23]

Morality in scripture is not made up of rules but of a certain manner of life defined by the situation of being the people of God, of being predestined, and this is indicated by the frequently employed phrase "worthy of." It is a matter of living in a way worthy of the gospel, worthy of the Lord, worthy of God. Now this is nothing other than the expresson of faith.[24] Faith is the birth and the life of the new man, who is permitted to do and who will do what is good and pleasing in the eyes of God, for it consists in laying hold of and assenting to the divine justification. This new man can only do good works, but then how define in an ethic that which could be considered beforehand as a good work?

The situation is further complicated, and this impossibility confirmed, by the conclusion now reached by specialists in the Old Testament, that ultimately the concepts and commandments which we find there do not have a moral content in the strict sense of the word. The law is not a moral law, and the commandments which go to make it up have quite another orientation and significance; namely, the creation of a certain relationship, the staking out of a certain domain, the proposal and possibility of a certain autonomy, an orientation toward life or toward death. That is not morality. "Justice," likewise, does not qualify in the moral category. It is a power, a mark of salvation, a gift, but without moral content.[25] So in any case it is out of the question to seize upon these commandments and this law in order to use them either as a foundation or as a content for morality, for it is really we who put our moral concepts into it. We interpret that law through the prism of our human morality.

And yet, in spite of what we have just said, in spite of the precedence of life over acts (or possibly because of it!) and contrary to what is constantly being tried anew, there can be no question of an ethic of "models." We shall take up elsewhere the problem of the imitation of Jesus Christ, but our point here is the impossibility of forming an ethic organized around models to be imitated. The "saints" are not a basis for Christian ethics. The latter flows from such categories as have been formulated, for example, by Bergson and a number of others: open ethics, ethics of creation, of values, etc.—grace being the final reality of the life of each of the men of whom the Bible or the church speaks. The retracing of the path of Peter or Paul, of Luther or Calvin, is strictly impossible.

The outstanding people of the Bible, the saints, can in nowise be models, because their all resides in the word which God has pronounced concerning them.[26] The action means nothing apart from the person who performed it. Hence one cannot consider the act, pass judgment on this act for example, and from that go back to the person to judge the person by his act. God alone can do that. We are obliged to take precisely the opposite avenue of approach; namely, that the knowledge of the person is alone decisive, and that the act in question is deserving of consideration or rejection because such and such a person performed it. The act is nothing but a sign of something deeper. It has no existence nor content of itself, whatever our opinions of it might be. The acts of the Pharisees, though "good," were condemned by Jesus Christ because the "inside" was bad. There can be a complete variance between the person and his acts and at that moment we could only know it from a knowledge of the person. But that again only God can do who reserves the judgment to himself. It is not our business to judge according to morality or any other criterion. We wanted merely to bring out the impossibility of moral judgment by emphasizing the lack of any possible objectivity in the affair, since the deed can never be considered in its objectivity but only in its relation to the person who performs it.

According to God's will, it is not a question of doing good but of embodying faith, which is fundamentally different. It is not a matter of doing works but of "bearing fruit." The question of the fruit is really a question of the tree which bears it. As a result, it does no good to define a morality, to decree the actions to be performed, or even to give the scheme of a "Christian life." Anything we might do in this direction remains necessarily external to man. Man, in fact, finds himself in one of two possible situations. It may be that (1) he has not received the revelation, has not known the grace which is afforded him; and in that case how could he understand the meaning of the requirement of God's will? What reason would he have to take seriously the necessity of a life of this kind? In whose name would he perform those acts, those works, which we might prescribe for him or demand of him? Or, (2) he has known the love of God and the salvation which is granted, and in that case why impose something on him? Why propose a certain kind of life to him? Why then, says Paul, continue to impose commandments, " 'Do not handle, Do not taste, Do not touch' (referring to things which all perish as they are used) , according to human precepts and doctrines?" (Col. 2:21–22)

He who lives in the covenant of his Lord by faith has no further need of these orders, of these prescriptions for the Christian life. He knows what he has to do. He knows where he is going. He knows who is leading him. He should of himself, through his own resources and in his own responsibility choose his path and his works. Thus in both cases Christian ethics is completely vain and useless. One can even say that it is much more so than any other ethics. For, once again, a given morality can justify itself in people's eyes from some common standpoint which has a validity acknowledged by all: from the standpoint of reason, of group loyalty, of a manner of life, of instinct, etc., and on that basis it has a value in and of itself. And even if it is not lived by anyone, even if it stands as a solitary monument to the effort of one man, it remains as a testimony to the man and perhaps as an accusation against those who have not chosen to follow it. Then Christian morality is not in that situation.

Either Christian morality is not lived—then it is nothing. It bears no objectivity. It has no authority in itself, because it is not the word of God. If it is not borne by men, incorporated into lives, it does not even have the value of testimony and of judgment with which we credit human morality, for the sole testimony accepted by God is the living man. The sole judgment is that of the word.[27] *Or else* Christian morality is lived. But then it does not exist as a morality; for he who lives it, lives *by* it. He does not follow commandments nor achieve objectives. He lives by the word of God which nourishes him, guides him, and carries him. And when his acts are in conformity with the Christian morality set up by a theologian, then so much the better for that morality! That life, and nothing more, is the justification for the work of the theologian. For, from the fact of the action of the Holy Spirit, each one's work is thoroughly personalized, as well as his life. He is no longer just any man, this person laid hold of by grace. He is no longer one of the mass of mankind.[28] He is a person.

There is no other foundation, no other rationale for the person than to be laid hold of by the personal act of God who says, "Thou . . ." But this personalization causes each life to become singular. There is not one Christian life. There are as many Christian lives as there are Christians. There are not Christian works, except insofar as the Holy Spirit pushes a man to make decisions and to fulfill holiness. Thus one lives in a world endlessly deployed along paths which open up step by step as one follows them, without their in any sense being mapped in advance. One lives in ever-surprising novelty. There is not, to be sure, an absence of continuity, breaks between yesterday and today; but today's innovation could not have been deduced logically and rationally from yesterday's decision since it does not obey a human logic, a rational conduct of life. It follows a deeper logic, a more secret truth, which unites yesterday with today but does not let one guess what will be tomorrow.[29]

To the extent to which the Christian life is a life of obedience, in which, therefore, the only possible norm of moral action is that which comes from elsewhere, from his future, from God—to that extent there is implied a renunciation by the Christian of every objective moral system set up in advance; for his resurrected life is not at his disposal, but is a gift at every instant on the part of God. And that is all the more true since the gospel never gives the means for fulfilling the will of God. For example, according to Bultmann's observation, the gospel does not tell us how to love, but only that we should love. The how is in the category of our freedom, which God grants us precisely to express the true love, but that love is determined by the indication of him to whom it is addressed, in a commandment which is addressed to us by God.

Since the Christian lives in newness of life, he must express this in his invention, and if this newness bears on the how of living, or on the what of living, that is because there is a power in the work which is not the application of a norm.[30] The innovation of the faith is a ceaseless invention of new ethical forms. A Christian morality, then, can have a terribly dangerous effect when it prescribes, foresees, channels, schematizes. It can dry up the invention of faith. It can mire the action of the Holy Spirit. It can be the cushion of idleness which leads a serious Christian to say, "Here is the sum total of the expression. It is well-put, well-reasoned, and in conformity with the will of God, and when I have done that . . . why should I look farther? Why risk getting lost on new roads? These, guaranteed by the tradition of the church or by the intelligence of the theologians, are enough." In this way the pattern supplied by ethics can divert the faith in Jesus Christ from its creative power and rob it of that which is most precious and essential, without which the church goes to sleep and the Christian life also finds itself left behind by the world, which for its part continues to develop. For the ethical invention of the faith is not located in heaven, but indeed right on this earth, in this place in which I am located. To a certain extent it is the response given by man to the confrontation between the Holy Spirit's requirements and the concrete situation in which he finds himself.

The requirement of the Holy Spirit is, if you will, unchangeable and eternal, but only in the kingdom of God is it to be fulfilled by man in its entirety, without any change. At present, it can only be embodied very partially, very crudely, and in accordance with changing forms, for man changes, and the situations in which he finds himself also change. The responsibility of this particular man, the work which is demanded of him personally, is precisely to discover how the Holy Spirit's eternal requirement can be embodied in today's (not yesterday's) world, in the events, the conflicts, of the present time. And because times change and conditions are never the same, the works of the past can be of very little use to us. There is no point in trying to make them permanent nor in trying to reproduce them. Still less should we expect the Holy Spirit to dictate to us the forms of the embodiment, the "how." It should be sufficient for us that the Holy Spirit makes contemporary the full authority and the full truth of the word of God, that he clothes us with power and that he assures us of the presence of Jesus Christ. Beyond that it is our affair, our responsibility. And it is—alas!—this newness, this presence of the man, that a too well-done Christian ethic can prohibit.

To be sure, the Christian life, according to the Bible, is externalized in a series of decisions, and that already resists any construction of an ethic. But this peculiar impossibility is even more marked when we realize what kind of decisions they are.[31] Normally, these decisions lead to an opposition to the world, with the values, principles, and decisions of the world, such as we come to know it in John and Paul. Now this opposition can neither be hardened, nor codified, nor schematized. If it results from an ethical decision taken in faith, if it thus leads to persecution, then "blessed are you when men shall revile you and persecute you . . ." But if it results from an a priori ethic, from taking a stand on the basis of principles, then "woe to you hypocrites . . ." In addition, these decisions are in contrast to global, generalized, macrocosmic views, to which—alas!— theology has often accustomed us. It is always a matter of prosaic decisions, of microscopic adjustments, which cannot (because of this characteristic) be the object of any blueprint, of any prior decision. Otherwise we would lapse into casuistry.

These decisions are contrary to instinct, to impulse, to the demands of the natural man. The whole Sermon on the Mount is there to attest to that. The requirements which Jesus places before us are not justified by any ethical reasoning. They are not *moral* decisions. And just for that reason we cannot use them as the basis for a formal ethic.

We cannot put an ethic together out of a systematic contradiction to nature without its being nothing but an asceticism and a fresh distortion of Christian morality. As Karl Barth has said, what man should do and should not do is not described for him by the ten commandments or the Sermon on the Mount, but he must hear it by a personal order of God.

In continuation of the above lines of thought, that which should show us the extent to which Christian ethics is impossible is the intervening of eschatology. It has been said that the ethos of the New Testament is one with the promise of the breaking in of the kingdom of God into the world.[32] This presence of the eschaton means that we are free with respect to the world but committed in the kingdom of heaven. The life of the Christian is necessarily a life of "the end of the ages." It is already located at a critical distance from the world. This insertion into the kingdom leads to an "unworlding" (Bultmann). But it is quite obviously impossible to construct the ethics of a life lived in terms of the last things, just as it is impossible to transcribe in ethical form the already current presence of that which will be reality only at the end of the ages. We confine ourselves at this point to a mere indication of the problem, which we shall examine later on.

But over against the impossibility and futility of the Christian ethic, it is also necessary to recall the danger of that ethic. The moment the Christian life and the revelation concerning that life are put into a developed system it is obvious that there can arise from such a system the good conscience, as all pharisaism has shown. It is clear that the moment one knows in advance what is good and virtuous the temptation to judge, and consequently to offend against charity, is constant. We have already indicated it and here we must go into it more deeply. Let us remember in this regard the importance of the commandment not to judge others, and especially let us recall the passage in the letter of James (4:11–12) which gathers up the entire teaching about judgment. Not only does the author remind us that it is a lack of charity, that it is a putting of ourselves in the place of God, because only God can judge, but he adds a very important element which directly concerns us. To judge one's brother, he says, is to judge the law. That is to say, in the name of a constructed ethic which allows us to pass judgment on our neighbor, we are judging the very revelation of God. How can that be?

The thought of James appears to be as follows. Whoever is converted to the Lord has received the commandment of the Lord in his life and in his heart. His heart of stone has become a heart of flesh. He has within himself the law itself of Jesus Christ. He is the representative of it. Now, as James said in chapter 1 of his letter, this law is the law of liberty. That is to say that since he has been liberated in Christ the neighbor is under the liberty itself of Christ, and therefore his conduct is none of our affair. You absolutely cannot judge him. If you pretend to judge your brother it is the law itself that you are judging, since the law, the commandment of God, now resides in this brother. Now if you are judging the law you are not keeping the law. Hence, in the fact of the judgment it is you who become the transgressor of the law. To judge others is to prove that one is himself ignorant of the liberty in Christ.

We said that the elaboration of a Christian ethic involves, more or less inevitably, this danger of judging, and we can say it at the spirtual level as well as at the level of the experience of history. Every time Christians or the church have been led to formulate a precise, objective ethic, every time the theologians have derived concrete decisions from theological principles, very rapidly one comes to the point of passing judgments in terms of the actions of one group or the other, consequently of separating people into good and bad, and finally of giving up all evangelization, since this judgment has been given the precedence. It is in that sense that ethics presents a permanent danger to the church.

So, if one takes into account all the obstacles against the possibility of the formation of a Christian ethic placed there by the truth of Jesus Christ himself, if, second, one thinks of the judgment which the word of God brings to bear on all morality, then one can say that at bottom Christianity is an "antimorality." Not only can it not give rise to any morality which would be faithful to the revealed truth, but it is also destructive of all morality. Morality, whether Christian or not, necessarily collides with God's decision brought to pass in Jesus Christ, and which locates the life and truth of man out beyond everything that man can formulate, know, and live.

As soon as a morality, Christian or otherwise, is established, it runs into that obstacle and is broken upon it. Of course it can ignore it. It can deny it. It can act as though it didn't exist. But that attitude, normal for unbelievers, is impossible for the Christian, who finds himself as a result in a situation of permanent contradiction. He should never forget that revealed truth is antimoral, and that as soon as a Christian morality is developed, just so soon is it called into question and, before long, destroyed by that very revelation, the living revelation, which it had taken as a point of departure, as a fulcrum, as a rationale.[33]

Historic Formation
of Christian Moralities

13 If there are diverse secular and pagan moralities, there are likewise numerous Christian moralities, according to the changing times, as we were saying above, but also according to varying theological outlooks. With every change in theology Christians felt the need to formulate a new ethic.[1] But our plan is not to offer a review of the different Christian moralities, nor their history. Still less could we hope to construct a morality by making use of materials drawn from earlier Christian moralists. They are definitely superseded. The situation here is entirely different from that for dogmatics. For dogmatics it is normal and right to consult the earlier theologians and to understand their peculiar expression of the revelation of God. The work of the moralists, on the contrary, has no further significance for us. This is not because they were less qualified than the theologians! It is not because their work was less "valid," but because if it was a genuine ethic it was necessarily related to a certain social, political, and economic situation which is no longer ours. Their conclusions (if not their point of departure and their method) are thus entirely outmoded. It might be interesting to study them as examples, or in order to take stock of the Christian tradition, but no more than that. Hence we cannot think today of looking for the ingredients of a Christian ethic in Augustine, or Ambrose, or Calvin, or Luther. If then we here raise the historical question it is in an altogether different outlook, with an altogether different purpose.

We firmly believe that in the final analysis it is impossible to construct a Christian ethic. How then did Christians and the church come to erect one? How did this necessity gradually impose itself at the beginning of the church's life, and how and why did it increase? How did it happen that Christians themselves came to treat this problem of conduct and of works as ultimately the most important problem—to the point that the latter ended by inundating theology itself in such a way as to bring about a theology of works and the Roman heresy, and to the point where non-Christians no longer considered or borrowed anything of Christianity but its morality? It must be acknowledged that we have here a very serious problem!

The letters of Paul and the letter to the Hebrews witness that, beginning with the first and second Christian generations, the moral problem presented itself in concrete terms. The extracanonical writings show this even more.

Obviously, we need to remember that at the outset the Christians were Jews who recognized Jesus Christ as the Messiah. As Jews they were heirs of the vast labor carried out in Judaism for the knowledge and recognition of the will of God made explicit in the commandments. Morality was already caught up in that tension between the unlimited requirement and the limited commandment (Ricoeur), and this is true in particular of the work of the Pharisees. Maledictions on the part of Jesus and the break which he displayed had not been enough to liquidate that heritage, for that heritage represented the highest ethical experiment which man had ever made. In spite of the desire to oppose the law with grace, was it possible to eliminate that research and that structure, which stood for the greatest possible approximation, from the human point of view, to the practical application of the will of God on its ethical side? Such elimination was the more difficult in view of the fact that in starting out with the unique gift which is salvation through grace one still had to live in accordance with the will of God (sanctification), and at that point one ran precisely into what the Pharisees had attempted: to fulfill the ethics of the prophets in an ethics of detail, to live one's daily life unreservedly on the basis of God's statutes.

This unto-the-very-end principle transforms heteronomy into an obedience which is integrally assumed and integrally willed. One should ask oneself, what else is there to do? For the very question which the Christians were to encounter in the conduct of their lives was exactly the question which the Pharisees had encountered, and to which they felt the greatest possible obligation to find an answer. It is wholly superficial to treat the Pharisees under their literalistic and legalistic aspect. Their quest was to *live* the law (hence currently) and to join together a religion of the law as the will of God, a religion of the soul (Herford), and a practice. The temptation will come very rapidly to take up once more the principal implications of pharisaism, scruple, concern for carrying out the commandments, a striving for moral holiness, avoidance of the corrupted environment, and necessarily merit. The Pharisee is to represent one of the endlessly recurring temptations within Christianity, and Paul's critique of the righteousness which is of the law, however basic, will not be enough to put Christians constantly on guard against that ethical possibility which is most difficult to fulfill, and yet at the same time most tempting for a scrupulous conscience.[2]

We encounter two essential questions at the very outset. First of all, we see according to Paul (the two letters to the Corinthians and the letter to the Galatians) that the morals of the Christians of the first generation were not beyond reproach, drunkenness, profligacy, lying, calumny, jealousy, magic, etc. How could it happen that Christians who are supposed to live under the guidance of the Holy Spirit should in real life behave so badly? These Christians are in need of instruction on the conduct which they should

normally maintain, and need in some instances to be repri-
manded. The time has come to show them that their actions
cannot have been inspired by the Holy Spirit. It is necessary to fight against the idea, surely current at this time,
and which reappears constantly throughout the history of
the church, that "since the Holy Spirit is guiding me, then
everything I do is good and legitimate before God." They
need to be reminded that they are behaving exactly like the
others, like the heathen, and that their faith does not show
in their human reality.

In addition, alongside the struggle against scandal and
moral fault, Paul had to reply to ethical questions which
were put to him. The examples drawn from the letters to
the Corinthians show clearly that from the very inception
of the church it was the custom to ask questions of the
theologians and of the "pillars of the church." The most responsible Christians well know that they cannot resolve the
problems with which they are faced (and which are ultimately moral problems) without the advice of those greater
than themselves. Hence, already the ethical consultations,
which subsequently multiplied in number in the Middle
Ages and which were to give birth to the institution of the
Director of Conscience, get off to an important start.

Paul, then, finds himself led by these two concerns to develop a morality for Christians. He gives advice, and even
orders, though he maintains a prudent reserve in this area,
and he does it by constantly going back to the sole authority, by constantly basing his teaching on the person of Jesus
Christ. But whatever his precautions it is still true nonetheless that what is beginning is the construction of a morality,
especially when we think of the recipients of this instruction, who think of it as an ethical command. Without
doubt, if Paul insisted so strongly on the opposition between the law and grace, that was not only, according to
the traditional and obvious interpretation, in order to mark
the contrast between the ministry of Moses and that of
Jesus Christ, between the old covenant and the new.

There also shows through in the letters the concern to struggle against moralism, even that founded on Jesus Christ, which was continually coming up, beginning with the first Christian generation. For they were concerned about their conduct and they needed to be enlightened. They were also concerned about the conduct of others. In fact, in these communities there could be no lack of judging the other person and of judging each other. There again the letters inform us on the evil practice. The injunction not to judge recurs continually (e.g., Romans 2:1–14; 3:4; 1 Corinthians 4:5; James 2:4; 4:11). Now obviously this judgment relates to the other person's behavior. So the moralizing tendency was already very strong, all the stronger since it was necessary to struggle against those who claimed to be Christians and who were behaving badly, and probably also against the dissolute morals of the hellenistic society of that time. They had to separate themselves from the surrounding milieu, to become the saints that they were by the grace of God.

The second question which arose was: How can a man who is born anew, who has received the baptism of the Spirit, fall back under the power of sin? How can it happen that liberated by Christ he is still under the power of Satan? The letter to the Hebrews reflects these stern debates. Can a man who has sinned still be considered a Christian? Does a man who commits evil still have the faith? "If we sin deliberately after receiving the knowledge of the truth, there no longer remains a sacrifice for sins, but a fearful prospect of judgment, and a fury of fire which will consume the adversaries" (Heb. 10:26–27).

We know that this debate was to come up again with respect to the martyrs. Those who gave in under suffering and renounced Jesus Christ, are they still Christians? Theologians were divided on the question. But the problem set forth in the letter to the Hebrews is less precise, for it reveals a concept of sin which is not exactly the same as that of Paul. What is in question is indeed a particularized moral fault, a transgression of an ethical kind. But that, then, presupposes a clear and exact knowledge of what a Christian ought to do, of the way in which he should conduct himself. It assumes a code whereby it might be determined who has transgressed, that is, who has sinned, who therefore is cast out. That is indeed the sense exhibited by the orientation of the letter to the Hebrews, while the writings of a slightly later period which emphasize the moralizing direction of Christianity at the beginning of the second century were never canonized. Hence one can see in this a certain mistrust on the part of the churches and their leaders, a certain suspicion of moral investigation. The moral writings were indeed acknowledged, were well received as studies in edification and piety, but they were never canonized. That is very significant.

Now this led, in the succeeding century, to the raising of general moral problems, and the ecclesiastical authorities, the bishops, were led to make decisions in these areas,[3] the question of divorce, of remarriage, of usury, of the use of money, of the oath to the emperor, the prohibition of certain professions, the prohibition of becoming a soldier or a magistrate, the prohibition of attendance at public entertainment, etc. The questions raised begin no longer to be purely private ones, but include social and political conduct as well. The authorities give advice, impose sanctions, address reprimands. Thus through the process of usage there was built up a sort of moral framework, a routine into which the Christian would settle himself quite normally.[4] In conjunction with all this, there was instituted penance in the second century, which resolved the problem raised by the letter to the Hebrews. He who commits a moral offense after baptism should submit to penance (confession and expiation of offenses committed, which may be public, exomologesis) . After that, the guilty person is reconciled to God. That is not only aimed at the moral offense, but *also* at reconciliation.

In the second century this is not yet an institution, and neither is there a true doctrine of universal morality. Things are to change in the third century. For one thing, the "edict of Calixtus" institutes penance officially, precisely for moral offenses (adultery and fornication), and attributes the power of absolution and of restoration to communion not only to bishops, but also perhaps to confessors of the faith. This will open up what is called "the penitential question." At the same time the theologians began to involve themselves directly in Christian morality and they introduced the questions and teaching of Greek philosophers into Christianity. Up to that time it could be said that only Marcion had constructed an ethics which was also an asceticism (the body as an enemy, fasting, abstinence, prohibition of all sex relations, etc.) and which was incorporated into the whole of his heresy. Shortly afterward another heretic, Montanus, set forth in his turn precepts of a complete ascetic morality. Again let us emphasize that Tertullian was to be drawn progressively toward heresy by the moral problem. The moral laxity of Christians and the edict of Calixtus seemed to him scandalous. The Christian life should be a pure life. He also constructed an ethics, but failing to overcome the flabbiness of the church, he who had fought so resolutely against heretics himself fell into the Montanist heresy through his agreement with it on the ethical question.

With the apologists borrowing part of their doctrine from the Stoics (and moral instruction was developed largely by them), redemption consists essentially in the knowledge of a morality which is correct from the philosophical point of view. The philosophers are placed on the same footing with the prophets. Morality is then put in the forefront. It is constructed of course out of the "Christian virtues." It is the sum of all the rules of the Christian life. The apologists hoped by that to convince the pagans, since this morality is very similar to the Stoic morality which great numbers of the pagans respected. The Christian virtues are the very ones preached by the philosophers. On this point the apologists were themselves openly heretical, and it is not without interest to bring out that Christian

morality as a system was first formulated exclusively by
heretics and was tied to very serious theological errors.

The influence of the philosophers in this sphere continued to increase in the third century. So things were changing. Until that time the first Christian ethics had tried to
be specifically Christian, to be a morality scrupulously
drawn from the biblical texts, and that tradition was to be
continued by the anchorites and eremites. But in the church
at large, and with the theologians, morality, following the
apologists, is to be based primarily on a philosophy.

And in continuation of the same tendency Christian morality is to be derived from the works of the theologians
and the decisions of councils and popes, which moreover
were quite often influenced by worldly and political motives. In particular, whereas the tradition from the first century on had been hostile to military service for a Christian,
the Council of Arles, just after the recognition of the church
by Constantine, decreed excommunication for Christians
refusing military service!

It is self-evident that the significance and even the origin
of Christian morality are now altered, for it is to receive
its form and authority from an external doctrinal authority, namely the pope. Henceforth there is created a good
which is fixed with respect to everybody by the ecclesiastical authority, and from that time forward the objectifica-
tion of the ethical situation cuts the relationship between
faith and works.

From these beginnings, and in the centuries which followed, the importance of ethics never ceased to grow. It is
no longer necessary to cite names and list works. There was
no theological question which was not broached from its
ethical aspect, nor a dogma from which moral conclusions
were not drawn.

This expansion of moral systematizing (both in casuistry
and in philosophy) can be explained by three motives.
The first is, without doubt, the motive of the cure of souls

and of spiritual direction. The priest constantly encounters the question asked at the beginning of the church, at the day of Pentecost, according to Peter's testimony: "What should we do?" I believe in Jesus Christ, but what must one do to live that faith? And one adds under one's breath: "Am I sure of being saved? For after all, I believe but I behave badly . . . ; by faith I am saved, but my behavior I deserve to be damned." It is a problem of morality. To the first question the faith answers by facing man up to his responsibility and his individual decisions. There can be no other statement than that of Peter: "Repent. . . . Be baptized. . . . You will receive the gift of the Holy Spirit. . . . Save yourselves from this perverse generation." So confronted with that proclamation each one has his own personal and irreplaceable decision to make.

To the second question the faith responds by reference to God's free grace. He can save thee in spite of all. There is no work which can reassure thee of his decision. But the love of God shown forth in Jesus Christ assures thee of his goodwill toward thee, and it far outweighs all moral failures. Faith in that is thus the sole condition of thy salvation. But that faith consists in giving thyself over, bound hand and foot, into the hands of God, in awaiting his decision with humility, confidence, hope, and love, and in accepting it in advance, no matter what it might be, knowing that it is just and good. Now these two answers are not at all satisfactory to the natural man. He needs to be reassured. He needs to be guided. He needs clear certainties, and to be released from his responsibilities. He does not at all want to spend his whole life faced with these two questions, which come up ever afresh. He does not want to start from zero with every decision to be made, to begin again from the groundwork of faith and to assume his whole responsibility. He does not want to remain uncertain about this salvation which he desires to possess. When all is said and done, he wants to be reassured about his destiny. So he demands to be told clearly what his duty is. He wants to know his duties and obligations exactly, the "conditions" of salvation, for to be thrown back on the pure grace of God seems to him frightening. That is what the crowds in the church required.

As long as the number of Christians had been small, it had been possible to curb these requests, to hold to the right line of individual responsibility. But with the increase in numbers the problems are multiplied. Priests have hundreds of moral "cases" to counsel. They need guidelines.[5] The requirement of ready-made solutions, of prepared answers, increases with the number of the faithful, and the increase becomes inordinate when people enter the church without passing through any true conversion, when the state interferes, and in persecuting pagans forces them to embrace Christianity. Under those circumstances the problem becomes one of a general conduct. One can no longer seek for each person the spiritual meaning of his acts and his works. One can no longer rely on each person's decision of faith, since he does not have faith. What can one expect of people who accept Christianity formally because they want to escape death, and are ignorant of the whole of Christian doctrine, have no spirtual experience of grace, and retain in their hearts loyalties to pagan gods, and in their morals cling to ancestral customs and beliefs.

If the first movement toward the formation of an ethic went along with a pastoral concern to reassure uneasy souls, the second movement is connected with the necessity of settling on stereotyped modes of conduct to be known as Christian conduct, as a standard by which to judge individuals and to keep them in hand, since it was impossible to control their consciences. From that it was a short step to the conviction that one can make progress in reverse from the exterior to the interior, from morality to religion, and that by making a man act, talk, and behave in a given manner, in a manner called Christian, one could lead him by habit, by outward training, to adopt a moral conscience which would become Christian, and to receive from the outwardly imposed conduct inward religious motivations.

Now this brings us to the second motive which impelled the church toward the formation of a morality. The adoption of the religion by the state and the entrance into the church of the pagan masses ended in the formation of a Christian society, in short, of Christianity. From that point on, Christianity is no longer an individual but a collective affair. Christianity is no longer lived in a church which is itself inserted into a hostile or an indifferent society. Church and society are now superimposed on each other. All the institutions of society must be Christian. Since it is impossible to change all the institutions, derive them from theology, create them out of whole cloth from the standpoint of revelation (which had been attempted in the church to some extent), one is very often limited to Christianizing the existing institutions, sometimes in a very formal manner. Hence knighthood, the guilds, peace leagues, the monarchy, etc., but that raises immense ethical problems. At the time when the church was gradually being constituted into a society it had been necessary, then also, to create institutions and a morality, but it had been possible to retain a certain balance between institution and event, between the action of the Holy Spirit and the moral or judicial rules. That is no longer possible when it is a question of a whole society. The latter reacts, in fact, like any other society. We have pointed out that each group requires a morality and progressively establishes it. That society which was in process of formation from the eighth to the eleventh centuries could not escape the sociological rule.

In the period covered by the Merovingian and then the Carolingian dynasties all the moralities, both Roman and Germanic, had collapsed. Nothing was left of them, and when new institutions appeared a new morality was needed as well. Man living in society cannot avoid setting up a morality. But since the people called themselves Christians, since the church was exactly coexistent with society, since society's center of interest (brought about by the predominance of the church's activity, the intervention of the state, and monastic instruction) was Christianity, the morality put together from quite diverse and doubtful sources was called Christian. One then strove for a synthesis between the two contradictory moralities, the sociological morality and the morality impelled by the Holy Spirit. The entire moral work of the scholastics bears the imprint of this attempt at a synthesis.

Finally, the third motive, growing out of the preceding one, for the organization of a morality is the express desire, not always but indisputably explicit, on the part of the church openly and perhaps unilaterally to manage the entire society. This will to direct, which is particularly explicit in the economic and political spheres, has had its repercussions on ethics. The latter becomes a very effective means of managing people. To impose more and more rigorous, more and more precise, modes of conduct and works, to maintain ever stricter control over the carrying out of religious and moral duties (and the inquisition was that also, as well as an aspect of the struggle against heresy) was a means of insuring the church's authority and the uniformity of society. The latter could not be definitely incorporated into the system of the church as long as people could exhibit diverse modes of behavior and give themselves over to their own moral promptings. This was all the more important since the Christian society was spread over many diverse peoples. It was necessary to achieve, over and above particularities of morals and of local ways of life, a unity of Christian conduct everywhere alike in its virtues and works, just as the institutions of the church should be everywhere alike over and above the diversity (becoming more sharply defined) of the institutions of the world. By thus controlling actions, the church could claim to control hearts. But this presupposed an enormous doctrinal development, and the formation of a systematic Christian ethics.[6]

The result of this evolution, of this mastery over behavior and intention on the part of the church authority, was extremely serious. The formation of a totalitarian and authoritarian Christian ethic, that is to say, one that is imposed and which provides ahead of time for all individual problems, has not remained an external fact, an epiphenomenon. It has altered the entire life of the church and of Christians. We must note, first of all, that this morality created, in a word, for sociological reasons and following a procedure identical for all moralities, is in reality a sociological morality. It is one morality among others. It takes its place among the moralities of the world. It can be analyzed as one of them. Attempts will be made, of course, to distinguish it by its content, to point out that chastity, love of neighbor, etc., are peculiar to Christian morality. To which one can reply quite easily that such is not the case, that many others have known these values, and that there is nothing peculiar to Christian morality. This is entirely exact in the line of development followed by the church.

It is wholly true that the morality thus constituted between the fourth and the thirteenth centuries is a morality of the society, that it should be examined in the same manner as every human morality, and that its foundation does not necessarily bear witness to the intervention of the Holy Spirit. Now this is always more or less exact. We must always remind ourselves that no matter how faithful we may be, no matter how much we try to remain bound by the will of God, to respect the freedom of the Holy Spirit, still the moment we give expression to a Christian ethic, the moment we systematize it (and we cannot do otherwise), the moment we actualize it (and there again we cannot do otherwise), we bring to light a work which depends upon psychological and sociological conditions, which is therefore subject to human analysis, subject to being treated as a morality on the same footing as the others. Just as, from a certain point of view, Christianity is one religion among the other religions, although it is the opposite of a religion—so also, from a certain point of view, Christian morality is a morality among the other moralities of mankind, even though Christianity is an antimorality.

The most loyal of Christian ethics, however far removed from the moralities, is still *also* a morality. The serious thing is that the ethic developed by the church was a human morality *in the first place*. It submitted in everything to the formative processes of morality. It submitted to the laws of sociology and to the temptations of philosophy. It did not know the principle of standing apart, of interpreting the exclusiveness of revelation. Hence it was a morality like the others, and one would not be able to find fault with it if it had not been for the imposture of adding the adjective Christian. For Christians and the church to declare bankruptcy, for them to say: we simply cannot translate the requirements of the faith into ethical terms, that is normal and possible. For them to resolve, in that case, to follow in one way or another a morality of the world, that could be sad but understandable. But that they should elaborate, for worldly reasons, under worldly conditions and prompted by the world, a morality which they baptize as Christian, that is an imposture. It has been called that because the conflict was intolerable, the contradiction between the morality and the faith, or between the sociological requirement of morality and the requirement to incarnate the faith. To attach the adjective Christian to the predicate morality was a facile but deceptive way of seeming to resolve the tension.

In constituting itself in this fashion, Christian morality ceased entirely to be what scripture shows us as the life of the Christian man. From the fifth and sixth centuries onward, it was no longer a matter of God's action for man and with man in his history. Ethics are no longer based directly on the Bible. They are no longer placed in indissoluble relationship with theology. One sought other foundations and other sources. And so we find in works on morality beginning with the ninth century two principal types. On the one hand there were treatises on Christian morality based on principles. On the other hand there was a moral typology of exemplary models. For the first, the movement

is more philosophical, for the second, more "historical."
For the first, one began with a sort of consideration of theology on its philosophical side. To be sure, out of scripture
(but leaving it behind, and in detachment from it) theological systems were created which obeyed a kind of internal logic. That is to say, that one deduced principles
from the biblical texts from which conclusions were drawn
and organized into a system. In appearance, the principles
could be biblically sound, and might even translate biblical
formulas directly. But the error consisted in transforming
the word into a fixed formula, the living and contemporary
act of God into a principle. From then on, no matter how
correct the formulation might be, it turns into a lie and the
power of death.

If a theology might be conceived which would do justice
to the word and to the act, it is almost impossible to conceive an ethic which could do that. The latter inevitably
reduces everything to conclusions from principles, and it
has often been under the influence of ethical necessity that
"Christian principles" have been set forth, in the Middle
Ages and since. But just as soon as principles of conduct
are proposed, just so soon does one discover that the conduct deduced from them is quite different from the total
and living movement which scripture reveals as the life in
Christ. In any case, one should take note of the fact that
Christian morality was instituted upon, and out of, principles which were both intermediaries and screens between
scripture and the life of the Christian. These Christian
moralities with their principles best met an intellectual need
and the necessity for having clear commandments.

Along with this, during the same period, another type of
Christian morality was created which answered even better
to the needs of piety. That was the morality of models and
of exemplary people, that is to say, the martyrs and the
saints. Here we are dealing with moralities of a historical
nature, in the sense that they indeed preserved the biblical
idea that the important thing is the life of man and his his-

tory. But, while scripture shows us the action of God in this life and this history and that it is that which translates itself concretely in a noteworthy behavior, this morality of models displays the man as noteworthy, and since *he* turned to God, if one is to imitate his behavor one will on that account also make contact with the will of God.

This moral trend, then, is based on the past of Christians, and it claims to relate to real happenings. History becomes didactic. Man needs to be shown both his own image and the image of the Christian in the description of the past. Just as the morality of principles drew upon ancient philosophies, so the morality of models drew upon certain historians. It is obvious that the Greeks in part, but the Romans more often, had this didactic concern in writing history. If they did not write expressly to establish a morality (like the Chinese historians from the third century B.C.), at least they wrote with the idea of furnishing moral examples. This tendency was accentuated from the third century A.D. onward, and the hagiographers took their place in the same trend. Thus, with the morality of principles one departs from the will of God by eliminating history. With the morality of models one departs by reducing history to man, that is to say, by registering this "Christian morality" in the order of the fall and of necessity. It is not enough to have rediscovered history to be in the truth!

Moreover, at the same time that this ethic was in process of construction it had the irrepressible tendency to become autonomous. We know how Melanchthon already began to separate ethics from dogmatics, but it is in the eighteenth century, with the enlightenment and pietism, that ethics sets itself up in a separate domain, having for its focal point of interest either the natural moral conscience or the psychology of the person who has been born again. It is important to note that this autonomy is the more or less inevitable consequence of the construction of a Christian ethic. Kant merely pushed to its ultimate conclusion what was there from the very beginning. It has never, in truth, been possible to construct a Christian ethic without the importation of foreign material: Stoicism, Aristotelianism, rationalism, and in our day in order to create the well-known Christian social ethics, Marxism pure and simple. But this has had catastrophic results from every point of view. It has reduced Christianity in the eyes of men to a mere identity with this morality. It has put forth a morality adaptable to a particular class of society (which is why the "Christian" morality has turned into the "bourgeois" morality), and it has solidified theological heresies.

We confine ourselves to stressing the last point. It is obviously very difficult to know which is the cause of the other. Paul shows repeatedly that a theological error brings with it a false and bad moral behavior.[7] It is possible that heresy played a determining role in the formation of Christian morality. We pointed that out above. But the existence of ethical development also appears to have influenced the theologians, and to have led them to take objectively good behavior into account in their understanding of revelation. A first, and very important, aspect of this theological influence is surely the transformation of the personal into the impersonal. The relationship with God is a personal relationship. It presupposes dialogue, and that God constitutes us as persons in order that we might become capable of responding to him and of doing what he asks. But this personal relationship is both formidable for the individual and dangerous for the order of the church through the possibilities of excess and of discord which it introduces. So one transforms it into a system of relations which are predetermined, established by the theologian, who lays down the norms and significance of the God-man relationship. Then there is no longer need for individual encounter. It becomes an encounter of humanity in itself with divinity.

This impersonal systematization is possible once the will of God has been codified into a moral order, and one need only fulfill the latter in order to carry out that will. The will need no longer be spoken nor received personally. In this way one economizes on the encounter with God and on the resulting discord. Thereby, also, the task of the Christian educator is made easier since the conversion transition is no longer necessary, and one need only introduce the child into the moral order. This regularizes the relation with God so that the future of this soul becomes predictable. But from the point of view of the concept itself of God this entails a very serious alteration. By it one does away with God's freedom and one pretends to have an intrinsic knowledge of his will.

If, in fact, we formulate a good which is ours, a good which expresses God's will in permanent form, that implies that God is an object whose will is not living but is crystallized once for all, unchangeable to eternity, and that we know what it is. We are then faced with a conflict between God and his will, a sort of subordination of God to the good. Again, an objective good existing as law binds God and prevents him from acting, except as we have decided— *we,* for ultimately the most faithful ethical expression is still our work, and it is in accordance with that work that we would claim to require that God act and judge. God, in that case, can enter into our system of thought, into our theology, as a neutral element. There has to be this neutral element on which and from which we reason, without which the whole system of ethics would be impossible!

Conversely, moreover, this concept of morality involves one's refusal to be called into question. When the good has been defined, decreed, so that we know exactly what we have to do and there is no longer any decision on our own responsibility, but a directive set forth for us by the authorities of the church certifying that such is the commandment of God, then if we perform it how can we accept the destruction of the guarantee, the calling of ourselves into question by the revelation? How can man know himself to be a sinner if he has done everything that he should do? How can he know himself to be poor if he can display his good works and his virtues? But if he doesn't know himself to be a sinner and poor, what need does he have for salvation in Jesus Christ and for grace? Such, in a word, is the most serious theological question raised by this development of ecclesiastical morality. One is brought inevitably to a theology of salvation by works and into opposition to salvation by grace. There is no way out of the dilemma (the moment the ethical system is set up and applied). Either works are necessary, but then salvation is not tied to pure grace, it is tied to works (whatever may be the theological formulas of cooperation, or divine foreknowledge, etc.); or else salvation is granted by grace, but then works are of no use.

For the life of Christianity the performance of works is absolutely and rigorously necessary. This reduces the importance of the death and resurrection of Jesus Christ. If works are indispensable for salvation the death of Jesus Christ is rendered vain, since man can of himself (only with "help") fulfill the will of God reduced to morality (whereas the entire Bible says that no one but Jesus Christ is capable of performing that will), and if man is called to *do* his salvation by his works, then the obedience of Jesus Christ and redemption no longer makes sense. Thus one can see that, in reality, nothing is left of Christianity.[8]

We shall not pursue the specifically theological questions. It is sufficient for our purpose to have indicated briefly how the development of Christian morality was associated with the particular development of a heresy. Could the situation have evolved otherwise? We cannot say. Still, it is quite important to remember that when the biblical affirmation of salvation by grace through faith was put forward and proclaimed anew, the entire moral system of the former church was by that same token under attack, as was the principle of the uniformity of the morals of Christianity and the principle of the directors of conscience. Also, the form of the reformation of the church was altered, for it must not be forgotten that there were reformations of the church before Luther. At least three times important transformations and rectifications were effected, but the path chosen was always moral and institutional, never theological and spiritual.

The importance which morality assumed in the church is, in fact, quite well brought out by the type of the reforms undertaken in Christianity from the sixth to the sixteenth centuries. There were substantial and successful endeavors at reformation, but reformation was conceived as a moral improvement in the lives of Christians (and the clergy first of all) , and as a perfecting of the institutions of the church. The immense enterprise of the Gregorian reform is typical. This brings us back once more to underscore the reversal, due to the influence of morality, whereby one must begin with the exterior, with actions, with behavior, in order to reach the inward man and to change his heart. But the modification of the exterior assumes an expansion of the authority, an improvement in the organization, that is to say, a judicial structure and a judicial morality. Thus one has always attacked what one wished to change in the church by the expedient of the judicial, and it cannot be otherwise once behavior and society are considered to be the essential thing.

Private and social morals were an obsession with the Middle Ages at a time, it is true, when manners had an immoral vigor which posed unusual problems for the church. It would appear that to begin at the beginning with theology, the cure of souls and spiritual instruction seemed too long and uncertain a route whereby to arrive at the reformation of this great body of the church and of Christianity. The other path was shorter, more effective, and better adapted to the purpose at hand. What is new with Luther is not the idea of reformation, but the style, the will to reform the church from the core out, that is to say, from her *spiritual* life and her theology, treating morals as something which would follow. Only, the question is serious, the reformers, having reaffirmed the authentic content of revelation, did not, in spite of appearances, develop an ethic to follow their theology.[9]

The Necessity
for a Christian Ethic[1]

14 And yet a Christian ethic is indispensable.[2] Not only is this true at the level of the individual conduct of each person's life, but the formulation itself of an ethic is necessary. What is it, in fact, which happens when a morality is not expressed? An example of this is seen in the Reformers, who seem to me to have failed in the enterprise of formulating an ethic, and who left the field wide open. The faithful and their pastors, just because no morality had been set up by the theologians, fell back directly on the Bible, on the law, on the moral texts of the Old Testament and on the exhortations in the letters. They applied, or tried to apply, all of it directly, taking it at the letter of the text. Doubtless that was all very well, but it had deplorable consequences. To the extent to which each of these biblical statements was taken directly to be the word of God, and as such was obeyed as it stood, one came up with a completely fixated ethic, maintained for its own sake over and above all the tangible conditions of human life and the evolution of society. It was expressed in an attitude shriveled to fit an unalterable situation, and in a rejection of everything which threatened to change it.

The Puritans undertook the superhuman and impossible task of establishing a veritable monastic conduct in the world. But that assumed that the world is not evolving and

that, once fixed, the situation remains identical with itself. One confused, then, the definitive seriousness of theological formulations concerning the truth of revelation with
the moral commandment, which was no longer distin-
guished from them. Once adopted, the ethical structure is
just as untouchable as the theological proposition. It
hardens and becomes more and more negative and prohibit-
ing. Now this takes place precisely because the morality is
"unconscious," because no thoughtful reflection has been
devoted to morality, and one has believed it possible to in-
scribe the commandment of God directly onto life, as a law
(which, as a product of the theology of grace, is the last
straw!). The formulation of an ethic in the church is necessary precisely to maintain its relative character.

A primary stress must be placed on the very important
fact that a ceaseless reference to grace or to the Holy Spirit
(as in the Lutheran *Berufsethik*), that a purely transcendent
theology, can leave a person completely disarmed in the
midst of the world, and can bring him to a kind of moral
indifferentism. This all becomes equally possible from three
standpoints, or derivative justifications: (1) spiritual pietism, which claims to put a person under the direct, immediate, and continuous guidance of the Holy Spirit; (2) indifferentism toward the world's problems on the ground
that the relative is unimportant; (3) the bringing to bear
of an excessive interest in the world's problems, on which it
is thought *Christianity* has nothing directly to say, and in
which the Christian should therefore involve himself according to the modes of action, the options, the solutions, established by others on the moral and political fronts.

These three heresies, which tend to destroy the continuity
between the life (renewed through Christ) and its manifestations in action, clearly show the degree in which a
Christian ethic is indispensable. Whether it be with respect
to a concrete problem or with revelation as the point of
departure, whenever a faithful member or an assembly of
the church proposes an ethical mode of conduct it brings

about a calling into question, a debate, a dialogue (that is, in a certain sense, a truly ethical situation). And, whatever solution is adopted, one knows that it is relative, that it can be called into question, that its justification can only be looked for in God, and that this mode of conduct is not situated under the sign of our own justice, but only in the hope of a blessing. Every ethic formulated in the church wears by that very fact its relativity, its need for constant renewal, for one knows very well that it is the product of a human search; whereas the ethic which pretends to be the immediate application of the commandment claims to be unalterable because directly inspired by God. Now an ethic (we shall study it later) stands in relation to the concrete (hence always subject to change) circumstances of life. It must follow them. Otherwise it is not an ethic. Thus the first conspicuous service which the clear and precise formulation of an ethic renders to the church and to Christians is to remind them of the relative, ever fluctuating, character of morality,[3] which service can only be rendered once the ethic has been expressed as such, and which is impossible as long as it remains implicit. Moreover, one needs to ponder the corollary of what we have just pointed out. In contrast to the attitude of the Puritans, and to the Christian moralism which took its place in the nineteenth century, we have witnessed a rude theological reaction, in such terms as: "They have tried to reduce Christianity to a morality. Morality is nothing. We need a return to the center, to the kernel of the gospel, to theological truth. Let us have done with moral preachments. Let us preach only Jesus Christ and him crucified." This, too, is all very well, but that blinds Christians to the importance of the incarnation of the faith and of putting it into practice.

It is not enough to have a good theology. The latter must also lead to good action, and that does not take place automatically. It is not self-evident. Theology in that case can become ever more rigorous and unbending (and by that fact it can, in addition, forge strong personalities), but it avoids all involvement with the tangible. The faithful, once again, are left to themselves, and in most cases will follow the average behavior of those around them. They will obey the promptings of the group and of the milieu. In fact they are defenseless, at the same time that they are quite consciously Christians. The pastors themselves are in that situation! That is what explains, for example in France, with the theological renewal and the earnestness of preaching since 1930, the inconsistency and absurdity of the political and economic positions adopted since 1945.

In reality, one is content to follow sociological trends in a total inability to criticize them, to control them, and to liberate oneself from them. We must not suppose that a faithful theology is sufficient in itself to create in the hearer an aptitude for life in the world. Ethics is there as a sort of preparation. It does not have the right to furnish solutions for every problem, solutions which would be imposed with authority. It can only be the reminder that the specific conduct of the Christian is the indispensable consequence of his faith. It should at the same time be the equipping of the believer with an instrument of reflection and explanation concerning himself and his problems. Finally, it will be a reminder that the earnestness of the theological commitment should be registered in an earnestness of commitment in the world, and it will establish, for the particular time in which it is valid, the conditions and limits of that commitment. But it cannot go beyond that. This preparatory task is modest but indispensable.

Karl Barth has a striking formula on this subject: the task of ethics cannot be to decide on the content of God's commandment, nor to judge man's action, but to describe the limits of God's commandment and of man's corresponding action.[4] We are indeed faced with one of the principal functions of that ethic, which cannot formulate the imperative addressed to a man, nor fixate the will of God for all eternity, but in displaying the continuity of the revelation it can remind man *where* the commandment granted *hic et nunc* enters in. And this presupposes that one places himself in the practical, historical situation of the faithful and of the church. Of course, the devotees of the absolute will say that we must not allow for weaknesses, and that we should take pride in the power of the Holy Spirit. It is no lack of faith to remark that we are not in the kingdom of God, that the church *also* is a human society and by that fact subject to the laws of sociology, that the Christian participates in history, and that it is within this history that he is not only to preach the gospel by his word but also to witness to his faith by his life.

If we bear these two facts in mind we shall be led to the following conclusions: The church is a human society. So, according to what we have recognized above, this society, even when it did not want to, instigated, produced, and secreted a morality, not as Christian but as a society. The church could hardly do without regulating the relations of its members by an ethic, and the faithful among them bring about ethical situations (novels about the church have shown this a hundred times!) and behave as ethical subjects, sometimes with very little Christianity. Now it is much more dangerous for the church to follow an unexplored, instinctive morality. We have indicated that above. Because it is a society it has to have a morality. Because it is a Christian society it needs, not a Christian morality (we have seen the impossibility of that term), but a conscious morality, aware of its relativity, humble and under condemnation, in the service of the faithful and not imposed upon them.

These four characteristics are, in a word, the mark of its Christian authenticity. The surprising thing is the fact that the principal preoccupation (the definition of the good) of all the traditional ethics is here ruled out. Ethics for Christians cannot set out in search of the good, "for the question of good and evil has been resolved and liquidated once for all in virtue of God's decree, through the death and resurrection of Jesus Christ. Hence theological ethics cannot go back over this ground, since the decision has already taken place. It can only *accept* the decision." [5] We have also said that the believer participates in history, and that it is in thinking of him as participating in history that we should formulate an ethic. But that means that the latter will constantly evolve. Morality should express our way of being present to the world. Hence it should vary as the world changes. To take the Christian morality of the thirteenth century and to pretend that Christians today should live according to its precepts is an absurdity. There can be no morality except a contemporary one.

Bonhoeffer and Barth stress the fact that it is just in this situation of the Christian participating in history that ethics becomes both necessary and possible. It is in this sense, for example, that Bonhoeffer shows that ethics is not a declaration of pious desires, but a *"Mit-leben,"* linked with persons and with the unfolding of their lives. [6] And Barth says that ethics consists in following the history of the relation of God and man in the redemption. [7]

But that implies, in addition, that ethics necessarily involves a relation with the given fact of the world. Niebuhr rightly criticizes classical orthodox ethics which, since it is exclusively biblical, nowhere makes contact with current reality. But where and how can this relation be brought about without its truth's being altered, without the revelation's turning into a possibility immanent in a historical process? In France, the accommodation to secular culture is particularly noticeable, and this leads to an abandonment of the truth. It seems impossible to avoid falling into one or the other of these errors in the quest, and Niebuhr's attempt is not convincing! In reality, this enterprise is only possible to the extent to which the ethics is conscious, known, intentional, and explicit, and also to the extent to which it relates to a society with which one is familiar in its concrete reality, in relation to which one locates oneself, and not merely in which one acts from one day to the next without examination or self-determination.

In other words, an ethic needs to be formulated for the faithful so that they can truly be present to the world in which they live, and not to a past or unreal world. To achieve this formulation one must proceed first of all to a true and tangible acquaintance with this world and to a diagnosis of its condition. That cannot be done apart from ethical research. It is in this situation that ethics is one of the constituent elements of the response which man is called upon to make to God. God in his absolute holiness speaks to man. He reveals himself as the God who saves and the God who demands, and he makes man capable of speaking, of responding. He makes him responsible. The dialogue inaugurated by God must be carried on, but just as the word of God is action, so also man should not be content to respond to the Eternal in speech alone, which would merely be words. Man's word is that of a responsible man. It is commitment. It presupposes a life given in this response. Faith is the response, but faith immediately implies a living attitude which transforms one's entire behavior. "Man must make his response through his particular situation in the created," Haering so rightly says.[8] Thus ethics appears as an indispensable sequence to our situation of being summoned by God. We cannot escape our status of being responsible, and we can only assume it by going ahead with our moral quest.

In any event, when man wills to live according to the word of God, or to incarnate his faith, it is a matter of a mode of conduct, of the carrying out of certain works. Whether one likes it or not, when it is a matter of a way of life, of decision concerning that life, of actions to perform, of a work to be done, it is a matter of ethics. The latter can be as rigid as one wishes (the commandment) or as flexible and indeterminate (self-affirmation, respect for the other person) , and it is still a morality.

We shall see, of course, that the Christian life is not morality. But the Christian life should be described, and in this sense it is an object of morality. But might not one quite simply live this Christian life? The spontaneity of faith is essential. That is true. Still, once again, we need to have a care for the concrete situation of the Christian. For one thing, experience shows that faith does not express itself spontaneously in works under all circumstances. The hortatory texts of Paul's letters and the letter of James are very explicit on this subject. Faith needs to be invited, stirred up. It is not a question of setting before it ready-made works in which it becomes incarnate automatically. This laying out beforehand of works to be performed is strictly the prerogative of the Lord, who has prepared the works in advance. But the role here of ethics is to appear as a call, a requirement, a spur. It has a possibility, a chance of being heard because it speaks to faith. And herein a recurring problem for morality finds its solution: How can a morality possess authority? how can it be heard by the person to whom it is addressed?

In the world there are numerous answers to these questions: the weight of society, reason, the authority of a witness, etc. But in the case of the Christian life the answer is simple. This morality has authority in the degree in which it derives from faith and relates to the revelation of God. But that authority only exists for the person who recognizes that it is in fact a testimony of the faith of another, and that it does in truth relate to the revelation, that is to say, the person who himself lives in the faith.

In this situation, Christian morality can only be indicative and not imperative, hortatory and not dogmatic. It will consist in the application to the particular and concrete situations of Christians of the requirements and promises of the faith in Jesus Christ concerning the behavior, the mode of action and of life of the new man. The latter, in fact, has always to learn to live both in the liberty of the faith and in the human situation in which he finds himself.[9] This morality has a chance of being heard and taken seriously because it is addressed to the faith of this man. It will be true just because it calls this man's faith into fulfillment. It will cease to be an empty word because it is an answer to the expectation of that faith, which is in need of a dialogue and a clarification in the church, of a spur to enter into action. This ethic's proclamation of requirement can henceforth be heard and carried out because a man, as a result of his faith, will have taken it seriously, and because the Holy Spirit, on account of this man's faith, will have granted him sufficient strength to live it.

But even over and above the spur which it should be, ethics ought also supply the lack on the part of Christians of the initiative and willingness to strike out on new paths. We were saying that the Christian life should be a constant renewal, a creation of abundant novelties expressing the richness of the Holy Spirit. Now, here again, experience teaches us that the most serious Christians lack imagination. They do not know individually or spontaneously how to manifest their faith in new ways. They slip very easily into grooves, into habits. The Christian mode of life of their fathers is enough for them. The work, the organizations, which had been the fruit of faith a generation ago are piously maintained. The political attitude adopted twenty-five years ago as a living expression of a Christian decision will be stoutly persevered in and reaffirmed. The pathway which we opened up at the time of our conversion or during our adolescence appears to us to be entirely straight, completely mapped out, and we are content merely to follow it. Now in all that, we neither realize the renewed freshness of the Holy Spirit's inspiration nor the change in circumstances, each of which would require that our faith discover an entirely new answer.

To be sure, ethics is no substitute for individual decision. It cannot be put in the place of the Christian, nor be a screen between him and God, but it can bring support to a lack of discovery. It can set forth "models," not in the sense of examples to be imitated, but in the economic sense of the word. These models would be examples of possible forms of expression of the faith (and not ready-made solutions), as a point of departure from which a person could reason

and come up effectively with something else. So here ethics
is an aid to the weakness of our faith. Under these circumstances ethics seems to us to have a critical function of
fundamental importance, namely, it should bring us constantly to ask ourselves the question whether we really have
come out from under the reign of the law.

We have no right, merely on the pretext that we believe
in Jesus Christ, to assume that we are automatically freed
from the requirements of the law. We quite readily acknowledge all the themes of Paul and the Gospels that once
we are in the faith we are no longer under the law. That is
a certainty, but how sure are we that we really are in the
faith? This can neither result from a purely subjective
conviction nor from intellectual knowledge. One of the
deciding factors resides precisely in our confrontation with
the ethical requirement. In fact, the ethical requirement
is placed before us in order to teach us ever anew that the
life of faith is not incarnated this side of the law, but
beyond the law. The example given us by Jesus Christ in
the Sermon on the Mount, saying: "You have heard that it
was said to the men of old . . . But I say to you," is
neither that of an absolutizing nor of a spiritualizing of the
law. It is the example of transition from life under the law
to life in the faith. Now there was never any question here
of doing less than the law required. It was a matter of going infinitely farther.

Ethics cannot describe for us the whole of this infinitely
farther, which is, in fact, left to the spontaneity of the life.
But ethics has constantly to remind us of the lower limit,
within which we are, for all practical purposes, under the
law, which means that the question of faith is continually
posed by the critical functioning of ethics. Faith does not
free us from the law in order to allow us not to carry it out.
The tithe affords a very simple example. The tithe was one
of the requirements of the law. Life in the faith liberates us
from that requirement, but not so that we may avoid ·pay-
ing the tithe. To the contrary, it faces us with the problem

of the total dedication of our possessions to God which should be translated into an actual gift of much more than the tithe. Ethics, in reminding us of the simple requirement of the law (and of course ethics is never reduced simply to the law) should cause us to ask ourselves whether we are living in faith, as long as we are declaring verbally that our goods belong to God while in reality that is translated into very small gifts, well below what the law asks. This criticism of our Christian life which ethics effects makes us ask ourselves whether, perchance, we might not still be under the law, and whether we have yet in our lives traveled the whole road that the law, as a schoolmaster, set before the Hebrews. But this criticism, this call to endless discovery, does not do away with continuity and permanence, quite the contrary.

Crespy rightly stresses that Christian ethics is at one and the same time an invention and a custom. This importance of ethics as continuity is not at all contrary to what we have just been saying about the importance of invention in the Christian life. If that life were never anything but an invention, if there were no habits, no customs, it would be a disorder—a disorder which reappears in all the spiritualist and illuminist movements. Now we have seen that there is in fact a continuity in the work and the will of God. But morality, conversely, cannot be only a custom. It needs constantly to be enlivened, transformed, and renewed by the invention which comes from the Holy Spirit.

This permanence, this continuity, this custom, which ethics should insure, brings us to reflect on another meaning of the latter. It is still a support for the faith. It is too easy to say that the Christian should live according to the present command of God. That is true. But we cannot overlook the fact which is well known in the spiritual life, the silence of God. And if we make mention of it, it is not on the basis of man's spiritual experience (although that would by no means be negligible), but it is also because scripture itself tells us of this silence. How often did the prophets lament the fact that God was far from them, and how often do we find in the Old Testament this declaration: "The word of the Eternal was scarce at that time." Jesus himself knew that silence on the cross. So it is too simple to say, "It is sufficient to live according to the commandment that God speaks *hic et nunc.*" And when God does not speak? When God remains silent? When we go through that dryness, that aridity, when nothing makes sense and God seems infinitely far off? When we are only aware of that unilateral aspect of truth that God is in heaven and we are on the earth? Do we cease on that account to be "Christians"? Do we stop living as Christians? Do we simply stop living? Yes, and yet we have to try to live, even under those conditions. And then? Then we need the support of our neighbor and of the church.

The neighbor will have to bear witness to us again of that same grace of God. The church will have to bear witness to us again of that same truth of God. That will be done by the cure of souls and the confession of the faith. And that again will be an intervention on God's part. But for the conduct of life? For the decisions to be made, which must still, even in this manner, be decisions of faith? Very well! Without doubt it will be the ethics presented by the church, it will be the morality lived together by Christians which will be there as a help, as an example, as a way opened up, and which will simply be followed during this period of absence and of questioning. So there is a sort of function as temporary substitute which ethics fulfills, but without ever going beyond that role, that is, without ever pretending to impose itself when the believer has been caught up again by the immediate truth of the word, and without ever wishing to enter into competition with the living word.

In that moment ethics forms part of the great movement of remembering which the Bible describes for us. When man finds himself in the silence of God he remembers. Among the many passages let us take the one in the Lamentations of Jeremiah (3:21, 24). God no longer speaks to his prophet, so the latter says, "I will remember, . . . I will hope." It is Jeremiah who makes the decision: "I will remember," for God's acts in the past are not effaced. The past of God's acts is the truth. Because God spoke in the past, that does not make his word less true today. Because I no longer sense God today, that does not mean that God has changed. Because God does not act, that does not mean that his love has wavered. Jeremiah wills and he remembers! He affirms, against all his present experience, that the Lord continues good, because of that word of God which he knew in time past. More than that, Jeremiah affirms, "I will hope." That is not only oriented toward the past, but also toward the future. He hopes against hope. He lays a bet that God is steadfast and that he does not change, and out of that decision, out of that "I will," everything becomes good for Jeremiah, the very silence of God, the yoke, the humiliation, the solitude, all of that now appears to him as the interior of God's love. This example can help us understand part of the role of Christian ethics, which will help a person to keep going even when it seems to him that God no longer speaks, because this ethics contains, in spite of everything, an echo of the truth which once was spoken by the Lord to his church.

It seems to us that at the juncture of the preceding indications there can be seen still another authentic role for morality. It is there to remind us that the Christian should act without waiting for the clear and explicit orders of the Holy Spirit. In the Acts of the Apostles, Peter and Paul are seen making their decisions which established plans of action, undertaking voyages, or "evangelistic campaigns," without the Holy Spirit's dictating to them clearly what they ought to do. To the contrary, Paul notes that after they had decided to go toward Asia the Holy Spirit prevented them from going there and sent them into Macedonia (Acts 16:1–10). The attitude which consists in saying that one acts *solely* at the instigation of the Holy Spirit (and this means a clear and conscious instigation, of which we have explicit knowledge) is a dangerous attitude, for it can easily lead to doing nothing, on the pretext that the Holy Spirit has not spoken. It also can lead to a carrying out our own desires, because the word of the Holy Spirit is spoken to us in a manner so secret that it is not subject to any examination whatsoever by one's brethren and by the church. But in that case how does one distinguish what is truly the Holy Spirit from one's own subconscious?

Paul enjoins that the exercise of the gifts of the Holy Spirit be subject to the control and to the service of the community of the church. Morality is precisely a means of such control, and at the same time it is a reminder of the necessity for action, of the possibility of the putting into practice and of the legitimacy of this embodying, even when it is not consciously in obedience to the order of the Holy Spirit; for the latter, we are often reminded, works secretly within us without our knowing it. And surely we cannot live that morality, that is to say, bring it into being, except to the extent to which the Holy Spirit renders it both necessary and possible for us. If we perform today what seems to be the putting into practice of the truest requirement of God, then we can rest assured that it is done through the power and the enlightenment of the Holy Spirit, even if we do not know expressly that he was present and was guiding our actions.

Thus this ethic can never go beyond the simple reminder that "man's doing should *become, be,* and *remain* that of a person who *acquiesces* in God's doing." But that conformity can never mean equality. That is to say that our action, which ethics should call for or incite, can only attest or confirm the action of God. It can never either *continue* it, nor *reproduce it.*[10]

This is especially important at a time when the Reformed Church of France is busying itself with ethical positions which claim to reproduce the action of God. "Man is not invited to take the place of God nor to meddle in his affairs. . . . The disciple cannot do of himself, nor for others, what Jesus Christ has done." [11] Thus ethics is the place of criticism. Far from being the science of the will of God, it is the examination, the calling into question at every instant, of everything that we have been able to try to do as Christians, of every response that we have been able to make to God.[12] Hence there could not possibly be a response made in advance. Ethics should include this prohibition of the a priori response, and thus leave complete latitude to enable the response that we are to give today to be different from that of yesterday, which does not mean that yesterday's was bad. That is what Karl Barth calls the law of repetition and renewal in ethics, which corresponds to the steadfastness and the perseverance of God. But that shows the degree in which it is impossible to develop a constructed Christian ethics.

We were saying that, insofar as the Christian life is expressed in decisions, it cannot be schematized nor codified. Hence ethics is an impossibility. But the other face of this same phenomenon has to be considered. These decisions, ultimately, are the work of God. They are not incoherent. The commandment of God is not a sequence of isolated, absurd revelations, for he who issues the command is the one, eternal God. Each prescription is linked with the other prescriptions because all are part of the divine order and cannot be separated. Every prescription is bound to the others by a hidden relationship which is the design of God.

In the same way, if human action is carried out in isolated decisions it is not dissipated and dissolved in them. Man's decisions are inserted into the continuity of God's work. So this permanence makes ethics possible. But more than that, it makes it necessary, for from this point of view ethics has a dual role. First of all it will point out the route of the ethical event. It will prepare for that event. This is indispensable for man.[13] Then, if the Holy Spirit guides us by precise orders, if he gives us no intrinsic knowledge on which to fall back, it remains in us as an imprint of that knowledge "after the Holy Spirit has passed through." There is an experience which is neither erased nor neg-

ligible. There is a memory of that guidance of the Holy
Spirit. This memory, as Soë rightly says,[14] has a positive
value (when the Holy Spirit speaks to us again he does not
find a *tabula rasa*), and a negative value (this "knowledge" can engender pride and indolence). But this knowledge needs precisely to be developed, recognized for what it
is, formulated in the continuity of God's design and retained as true until God causes us to penetrate into a further
acquaintance with his will. If we do not go ahead with this
effort at discernment and development, we indicate thereby
that we are not taking seriously the continuity of the design
of God.

Christian ethics also has the function of giving back an
importance to the relativity of the world. It is a temptation
for all Christians to minimize or to discard this relativity,
considering the revealed absolute to be the only thing of
importance. Kierkegaard, who showed clearly how the absolute commandment of God brings about an alienation between the world and ourselves, was led at one point to
think that therefore the human is scarcely important. The
new birth changes us, and that is true even if the change
does not express itself outwardly. The world becomes a
game played by children, lacking in seriousness.

Kierkegaard (after 1846) saw that this is not entirely
right and that the revelation brings us into a new relationship with the world, into another love which cannot be pas-
sive, and consequently which has to be embodied in ethical
forms. Without this the whole incarnation is called into
question. As Niebuhr says, revelation demands of us an impossible absolute, and this leads to a neglect of human
means, abandoning "road construction" to those who have
not realized the total dimension of what there is to do "in
order to reach the mountaintop." Ethics is there precisely
to bring down to the level of the tangible problems the demand of the absolute which the Christian experiences
within himself, and to oblige him to take seriously the rela-

tivity of human situations. For "the tangible responsibility in which the revelation places us prohibits us from giving up our interest in the world." [15]

Finally, ethics plays a decisive and inevitable role in recalling the essential quality of incarnation and action in the Christian revelation. If one looks closely at the famous parable of the house built on the rock and that built on the sand, it is clear that the essential difference lies in the doing. The doing, the action, is decisive. The admirable expositions of Bonhoeffer [16] show the degree to which action in the legalistic sense differs from its meaning in Christian ethics. In the "pharisaic" sense it is an expression of the "disunity," of the lack of harmony, of the person with himself, of the opposition between living and doing, of the ever more finely drawn distinction between a good and an evil, of the "whether . . . or . . . ," and lastly of judgment. For Jesus (and for the person who is in Christ) there is precisely no disunity, but a perfect unity of being, a simplicity of the world and of man reintegrated in God.

Hence there is not a choice between a good and an evil, for choice is only exercised in the knowledge of good and evil, which *is* sin itself (and for that reason we see that a Christian absolutely cannot agree to the formula whereby the only ethical situation is that of choice). Nor, again, is there any "judgment" (Bonhoeffer shows clearly the way in which judgment is sin because it presupposes that knowledge of good and evil). There is only *action,* an action which issues from the very root of one's being, and which harmonizes with the unity of being. "Jesus acts. He does not judge." Jesus' knowledge always takes itself out in action. Christian action is an action which is "pure," not calculated, not pondered, not aimed at a goal. It does without "knowing" (Let not thy left hand know . . .). It is the fruit of the innocence of the dove. It is *at the same time* prudence. Ethics is continually present as a reminder that a Christian life is the response to the endless paradox of innocence and prudence, of involvement and knowledge.

Furthermore, faced with this necessity, with this urgent need of an ethic for Christians, we are led to understand better that which was an impossibility.

Such an ethic can—and should—cause the conflict to jut out, to stand out, between the will of God and what the world calls morality. Hence, if a person finds himself so imbued with human morality that he can only consider that as final, there can be a conflict of duties. But there is no conflict if morality is put in its proper place. In addition, the role of ethics for Christians cannot be to pretend to resolve the seeming conflict of "Christian duties." That would be to lapse into casuistry. Furthermore, there cannot be a *genuine* conflict for the Christian, for there are no contradictions in God's will. That will is one and perfect, but it is not always obvious nor routine. The search for it requires an effort beginning with the new birth. There is an awakening to various possibilities but that does not create a conflict of conscience, for whatever the choice might be that we put into effect, we should fall back upon the grace and love of Jesus Christ. In any event, there could never be a right solution which would permit us to avoid this surrender to grace. It is just that trusting surrender which removes all the tragic aspect from the choices which we might make among the possibilities that the will of God opens up to us.[17] If the choice we have carried out involves unhappy consequences it is, in the last analysis, God who takes them on, which quite obviously does not mean that we are free to do just anything. It is, in any case, a matter of responsible, honest seeking the will of God in prayer and the study of scripture.

We have laid stress on the freedom of the Holy Spirit, and on the freedom of the God who reveals himself by the will and the word of the Lord. That is entirely true. But we absolutely cannot interpret the word freedom in the sense of inconsistency, of arbitrariness or absurdity.[18] Without any doubt, God can will and decide anything at all. He can change his action as he pleases. But he does not do so. The very revelation which he grants us shows us a remarkable continuity in his decisions. It has been possible to speak very exactly of a plan of action on the part of God. He has himself drawn up that plan, and he holds to it, just as he holds to his promises when he has made them. There are not conflicting decisions in God's action, following one upon the other without mutual relationship. If, at a given moment, they take us by surprise that is only because we do not understand them. Neither are there conflicts between the successive stages of the revelation.

God is the same, yesterday, today, and forever. He at no time deceives us about himself. That which he revealed yesterday is always completely valid. Therefore we can count on a steadfastness, on a continuity on the part of God. We are not at all given over to a despot who would toy with us. We know that that cannot be the case from the moment the center of the revelation which God has given of himself is that he is love. That implies precisely that he does not mock us, that he does not deceive us, that he leads us in a path which is right for him and for us, reasonable for him and for us, and not arbitrary nor capricious. Therefore, when we refer back to the revealed word, to the objective testimony contained in the Bible of the living relation which took place once for all, there is no contradiction. Whenever we try to understand out of the Bible what the will of God is in our own time, we are not doing something prejudicial to God's freedom, because he has precisely subjected his will to the limitation of that objective word in order that we may so understand it.[19]

Thus it is legitimate, even ordained, that we should lay hold of that past revelation and seek in it an ethical instruction for today.[20] And for that reason we should be well assured that there is no conflict between the objective revelation and the revelation *hic et nunc,* between scripture and the Holy Spirit, between the permanent will of God and his will *hic et nunc* for each one. The Holy Spirit illuminates and makes present, makes contemporary, that which

he himself taught in time past to the prophets and apostles.
He does not have "something other" to say to us or to add.
Therefore all self-styled revelation of current interest should
be subject to verification by the word revealed in the Bible,
and conversely all interpretation of the latter should be subject to the revelation *hic et nunc* of the Holy Spirit, without the possibility of there being any contradiction. Thus
within this limit one can surely enunciate an ethic out of the
word of God. The latter is an eternal word, and in the
Bible is objective, constant, unchangeable; but it does not
have a direct ethical meaning. It must be translated for the
sake of the conduct of the current life of the believer—
only, that eternal word is not applicable for man as the
word of God except it become current for him through the
action of the Holy Spirit; and the difficulty will be precisely that as a living word it cannot be incorporated into
an ethical system, yet as a word which God has acquainted
us with it should give rise to an ethical requirement.

As we have seen, this translation which we are obliged to
make has only a limited validity and applicability. But
since the word of God must necessarily be currently ac-
tualized we have to understand that the actualization should
be carried out not only with respect to the theological and
spiritual content, but also with respect to the ethical content. The problem is the same. But in the past half-century
this ethical ingredient has too often been forgotten. Now
the gospel of grace is nonetheless also the gospel of God's
requirement, yes, the gospel of his jealousy.[21]

While we were saying above, concerning the will of God,
that it cannot be known and that it only becomes controlling *hic et nunc,* that therefore it can neither be incorporated into a morality nor give rise to one, now we are forced
to add a quality which we have noted in morality for the
faithful, that it, too, is narrowly bound to the current situation.[22] The contrast between the two terms, "will of God"
and "ethics," is fully legitimate if, with a great many moralists and Christians, we pretend that there is *one* perma-

nent, eternal, and natural morality, *one* definition of the good in itself. But once it is recognized that ethics is essentially fluid at that juncture between the word of the Lord and the stream of circumstances, of social, political, and economic relations; once it is recognized that ethics can only be valid for the perhaps brief period during which things are stabilized, and that it should be modified in accordance with events, then we perceive the possibility —not the necessity nor the constant renewal, but only the possibility—of a coming together of the *hic et nunc* of the word of God and the *hic et nunc* of a valid and true ethic for man. For the current application of the word of God, which is too often interpreted as being only for the soul of the believer who receives that particular revelation, is valid as well for the church, and for that reason it contains an element of duration, a registration in the course of history, and is not merely a flash of lightning in the heart's dark night. But if that is all correct, then in conclusion a set of prohibitions is drawn up for Christian morality. It can no longer in any way lay claim to being an objective definition of the good. It can no longer in any way lay claim to possessing or knowing that good.

To conceive the existence of this ethic is by that very fact to assert that "all independent search for the knowledge of good and evil is excluded." [23] It can never be formulated as a way of being correct with God or of protecting ourselves from him.

> Ethics can never cease to bear witness to the reality from which it proceeds, to wit, the word of God. . . . In no case can it change direction, that is to say, it has no right to become surreptitiously a description of the Christian man,[24] such as he is or ought to be, or again, an empirical or idealistic exposé of the Christian life. It is not allowed to turn its back on the word of God in order to try to see what would or could become of the man who has received that word.[25]

It never becomes an imperative, for everything we have just said about the indispensable nature of morality does not do away with nor satisfy the impossibility of that morality. We have not set forth two principles which succeed one another in such a way that the second cancels out the first, but the two confront each other and cannot eliminate each other. If we accept these two situational components, we shall first of all be obliged to acknowledge that this ethic cannot be established from the standpoint of the structures of creation nor from the standpoint of the kingdom of God. It belongs to this world (to this eon), between the fall and the return of Jesus Christ. Hence it is not to be based on a supposed knowledge of the will of God for Adam, as though there had never been a fall, nor on the restoration of all things in Christ, as though that had already taken place in its fullness. In the second place, there can never be any question of a Christian ethic, as we have said. The only thing we can try to do is to describe an ethic for Christians that will be within all the limits indicated by a servant role, beneath the cross and in the hope of its pardon.

What we have said of the impossibility of formulating a Christian ethic and yet of the necessity of constructing one is met with again at the level of the applicability and inapplicability of that ethic. Surely, as Niebuhr remarks,[26] Christianity complicates dreadfully the situation of the person trying to answer ethical questions, because it places man in a last situation. Surely the commandment of Jesus is inapplicable. His ethic has nothing to do with the immediate moral problems bearing on the relativity of the arrangements to be sought in economics or politics, or of balances of power to be stabilized. Surely the commandment of total love is concretely unlivable. The kingdom of God cannot be lived as though it were presently in our midst. But there could be no question of manufacturing a morality for the sake of rendering the truth applicable. That is not its role. It is not a matter of finding a middle road, nor of setting up distinctions and compromises so that the "extraordinary" demand of Jesus might become ordinary. Now that is just the temptation of almost all those who have developed an ethic, and even of Niebuhr, when he makes love a principle and a commandment which remains an impossibility *as well as* a possibility.

Every attempt to bring this requirement to the level of man by the route of principles and values is a betrayal typical of morality. And yet the latter does not remain a pure impossibility. It is, in spite of all, included in the *"fiat"* of Mary, and by that fact it becomes a human reality, not solely in the unique and perfect fulfillment of the Son, for that fulfillment does not remain solitary. Niebuhr's phrase characterizing the ethical situation of the Christian as an "impossible possibility" is a happy one, and it is along that same line that the present studies on finitude and requirement are worked out. In a word, this ethic is not applicable *or* inapplicable. It is both at the same time, for considered solely at the human level it is without logic, foundation, or meaning. Considered as the life in Christ, the "whether" no longer comes to mind for the applicability is no longer our responsibility.

In conclusion, let us say that even if the entire analysis of the urgent need to develop an ethic, even if all the reasons advanced were worthless, still we would not be able to escape the necessity of undertaking the venture of that ethic, because we cannot escape the necessity of responding to these questions: What is the meaning of the fact of being liberated by Jesus Christ from the tyranny of things, and so of regaining the possibility of using them without being enslaved by them? What is the meaning of being committed by Jesus Christ in a true encounter with others, and so of regaining the possibility of serving them and loving them? What is the meaning of the fact of being enlightened by Jesus Christ concerning the destiny of the world, and so of regaining the possibility of serving God and of loving him with all one's heart, with all one's soul, with all one's mind? [27]

Notes

Part I   Origins

1. Hence we frankly take what one might call a
nominalist position. Commandment is not based on the divine essence but on the sovereign will of God. Taken in and of itself the
commandment makes no sense. It only has meaning because God
has spoken it and given it. But one must steer clear of certain
errors into which traditional theological nominalism has fallen;
for example, that in the last analysis the only virtue required is
pure obedience (how can that be if the word of God wakens us
to freedom?), that it is simply a question of moral perfectionism
(which is impossible if precisely there is no preestablished morality) and a question of a *hic-et-nunc* legalism (which is contrary to the idea of a commandment). These errors are not contained in nominalism necessarily. Quite the contrary! The error
which lurks on the other hand is that of the absurd: "The more
absurd God's commandment is, the more certainly it is an expression of the pure will of God." But there we are in the presence of a systematic aberration. It could hardly be a matter of
saying that the good is simply a label which God pastes to the
outside of anything at all. His word is a creative word, and when
he speaks the good exists as good. God is neither arbitrary nor
tyrannical. He is love, and when he expresses his will it is a will
of love. Hence the good given by God is good for us.

These two revealed truths maintain nominalism in its rightful
proportion. Every other attitude, even such a delicately blended
one as Haering's, leads to elevating the good to a lofty independence, possessed of its own inherent foundation and corresponding to an "authentic" natural order of things. It leads also to the
positing of norms of eternal wisdom which mete out the will of
God. Now it seems to us that scripture gives us a different view
of the majesty of God's freedom. (See Haering, *La loi du Christ,*

3 vols., 1959; cf. Haering, *The Law of Christ*, 3 vols., Newman Press, 1961–66, hereafter cited as *Law of Christ*.)

2. Bonhoeffer, *Ethik*, pp. 129 ff. (Cf. Bonhoeffer, *Ethics*, New York, Macmillan, 1955, pp. 142 ff., hereafter cited as Bon., *Ethics*.)

3. K. Barth, *Dogmatique* II, 2, 2, pp. 29–70. With few exceptions the citations will be from the French translation. (Cf. K. Barth, *Church Dogmatics*, Edinburgh, T. & T. Clark, 1957, II, 2, pp. 509–42, hereafter cited as *Ch. Dogm.*)

4. To claim to find any other origin than the fall for the phenomenon of natural morality is to run counter to all that the Bible can tell us. It is obviously permissible for non-Christians to give a quite different explanation, but it is surprising that Christians should be so seduced by the good which is done in the world that they would either try to find a reason for it in God, or would offer reconciliations between natural good and revealed good. Natural morality (good prior to God) leads constantly to doctrinal confusion (for example, the law of life and the law of love: Nichols, p. 107; cooperation and love: Peabody, *Jesus Christ and the Social Question;* the ideal, nature, etc., with the good: J. Bois, *Problèmes de la Morale chrétienne*), or else one places these moralities as extensions of one another (more recently De Vos, "Zur Frage der natürlichen Sittlichkeit," *Zeitschrift für Evangelische Ethik*, hereafter cited as *ZEE*, 1958, No. 6) ; and Reiner tries to show that anthropology is the bridge between the two (Reiner, "Ethik und Menschenbild," *ZEE*, 1958, No. 5). It seems to us that nowhere does the Bible authorize this concept of an autonomous morality establishing a good *according to God.*

With regard to the well-known passages in Calvin, in which natural morality and natural law come into question (again these expressions must be carefully understood) , it is certain that Calvin does not intend thereby to justify a good which man might boast of before God, nor any autonomous morality. But on this point he was under the powerful influence of his time. In the degree in which he was living within Christianity, or in which he shared the philosophic ideas of his age, especially concerning the nature of man, he was prevented from drawing from his theology the logical consequences in the field of natural morality and of natural law. But today, Christians who have based themselves on the existence of a permanent human nature which they used as a point of departure for the doctrine of a partial fall, of the possibility of a natural knowledge of the good on the part of man, etc., and who have imposed this interpretation on the biblical texts, should be embarrassed by the fact that scientific investigations tend to deny the existence of this "nature," unless it be in a sociological sense. In looking at the biblical texts, we are obliged to set aside these natural premises, which in the present situation do not appear to be confirmed.

5. *Christianisme social,* 1957, p. 830.

6. It seems to us impossible to accept Humbert's interpretation: that since knowledge, and not the good, is the heart of the problem, an exclusively moral signification is ruled out. In the traditional sense of morality, yes; but the problem of the good is precisely not a moral problem from the biblical point of view. It is important to remember that the good is there placed in relation to life, and evil in relation to death. Therefore it has to be said that this knowledge is brought to bear on that which gives life and on that which brings death, but always with the proviso that it is God who gives life! Once that proviso is admitted, then this "good and evil" is the most important thing, more important than the understanding itself, for it is finally a matter of an understanding which affects everything!

How can it be maintained that the question is one of discernment and knowledge, a question of that which makes a person wise, able, and prudent, when, unless one dismembers the biblical text, nothing allows us to say that Adam had no knowledge before his disobedience but quite the contrary? How can one maintain that the problem is not that of the good, when all through scripture the question is that of the good which God pronounces? Strictly speaking, Humbert's interpretation can only be maintained by setting the Jahwist and Elohist accounts in opposition to one another. It is surely one of the weaknesses of Ricoeur to have adopted that interpretation because it agrees with his reconstruction. But one should at least ask oneself the two following questions.

A. How does it happen that these two accounts are placed side by side? How explain the fact that the rabbis, who were not imbeciles, did not try to harmonize them? Why are they handed over to us unaltered as the word of God by Israel and Jesus?

B. Might it not, perchance, be possible that their confrontation, their mutual relationship, contains *one* teaching, *one* truth, on which each account throws light? In that case it would not be a matter of dissociating them and of putting them in opposition to one another (as Humbert does) but on the contrary of giving heed to them in their diversity in order to learn complementary aspects of one single revelation.

Here let us take note of the danger which lies in the concept of myth. The moment one characterizes this passage as myth one imagines himself qualified to rework it, retaining whatever pleases him, and rejecting whatever appears not to be the sense of the myth. That is what Ricoeur does when he selects in the account everything which diminishes the importance of Adam's act, whereby he is able to show that the myth is only a construction from the standpoint of a prophetic accusation against mankind, which eliminates the relation between the works of human civilization and sin. In particular, when he labels the destruction of Babel, the condemnation of Cain, the expulsion of Adam from Eden, as "recessive forms of the jealousy of the tragic god," and explains it by a "clerical resentment against the heroic greatness of industrial man," we are deeply grieved at such a discriminatory analysis which nothing can justify, and at the facility with which anything that casts doubt upon the thesis built up elsewhere is relegated to a footnote. (See Ricoeur, *Finitude et culpabilité*, 2 vols., 1960, Vol. II, 2, chap. 3; cf. Ricoeur, *The Symbolism of Evil*, New York, Harper & Row, 1967, Part II, chap. 3, hereafter cited as *Symbolism*.)

7. For Adam it was a matter of defining himself as an autonomous person, in the etymological sense, having his own law in and through himself. That meant that his behavior was no longer a matter of relationship with God. He knew the good within himself, without God's having to say it to him. While the entire ethical outlook of revelation is based on relationship (love), ethics based on man, with its point of departure in his knowledge of the good (that is, his intrinsic definition of the good), will necessarily be an ethic of nonrelationship, of the closed door. And Genesis shows us that at once: man's setting up a distance between himself and God, the rupture between man and wife. But to see things that way is, at the same time, to challenge the traditional categories of morality!

8. Bonhoeffer on the meaning of shame, p. 131 (cf. Bon., *Ethics*, p. 145).

9. It is obvious that we absolutely cannot accept the interpretation we find in Ricoeur (pp. 237–8, cf. *Symbolism*, p. 247) that, from the fact of disobedience, "Man effectively realized his likeness to God, which had remained as asleep during the innocence" . . . "Sin represents a certain promotion of the awareness of self . . ." "This similarity to the gods achieved by means of transgression is something very profound: whenever the boundary ceases to be creative . . . man for the sake of his freedom reverts to the boundlessness of the principle of existence . . . the era open to liberty through misdeed is a certain promise of the infinite . . ."

This interpretation of the break with God as being, in the last analysis, a progressive step for man, as he realizes his similitude with God, contradicts the whole of revelation. Man wants to be

God and thereby finds himself *destroyed*. Man wants to be free of God and thereby he is subject to death and evil. There is no promotion, no development of the human. And it isn't enough to finesse, as does Ricoeur, by saying that it is a matter of a "bad infinite," because what is debatable is the claim that there is an accession of something over and above what was there previously in the communion with God. Nor will it do to pretend to include the adventure in the "how much more . . ." of grace, and to look upon sin from the standpoint of "where sin increased, grace abounded all the more," for Ricoeur's explanation, in contrast to that of K. Barth, ends in justifying the sin instead of the sinner. When he writes that, thanks to Adam's disobedience, thanks to the sin described in the myth, "an irreversible venture was set in motion, a crisis of 'becoming man' which only finds its solution in the final process of justification," one cannot help being surprised at the idea that the man created by God had not been the true man, and that man will only come into being through disobedience, pardon, and a resurrection at the very end of human history.

If the second creation is superior to the first (about which we know nothing), that will be by a free act of God, and not by the cumulative effect of human history. Moreover, we have absolutely no way of knowing whether man created by God did not have in his submissiveness as complete a knowledge of the love of God as we are able to have in Jesus Christ. In any case, from no point of view is the work of God a necessity, nor even conditioned by disobedience nor by man's situation. We would be following exactly in the path of the heretics of the early centuries who adored Adam the sinner because it was thanks to his disobedience that we have had the unprecedented good fortune to be saved by Jesus Christ. Truly it would require an exceedingly great love of history, and an extraordinarily high appreciation of the works of man, to think it a piece of good luck that God has had to sacrifice his Son.

10. Cf. Bonhoeffer, pp. 129 ff. (cf. Bon., *Ethics*, pp. 145 ff.) .

11. It is this *exact* and *true* view of the origin of human morality, under its mythical aspect, which best explains the indissoluble and ambiguous connection between morality and religion. Even those who pretend to deny that connection always come back to it in a roundabout way whenever morality has to be applied. Thus it sometimes happens that the application of morality leads to a development of beliefs and myths of a religious nature in a system or society which wants to be nonreligious, as in the Soviet Union. Autonomous ethics are always an overlay for a concealed religion, as has been well shown by Soë, *Christ-*

liche Ethik, 1957, sec. 6. But it seems to us that this "religious" something which inspires morality, which builds it or conceals itself within it, is in no way an expression of the will of God. It is indeed a "religious" something in the human sense of the word; that is to say, it is part of man's overall attempt to scale the heights of heaven, to lay hold upon God and to bring him into submission, or again, to acquire divinity for himself—in any case, to substitute something else for the will of God.

12. We do not think that when Calvin rules out the total depravity of the reason he means to say by that that man by his reason is capable of discerning truth and the good, nor even that reason is the apt point of entry for receiving the revelation.

13. Cf., for example, Soë, sec. 2; Prunet, *La Morale chrétienne, d'après les Ecrits Johanniques,* 1957, chap. 4.

14. For example, an overtaking of man by himself in search of sainthood (cf. Blanchard, *Sainteté aujourd'hui,* 1954) —or in search of the good, Baruk, on the function of the good.

15. For example, Reiner, "Ethik und Menschenbild," in *ZEE,* 1958, No. 5, p. 284.

16. Thus the obviousness of the law of love for Niebuhr, *Ethics,* p. 114.

17. Cf. Quervain, *die Heiligung,* 1946, pp. 25 ff.

18. K. Barth, *Dogm.* II, 2, 2, p. 247 (cf. *Ch. Dogm.,* II, 2, pp. 747–8) .

19. Ricoeur, II, 2, p. 38 (cf. *Symbolism,* pp. 70 ff.) .

20. *Ibid.* (cf. p. 42) .

21. *Ibid.* (cf. p. 57) .

22. On this subject see Van Peursen, "Ethik und Ontologie in der heutigen Existenzphilosophie," *ZEE,* 1958, No. 2, where the author enters into a critique of existentialism from this point of view.

See also K. Barth, *Dogm.,* II, 2, 2, p. 241 (cf. *Ch. Dogm.,* II, 2, pp. 726 ff.) . At all points man is the transgressor of the divine law. The proof that man is a transgressor resides in the fact that man is always on the point of wanting to excuse himself, to exonerate himself. That is sin par excellence.

CHAPTER 2   THE GOOD

1. The question of the good is asked within history, and it arises out of concrete situations with reference to which God formulates his commandment. The whole Bible shows us this relationship. Hence, for example, there is no rule with its "exceptions." As Bonhoeffer so accurately says, "The good is not a quality of life. It is life itself"—but Christ alone *is* the life; and again, "to be good means 'to live' "—but God alone is the cre-

ator. (See Bonhoeffer, *Ethik,* pp. 166 ff.; cf. Bon., *Ethics,* pp. 185 ff.)

This relation between the will of God which is the good and his revelation in the Bible is strongly emphasized by K. Barth, *Dogm.,* II, 2, 2, p. 203 (cf. *Ch. Dogm.,* II, 2, pp. 700 ff.) in the following terms: *This God and the Bible,* what the one ordains and the other requires are therefore practically inseparable—if there is no abstract authority of the Bible, neither does there exist any abstract authority of God. If the Bible is not a living word of God except when it bears witness to fact, it is clear that every living word of God cannot be different from that which is attested precisely in the Bible. It follows from this that we are not only called to act by analogy with biblical circumstances, but it turns out that the God who spoke to men in the Bible is also our own God, and directly ours, thanks to their witness. The good revealed to them is also ours. We must act, then, as though living out a repetition and a confirmation of that which was confided to them.

2. Nowhere, biblically speaking, is it truly a question of a natural knowledge of the good. Haering well displays the opposite Catholic position in explaining how moral freedom presupposes the knowledge of the good, and the latter the knowledge of the true (I, pp. 169 ff.; cf. *Law of Christ,* Vol. I). And no distinction is made between man as he was created, man as he is, and man regenerated in Christ. On the other hand, he alludes irritatingly to the "normal" man. One finds oneself confronted by a metaphysical anthropology, based on the hardly explained conviction either that the fall did not change anything very much, or that the kingdom of God is already brought to pass. Hence man can see the good naturally and know it, but may sometimes by accident be blinded (sic, pp. 178 ff.), whereas in our opinion —and we think in revelation—man is by nature blind to the good, but can be enlightened by grace. At that moment he sees the good of God, apart from the sinful imitations invented by man.

3. Against this conception read J. Bois, "la crise de la Morale," in *Le Problème de la Morale chrétienne,* 1948. The arguments there presented appear to misunderstand, in the last analysis, the significance of the unity of the good and the will of God.

4. Soë, sec. 19.

5. K. Barth, *Dogm.* (German edition), III, 4, p. 159 (cf. *Ch. Dogm.,* III, 4, p. 327).

6. Bonhoeffer's statement on the good and the final reality which is God corresponds exactly to this concept of the good (*Ethik,* pp. 55 ff.; cf. Bon., *Ethics,* pp. 55 ff.); likewise Prunet, chap. 2, sec. 2, where he shows that a christological ethics pre-

supposes that there is no other good than the will of God. (See also K. Barth, *Dogm.*, II, 2, 2, p. 207; cf. *Ch. Dogm.*, II, 2, pp. 708–9.) There are two absolutely synonymous notions: one, God and the commandment of God are good, and two, the good is God himself in his commandment. One cannot dissociate the good of God and his commandment. All breaking down of the notion of the good to the detriment of one of its components, which is what the creators of ethics always do, brings about, according to Barth, the breakdown of the very notion of God and the commandment. It is certain that the notion of the good of God's commandment has an absolute primacy over that of the good, because the good is a predicate of the function proper to God. God is the whole of what is just and good; which means that the good has no preeminence whatsoever over God, but to the contrary it is God who is and who declares the good, and whether it is thus or thus. It is because God is love that he formulates the good for man, and that is his benevolence toward man.

7. On this read K. Barth, *Dogm.*, III, 54, 4, pp. 34 ff. (cf. *Ch. Dogm.*, III, 4, pp. 34–5) and de Quervain, pp. 223 ff.

8. K. Barth, *Dogm.*, II, 2, 2, p. 528 (cf. *Ch. Dogm.*, II, 2, p. 757).

9. K. Barth, *Dogm.*, II, 2, 2, p. 174 (cf. *Ch. Dogm.*, II, 2, p. 675).

10. We are reminded of the celebrated formula of Theresa of Avila: "I do not seek virtue, but the Lord of virtues."

11. On the concept of justice in the Old Testament, we take the liberty of referring to our *Fondement Théologique du Droit*.

12. Bonhoeffer, *Ethik*, pp. 55 ff. (cf. Bon., *Ethics*, pp. 55 ff.).

13. On these different points see de Quervain, *Die Heiligung*, Introd. and Part I.

14. On this contrast cf., for example, K. Barth, *Dogm.*, II, 2, 2, pp. 100 ff. (cf. *Ch. Dogm.*, II, 2, pp. 606 ff.). We do not mean to contend that this contrast is ontologically valid and permanent. We merely observe the fact that man in ethics looks for a deed, and that the gospels and the letters are talking, on the other hand, of a being, of a transformation of being, not moreover separated from the deed, but such that the deed comes second and as a consequence.

15. K. Barth, *Dogm.*, II, 2, 2, p. 249 (cf. *Ch. Dogm.*, II, 2, pp. 583 ff.).

16. On all these points see Soë, sec. 28.

17. K. Barth, *Dogm.*, II, 2, 2, pp. 29 and 104 (cf. *Ch. Dogm.*, II, 2, pp. 535 and 610).

18. On this subject cf. Soë, sec. 29.

19. Cf. Prunet, chap. 3, sec. 2.

20. In chapter 5 we shall examine the reconciliation or the op-

position of the two moralities in relation to what we are saying here on the reconciliation and the opposition of the two kinds of "good."

CHAPTER 3 MORALITY

IS OF THE ORDER OF THE FALL

1. There is a renewed tendency in contemporary Protestant theology to minimize the seriousness of the fall. Always, in one way or another, man tries to restore his own dignity and insists that there is something which escaped the catastrophe unharmed. He thinks to preserve a dignity and a freedom before God. He does not want to be a creature destined for death. This heresy is the work of human pride, which cannot tolerate everything's being dependent upon the grace of God. Nevertheless, there can be no room for discussion of the fact that by the break with God, the living God, man is thrown onto the side of nothingness. He is cut off from life. He dies inevitably. God's free act before man is not at all to have said that man henceforth would die, but rather to have kept alive this "man for death." If it were otherwise Jesus Christ would not have had to die. To deny that man is a "man for death" is to deny the incarnation and the resurrection, is to allow that there were many other possibilities, is to reduce the work of Jesus Christ to nothing.

On the seriousness of the fall, even Brunner for the orders and Bonhoeffer for the mandates recognize that these are not leftovers from the purity of the original creation and that *in themselves* they imply nothing divine. They can only be recognized as such by faith.

On this perversion of the cosmos see Prunet, pp. 56 ff. In the same work is found (p. 124) an accurate evaluation of the difference in the concept of sin in John and Paul in contrast to that found in later Christianity. With them it is a fundamental condition of man as shown by his self-justification and the search for life within himself. In later Christianity it is a failure to live up to rules, moral fault, stain which man can wash away, superficial and relative deterioration, spurious membership, guilty attitude, lawlessness (for example, in Arminianism, etc.), all of them notions which are to be found in contemporary Protestantism, even among orthodox theologians.

2. As K. Barth has well shown, in this state of separation the law of God, when it is known by man, is only an occasion for covetousness. The commandment of God is transformed by sin. To man in this state the law provides not a point of departure for a true knowledge of the good, but a sort of urge to "be like God," to self-purification, to self-justification, to self-sanctifica-

tion (K. Barth, *Dogm.,* II, 2, 2, p. 83; cf *Ch. Dogm.,* II, 2, p. 592) .
Within the world of the fall, the world in itself is not a source
of true morality but just the opposite. That is why the most severe attack by Jesus is against the Pharisees. If there is an ethics,
it is in consequence and in perpetuation of the fall (K. Barth,
II, 2, 2, p. 9; cf. *Ch. Dogm.,* II, 2, p. 517) .

Thus when Niebuhr *(Nature and Destiny)* insists on the
autonomy of ethics (natural), and insists that ethical research is
a human task, he is right! But while he takes that to be a favorable observation it seems to us to reveal only that in the knowledge of good and evil Adam became autonomous. The fact of
wanting to know good and evil is just what constitutes original
sin which separates man from God and thus can only confirm
what man seeks to deny (K. Barth, *Dogm.,* II, 2, 2, p. 139; cf.
Ch. Dogm., II, 2, p. 645) .

3. This observation is even more true if we allow as the translation of the biblical text: "man was created within the image
of God" instead of "in the image of God" (translator's note:
the contrast is between the suggested "dans l'image de Dieu" and
the habitual "à l'image de Dieu") . The usual translation, as
Crespy *(le problème d'une anthropologie théologique)* has quite
rightly pointed out, means that there supposedly was a sort of
quality of man as created, a quality of his nature. The Hebrew
text, to the contrary, seems to mean that man is in the image
of God in the sense of a promise, a setting of his destiny and of
his future. It is a matter of the intended purpose of man's being,
of the mission which God has assigned to him.

If that is the case, however, then from the moment man pretends of himself to guarantee the knowledge of good and evil,
from that moment he pretends to guarantee his own destiny by
himself. That, in effect, is the whole of what the Bible is constantly telling us with regard to man's pretention, and God does
not oppose that pretention directly and by force! Consequently
one can say that from the moment when Adam took of the tree
of the knowledge of good and evil he was no longer within the
image of God, and if the promise survives it is solely in Jesus
Christ, who is the only one now remaining within the image of
God. A further consequence is that one can draw no conclusion
about the situation of contemporary man from this idea of the
image of God, which in a way no longer concerns us apart from
the fact that Jesus is Lord.

4. It is a manifest error of Bonhoeffer's to suppose that it is
the modern world which achieves autonomy in the spheres of political life, art, and morality, and that only modern man has
discovered the laws of these spheres independently of anything

which Christianity might have to say about it. In reality, at least in the sphere of morality, we must remember that from the very beginning, and in all civilizations, this tendency to assert moral autonomy is constant, and it even corresponds to the situation described in the Bible. The only thing one can say exactly is that in contemporary society one finds conspicuously again the traditional situation, which has temporarily and artificially been concealed by a religious view of Christianity.

5. It is grace itself which is the answer to the moral problem, in the sense that it sanctifies man, claims him for God, puts him under his command; in the sense that, in proposing that he determine for himself the divine predetermination of which he is the object, it invites him to obey God's command. (See K. Barth, *Dogm.*, II, 2, 2, p. 8; cf. *Ch. Dogm.*, II, 2, pp. 510–11.)

And in this sense we are indeed in agreement with Niebuhr's thesis (*Moral Man and Immoral Society*) according to which life in society, objectively considered, is amoral (as far as Christian ethics is concerned there is no morality of society and only man can be the object of morality). But we do not agree with him if that implies that there could be no morality in society, and that customs and traditions would be outside of morality.

6. This natural morality is surely fragile precisely in view of its natural basis (Niebuhr, *Ethics*, 50). The study by De Vos (*ZEE*, 1958, p. 347) does not appear to us to have restored to natural morality either its universality or its soundness. But what seems to us most untenable in this study is the relation between natural morality and Christian morality.

7. "The permanence of the natural law is bound up with the unity of human nature; its relative variableness is also bound up with the relative variation of this same nature" (Sertillanges, *Philosophie morale de saint Thomas d'Aquin*, p. 113).

8. In spite of the nuances which he brings to bear, Haering becomes part of this when he states that "the fundamental principles of the natural law can be known with certainty by any normal man in possession of his reason because they are self-evident" (I, p. 374; cf. *Law of Christ*, Vol. I). It is a question here of principles; that is, of rationally knowable ordinances, which have nothing in common with the action of the Holy Spirit revealing the work of God in Christ.

9. What hasn't been written about the moral conscience! . . . "inward agent of the good," "judge of our actions," "instrument for hearing Christ's call," these are the least of its virtues! It is the "sense" which permits us to hear the word of God (Haering, I, p. 188; cf. *Law of Christ*, Vol. I). It is held that all peoples accept the existence of the moral conscience because Socrates made

mention of his demon, and because the Stoics saw *syneidesis* as a participation in the eternal law of harmony.

For a description of the formation of the moral conscience see Soë, secs. 5 and 7. Even so, he wonders whether Paul had not already had that interpretation, which we doubt. On the other hand he indeed notes that the moral conscience is a human phenomenon which has no reference to revelation. It is not the "place" where God speaks (sec. 9).

10. It is by an abuse of the texts that Haering can speak of the conscience in certain passages in the Old Testament (Gen. 4:12; 1 Sam. 24:10; etc.). What he attributes to the conscience is very clearly the fact of the presence of God. It is not the conscience which accuses, but the fact that in the presence of God man discovers himself to be a sinner, and only a very hasty view of the texts of Paul can possibly understand them in the current sense of the moral conscience. It is very forced to claim to deduce from Romans 14:20–23, that to act according to faith and to act according to conscience are one and the same thing, for in this passage it manifestly is not a question of conscience.

11. And the verb from which this word is derived confirms this meaning: *synoida,* that is, either "to know with another," "to be confident of, . . ." or "to know in oneself," to be conscious of . . ."

12. Roux, *Epîtres Pastorales,* 1959.

13. The notion of conscience in Baruk *(Psychiatrie morale expérimentale)* is quite close to that which we are describing here. "The moral conscience corresponds less to a commandment than to an interior judgment . . ."

14. *Dogm.,* II, 2, 2, p. 164 (cf. *Ch. Dogm.,* II, 2, p. 668).

15. We conclude this paragraph by calling attention to two studies on the problem:

Bonhoeffer rightly notes that the conscience is a phenomenon of duplication of the person, which in reality comes from the fall *(Ethik,* 134 ff.; cf. Bon., *Ethics,* pp. 161 ff.). The criterion of the conscience is man's agreement with himself, but that is the situation of sin. In effect, the conscience in no way implies a relation of man with God, and instead of leading man to find his unity by the covenant with God (act of grace), it claims to cause man to find his relation with God by man's inward peace with himself. This is the very reverse of the decision of God. Thus the conscience leads man to a self-analysis and to a radical failure to understand the will of God. It is the center of man's autonomy *(Ethik,* pp. 188 ff.; cf. Bon., *Ethics,* pp. 211 ff.) and hence needs to be overcome in its identity in order that man may submit to Christ. When that happens the phenomenon of the moral conscience gives way to the man responsible before God.

Second, and in the same direction, we are entirely in agreement with Ricoeur (II, 2, pp. 85 ff.; cf. *Symbolism*, p. 85) when he analyzes the relation of the conscience and of the "sight," *regard,* of God. "My own view of myself means the approximation of the absolute view by the consciousness of self. I want to know myself as I am known." "With guilt is born 'conscience': a responsible facing up takes on consistency in the face of . . . the requirement of holiness" (p. 138; cf. *Symbolism*, p. 143), but this conscience becomes degraded into a moral conscience which judges good and evil, which becomes in itself the point of reference for the good. Let the *in thy sight* be forgotten and the consciousness of a fault becomes guilt instead of sin. Now the conscience becomes the measure of evil in a statement belonging to total solitude (p. 102; cf. *Symbolism,* pp. 104 ff). Undetermined, the guilty conscience is also a closed conscience (p. 141; cf. *Symbolism*, p. 146). To become one's own court of justice for oneself is to be alienated indeed (p. 139; cf. *Symbolism*, p. 145).

CHAPTER 4 MORALITY
IS OF THE ORDER OF NECESSITY

1. The transition to the order of necessity is much more than a "tarnishing of freedom." Whatever the dialectical relation may be between the contradictory themes, they still are mutually exclusive. Where liberty is, there is no longer power of evil, because freedom subsists only in Christ. It cannot be said that sin opens an era of freedom (Ricoeur, p. 238; cf. *Symbolism*, p. 246). It cannot be said that the country which falls completely into the hands of the enemy continues to enjoy self-determination (Ricoeur, p. 150; cf. *Symbolism,* pp. 156-7) —comparison is not an argument. Whatever be the force of the proposition that evil cannot be as basic as the good, it still remains true that slavery—real, and not merely the thought symbol—is not freedom, and that the break with God leads to slavery which expresses itself in the order of necessity. Hence we cannot accept Ricoeur's explanation, including that of the slave-arbiter (II, 2, 145–50; cf. *Symbolism*, pp. 151–7).

2. K. Barth describes forcefully this entrance of necessity into the universe from the fact of the knowledge of good and evil. Not only can man make this distinction but he *must* make it. No matter where he goes and whatever he does he encounters good and evil. From all sides the *sic et non*, the reasons for acting and for not acting, the commands and the prohibitions swamp him. These forces join together to trouble him, to overthrow him, to

lay hold of him, *constraining* him to take now this direction, now that. His eyes now are open but like the eyes of a person suffering from insomnia. He is forced to choose, make decisions, learn from one side or the other how to conduct himself, seek to cut a path for himself through an immense forest of requirements, some of which he will accept and some of which he will reject.

In order to do all this, man will develop his own system of morality according to his own idea of the universal order. Never will he satisfy all the requirements which are laid upon him, and he will never really satisfy any one of them. Such is the similarity to God which befits the impious, the godless, Adam, man who did not want to begin by satisfying God. In turning against God, *man has been given over* like a hunted animal to the dogs, to the requirements which the world, life, men, exploit against him, and which he can never cease to level at himself. (See K. Barth, *Dogm.,* II, 2, 2, p. 79; cf. *Ch. Dogm.,* II, 2, pp. 586–7).

It is a commonplace to speak of the slavery of sin, but in reality this needs to be translated from the inward life to the totality of life in speaking of the order of necessity.

3. In spite of the increasing awareness on the part of the sciences (including the psychological and sociological sciences) of the existence of determinants in human life, the metaphysicians, moralists, and theologians persist in maintaining the freedom of man as a datum, as a fact of nature. They affirm it as a presupposition in the face of every observation and demonstration. Generally, moreover, the question is asked at the level of problems of conduct and of ethics. In Catholic circles this is expressed, for example, by the formula: "Man is free in the image of God" (cf. Haering, I, 145; cf. *Law of Christ,* Vol. I), as though there were no difference between man as he was created and man as he is now. But immediately one finds it necessary to introduce numerous distinctions, for one is forced to observe that this freedom does not exist. Then begins a whole casuistry on the "troubles of freedom" (Haering, pp. 154–68; cf. *Law of Christ,* Vol. I), from which, after all is said and done, one never emerges!

4. Cf., for example, Bergson, *les deux sources,* pp. 12–13 (cf. Bergson, *The Two Sources of Morality and Religion,* New York, Anchor Books, Doubleday, 1956, pp. 12–13, hereafter cited as *Two Sources.*

5. In spite of its greatness, the ethics of Kant is a special illustration of this belonging of ethics to the order of necessity, by the absolutizing of the law and by its impersonality.

6. Cf. on the psychological effects of the conflict between the acknowledged morality and social behavior: K. Horney, *la per-*

sonnalité névrotique de notre temps, 1960 (cf. Karen Horney, *Neurotic Personality of Our Time,* New York, W. W. Norton, 1937) .

CHAPTER 5   THE DOUBLE MORALITY

1. On this question one can cite, among other recent authors, Soë, secs. 4 and 31; Bonhoeffer, pp. 41, 79, 86, 178 ff., 430 (cf., Bon., *Ethics,* pp. 41, 77, 84, 177 ff., 231; de Quervain, I, pp. 203, 214, 264 ff., 275; Mehl, *Problème,* pp. 31–51; Ramsey, *Basic Christian Ethics,* 1954, pp. 192 ff.; Piper, *ZEE,* 1957, p. 125) .

2. Christian ethics cannot count on a natural morality of man, nor on a knowledge of good and evil that man would possess independently. It should guard against ascribing to man a knowledge of good and evil that man would possess independently of the fall, and against confusing man's own natural tendency with the will of God. (See K. Barth, *Dogm.,* II, 2, 2, p. 15; cf. *Ch. Dogm.,* II, 2, pp. 522–3.)

3. To say with Roux *(les épîtres pastorales,* p. 95) that Jesus Christ is the criterion of values is to say something absolutely exact, but which tends rather to the elimination of values than to their recognition.

4. But under those conditions the church should be clear precisely on this point. When she produces an ethic this necessarily has the character of ethics according to the world. The problem then would be that this should not be composed of values chosen by a given society and then converted into Christian ethics. For the central value of Christian ethics to be peace in the peoples' republics and equality in the U.S.A., and for authors uncritically to declare this to be the basis on which ethics is to be constructed, seems to us to be quite unacceptable!

5. It is only in this sense that we accept the idea that Christians have to choose among the world's values (Mehl, Ricoeur, "Discerner pour agir," *Semeur,* 1950) . That is true provided one knows that these values do not express truth, nor the specifics of the revelation to be lived.

6. On the other hand, we certainly can recognize a considerable value in natural ethics when this expresses "the finite mind's realization of its own finitude" (Niebuhr, *Nature and Destiny)* , when it is the recognition, explicit or not, of the insufficient and dependent character of life, when it witnesses to a lack, to an absence, when it expresses a normality which leaves room for a bad conscience in actual practice. Natural ethics can, in fact, be all of those things (but then this implies an abandonment of all pretense at attaining the good of oneself, or at a strict rational-

ity of norms). And in that case it testifies to the failure of the Adamic enterprise. Also in that case it can be taken with the greatest seriousness for the faith.

7. This idea of a useful morality approaches that formulated by Eric Weil (*Critique,* 1948, "Raison morale et politique") when he shows that the moral principle has the great weakness of never saying what needs to be done in practice, and of the overwhelming power to forbid certain procedures. The positive value which it points to is not positively defined. It will be necessary to have recourse to reason, which teaches what is and what is not possible under the given conditions.

8. *Ethik,* p. 97 (cf., Bon., *Ethics,* p. 101).

9. Whether one likes it or not, the choice has to be made between basing all on revelation or basing all on man. Man is the point of departure for all natural ethics. One can see very well the difficulty for Catholicism in the moral theology of Haering. He lays down true principles: "Moral theology can be nothing other than the doctrine of total commitment in the footsteps of Christ. Its point of departure can only be Christ." "One must not separate anthropology from Christology" (I, 95; cf. *Law of Christ,* Vol. I). But having said that he sets out to give an ontology of man, of natural man not regenerated by grace, and it is on that foundation that he rests the possibility of Christian ethics (pp. 97, 268). It is as part of nature that man brings true moral values to pass. In a word, the moment a compromise is sought between God and man, immediately the balance shifts to the side of man!

But in the contrast between the two moralities it especially must not be said that the one which comes from God is a religious morality. That is a dreadful confusion introduced, and it is only natural, by all Catholic authors (and lastly again by Haering, Vol. I, in spite of his excellent theological point of departure), but also frequently by Protestant authors, which is astonishing, so by Niebuhr (*Ethics*).

10. I am well aware of the difficulty of allowing for the existence of two moralities, and one that risks coming under all the criticisms leveled at Luther for his theory of the two realms. We shall meet this problem again later on. However, I shall insist on the fact that it is not a matter of a total separation, of a dualism, between two moralities, of which one is good and the other simply bad. Similarly, it is not a matter of renouncing all contact between God and his creatures, though it must be remembered that this contact exists only in Jesus Christ. On the other hand, to reject the existence of two moralities, to attempt to establish a monism at all costs, is to enter into an idealism which is

completely unreal. All doctrines claiming that human moral systems more or less contain elements of the divine good misunderstand the reality of the existing world, misunderstand the reality of politics, for example, and judge only by exceptional, well-chosen examples. Or again, they limit their vision to a single aspect of the real, rejecting with the greatest of ease everything which fails to fit in with monism.

On the contrary, we feel bound to keep in view the complexity of the real in its totality, and the moment we do that we discover that the biblical doctrine of two moralities is also the only one which corresponds to the reality of the world. An example, at once tragic and clear, of this contrast is afforded by the debate which took place on the subject of the condemnation of Eichmann. It is obvious that from the point of view of the survival of the human community, from the point of view of civil justice, as from the point of view of the natural human sentiments, Eichmann should have been condemned to death, for, as was said, to let a murderer go free is completely to overthrow the principles of justice and the laws of civilization. But over against that a Christian conscience has to ask whether pardon is a purely individual matter, or whether it also concerns collective crimes, and whether pardon should not involve Eichmann's release.

That idea was maintained by M. Gollancz, writing as follows: "Six million human beings have been killed, but what good does it do to kill one more? Will this action rip away the veil of hate and cruelty which Auschwitz has thrown over humanity? Eichmann belongs to God, and only God can judge him. We should not be guided by the mythical idea of compensatory justice, but by that of spiritual compensation, which is closer to us. The more hateful the evil has been the greater the mercy must be. The extreme wickedness of Hitler demands an extreme act of goodness. Only mercy and forgetting can bring a little light into our darkness." And Gollancz concluded with the suggestion that Eichmann be set free with this injunction: "Go and sin no more." It is obvious that the application of that morality would be disastrous for the collective life, but it is no less obvious that it corresponds to the requirement of love of neighbor, or more exactly the love of one's enemy. Here can be seen the contradiction between the two moralities, and we should note with melancholy humor that the morality of civil justice was sustained by a Dominican Father and that the morality of love of neighbor in God was sustained by an Israelite.

11. K. Barth defines extremely well the contrast of the problematical itself. The problem for general ethics, namely the

search for law or value, the quest for the truth or for the knowledge of the good, none of that is a problem for ethics which inheres in the Christian doctrine of God. Conversely, that which is no problem at all for general ethics, namely man's real situation *called in question by* his response to the ethical question, the real bond which unites him to the good, like the real distances which separate him from it, it is that which constitutes the burning question for Christian ethics. (See K. Barth, *Dogm.,* II, 2, 2, 12; cf. *Ch. Dogm.,* II, 2, p. 519.)

12. *Ibid.*

13. See the very classical treatment of the relation between morality and freedom in Haering, I, pp. 143 ff. (cf. *Law of Christ,* Vol. I) . And on the opposite side: from the fact of giving up his own choosing between good and evil the elect of God turns solely to the search for obedience. From the fact that he does not desire to be good of himself he submits solely to the will of God. The good becomes an event, and here the ethical question receives its answer in Jesus Christ. Thus we see the divine ethics affirmed *in contrast to all human ethics.* (See K. Barth, *Dogm.,* II, 2, 2, pp. 10–11; cf. *Ch. Dogm.,* II, 2, p. 517.)

14. Regarding the specific character of Christian morality, Niebuhr is right in showing that every time Christianity abandons this specific character it loses the ability to identify the ethics of the world; but then Christian ethics has to defend itself on two fronts, that of dualistic idealism and that of naturalistic monism, that of an optimism which grants validity to the world in and of itself, and that of a pessimism which reduces historic existence to meaninglessness. Such is precisely the specific character of this ethic, unlike any other. It is clearly expressed in the successive myths of ancient Israel. Likewise Christian love is at the same time different from moral love of the legal type, and love of the mystical variety (cf. Prunet, p. 25) .

15. It is certain that the confusion caused by a great number of theologians stems from the fact that the ideal duty and conscience can cause the natural man with a theistic outlook to conceive of God as requiring the good. But that is not what revelation teaches us. It sets forth God as acting toward us as he would have us behave toward others (Soë, sec. 4) . Typical of this confusion is J. Bois, *Le Problème de la Morale chrétienne.*

16. This similarity often causes confusion and temptations. As Hillerdal has pointed out (*ZEE,* 1957, No. 6), in many instances only a very little thing distinguishes the hortatory sayings of the New Testament from this or that philosophical or humanist morality. This very little thing is simply the expression "in Christ." What a temptation it is to omit that expression in order to arrive

at a *consensus omnium!* And if instead of omitting it one takes *it* as his starting point, then the distinction from all other moralities becomes radical.

A very characteristic example of this confusion is seen in M. Roux, *Epîtres pastorales,* p. 179. We shall have to deal with the problem again in speaking of the specific character of morality for Christians.

17. K. Barth has well described for modern times the influence of systematic ethics on Christian ethics, and the successive modifications by the latter on the ethical ideas of the world. (See K. Barth, *Dogm.,* II, 2, 2, pp. 14 ff.; cf. *Ch. Dogm.,* II, 2, pp. 521 ff.)

18. On the different possible relations between the two moralities (cf. K. Barth, *Dogm.,* II, 2, 2, pp. 15 ff.; cf. *Ch. Dogm.,* II, 2, pp. 522 ff.) : neither an apologetic nor a compromise nor a distribution of roles. K. Barth opposes differentiating between the two on the basis of the criteria of the world's ethics. But we also accept Barth's attitude which considers that ethics should examine the problems, intentions, and motives of general ethics for what they are, in order to accept them or reject them. Ethics should adopt a comprehensive and not a negative attitude while remaining essentially critical. (See K. Barth, *Dogm.,* II, 2, 2, p. 20; cf. *Ch. Dogm.,* II, 2, p. 527.)

19. From another point of view, within the outlook of communism itself, the theory of the short stretch of road is absolutely reprehensible, as we have tried to show in the report to the National Synod, 1959.

20. As Haering does, for example, in likening the heroic death of soldiers to that of the martyrs (I, p. 313; cf. *Law of Christ,* Vol. I) .

21. There we see the effort of the Christian to justify his morality. A validation of Christian morality from the standpoint of general morality is impossible. It is absolutely out of the question to try to attach the first to the second, or to claim to develop, extend or enrich the one by the other. There is no longer question of discussing the matter on common ground, as with partners. (See K. Barth, *Dogm.,* II, 2, 2, p. 12; cf. *Ch. Dogm.,* II, 2, p. 519.)

22. Soë, sec. 10.

23. It seems impossible to recognize an identification of the decalogue with the *lex naturae,* as was often done, and perhaps by Luther in the *primus usus legis,* for the idea that the decalogue is called upon to "maintain discipline among the unruly" implies life in a Christian society, as we have already shown. The decalogue is a law *revealed* to the *Jewish people* as the chosen people. It is not a general law for all, and it does not express what comes naturally to the human heart. Otherwise it is hard to

understand why it should be revealed on Sinai in the midst of thunder and lightning (cf. on this subject Bonhoeffer, 1st appendix; Niebuhr, pp. 106 ff. [cf. Bon, *Ethics,* pp. 271 ff.]) .

24. The constant effort of Christians in establishing a morality has indeed been, as Soë (sec. 30) indicates, a rejection of the tension between the command of God and the decay of the world. Man then can either flee the world (monasticism, for example) or relativize the commandment (the Lutheran *Berufsethik,* for example, which ends in making constant reference to grace in order to dissipate the ethical consequences) . Social Christianity also relativizes the will of God by denying the radical opposition between the order of the world and revelation.

25. On these four points: K. Barth, *Dogm.,* II, 2, 2, pp. 89 ff. (cf. *Ch. Dogm.,* II, 2, pp. 583 ff.).

26 K. Barth, *Dogm.,* II, 2, 2, p. 102 (cf. *Ch. Dogm.,* II, 2, pp. 608 ff.).

27. We find a curious application of this notion in 1 Cor. 5:9–12. Paul forbids the "saints" of the church of Corinth to have anything to do with immoral men, robbers, or indolaters. But he makes a distinction. If they are immoral men, robbers, or idolaters who are not Christians it is perfectly normal to continue to have relations with them. They obey other precepts, another morality. It is not for us to judge them. We can meet them in accepting them for what they are. Otherwise, says Paul, it would be necessary to leave the world (which God *never* commands as a permanent and final measure) . But on the other hand if it is a matter of Christians who behave like that then one must break off all relations with them, not eat with them, cast them out, because they have another rule to live by, that alone which we are to know as Christians.

28 Bonhoeffer, *Ethics,* pp. 5 ff.

29. We shall be maintaining a third essential consequence. The Christian recognizes the relative validity of the world's morality and knows very well that he cannot escape it.

30. Ellul, "la Théologie de la grande ville," *Verbum Caro,* 1948.

31. Haering is very characteristic of this Catholic tendency when, beginning with qualities of Christian morality, he clearly formulates the idea that every morality corresponds to criteria. Thus, "the morality of Christ, and every authentic human morality, is essentially religious in character" (I, p. 29; cf. *Law of Christ,* Vol. I) . He makes the same improper comparison when he writes that "it is the common conviction of all peoples that man hears God's voice and the voice of the good in his heart" (I, p. 188) .

In the end the entire debate turns on the question whether the norm of morality is written by God in the very being of man, and whether there is some identification between the natural motivation of the subject and the divine will (I, p. 351), which we expressly deny. It seems to us that scripture is very clear on this point, and that when Jesus repeatedly opposes the spontaneous conduct of man with his "but I say unto you" there is no identification between natural motivation and the command of God. Haering's attitude necessarily leads to the result that we are condemning elsewhere: in the degree in which every morality should correspond to the Christian scheme (since there is a natural morality coming from God) everything which fails to correspond is not a morality. That allows the liquidation along three lines of every effort to arrive at modern moral thinking (I, p. 34). "Right off let us put aside scientific ethics and those moral attitudes which sacrifice the human person to the group. . . . These concepts can in no way establish morality on a serious footing. They rather tear it down." The error of the premises leads to the inhumanity of the conclusions!

32. *Dogm.*, II, 2, 2, pp. 137, 150, etc. (cf. *Ch. Dogm.*, II, 2, pp. 641, 655, etc.).

33. K. Barth, *Dogm.*, II, 2, 2 (cf. *Ch. Dogm.*, II, 2, chap. 8) shows that the good defended by the state is certainly not the good which the latter could have created or preached of itself, but consists in the fact that the state insures a law and order which permits, makes outwardly possible, the preaching of the knowledge of the good willed by God. This state, in safeguarding the communal life of man, in preserving it from dissolution, makes the Christian community possible and consequently the eventual presence among men of the good according to God. It is a matter of a temporary order which does not carry grace within itself but which allows the expression of it. Consequently the morality of the world, like the law enacted by the community, is not to be neglected and despised by Christians. Christians cannot become the enemies of that which to be sure is a product of man's sin, but still less can they be content to bless these human inventions by letting them follow their own path, and by supposing that they purely and simply express the will of God (cf. Niebuhr, *Moral Man and Immoral Society*).

34. Soë rightly explains how in the end the Christian ethic always tries to reduce this tension (instead of introducing it), either by fleeing from the world or by relativizing the commandment. All social Christianity is characterized by this error (Soë, sec. 30).

35. Consequently Niebuhr's (*Nature and Destiny of Man*) criticism of Luther seems correct, when he concludes that Lu-

ther's position devalues every ethic of the world because all are characterized by sin, any distinctions among them being unimportant. But Niebuhr sometimes persists in placing the moralities of the world and the requirement of God as extensions one of the other. Luther's error, supposedly, was to apply to the collective life his exact view of the individual. The latter is radically a sinner and his justice is nothing but sin. From that point on the progress of knowledge and the search for freedom and social justice are nothing. In Niebuhr's eyes this is the failure of Luther's effort to link life in history to the response to grace. But as a matter of fact Niebuhr's effort to maintain at one and the same time the radically sinful character of man and the possibility of social ethical progress seems to us impossible to sustain concretely and in the last analysis to be very artificial. The meeting point which he sets up between nature and grace (mutual love and sacrificial love) appears to us as a return to the classical error of a concurrence between the work of man and the work of God. Once again, for Niebuhr it is a matter of saving the works of man by themselves, of showing them to be valid in and of themselves.

36. This concept of the double morality has nothing to do with the notion of the two realms in Luther—or at least according to the current interpretations of Luther's thought. (Of course this doctrine of Luther must not be confused with the doctrine which goes by the same name in medieval Catholicism.) There are two realms obeying different laws and moralities and the Christian is a citizen of two worlds, one world which is temporal and political, in which the state is the master—and a spiritual world. Private life—most fittingly molded by the spiritual—is then totally separated from the life in society. The Christian obeys a vocation but is not obliged to change the order of the world. The authorities of the state are charged with watching over this order and that is a function given them by God. The state should base itself on the law of God (*primus usus*) in order to attain that end and to establish the *justitia civilis* (see criticisms and interpretations of this in Thielicke, Bonhoeffer, Soë, etc.). Yet once more this idea of two distinct domains should be considered one of the fruits of Christianity. For Luther, who lived within Christianity, it went without saying that the secular offices, the state, the civil law, were "Christian," inspired by the decalogue and suited to the establishment of a *justitia civilis* conformed to the will of God. It is then normal to establish a spiritual domain of which the church has charge, and a temporal domain of which the state has charge. But the basic error is that of thinking that Christianity is a *normal* situation. In fact, Luther runs up against obstacles like the Jews and still more the Turks. Is he ready to

hand over the government of the earthly city to the Turks?

For us there is no division into two domains, into two realms. There is no distinction between public life and private life, etc. There is only one world in which we live with its forms of spirituality also. The domain of the church is powerfully conformed to the world: the church as a sociological body, Christians subject to political and economic influences, the contamination of the faith by religion, etc. And the church and Christians find themselves within this world. Within the temporal is found the bearer of the revelation—and not the spiritual—and that does not add up to *two* domains.

Thus on the one hand the Christian is called upon to participate in the activities of the world in which he lives, to recognize, not the justice before God, but relative usefulness and normality. It is normal that this world develop its own morality. But on the other hand the Christian is called to live in all its dimensions the fullness which has been given him, without distinction of temporal and spiritual, private and public, etc. The Christian faith implies for him transformations in politics, in business, etc., which are directly referred to the person of Jesus Christ. Thus tension is set up in *one* world (and not a separation), tension which does not mean rupture but not adherence either. It is a dialectical relationship which eliminates at one and the same time the possibility of the autonomy of the morality of the world and the possibility of the autonomy of the revelation in relation to the world. Moreover, it is possible that Luther may also have conceived the relation between the two realms as a dialectical relation.

Part II Morality of the World

1. We shall not be involved here in a philosophy of morality nor strictly speaking in a sociology. For a sociological analysis of the moral life we refer to the chapter bearing that title in *Traité de Sociologie* (Vol. II) conducted by Gurvitch. We have no difficulty accepting the outlines drawn up by M. Gurvitch, as well as his sketch of the types and forms of the moral life. We feel more hesitant about the relationship he indicates between these types and forms on the one hand and the types of civilization on the other.

2. To speak thus is not to reduce ethics to one of man's many activities. Ethics keeps its own special domain, as K. Barth has shown. (See *Dogm.*, II, 2, 2, pp. 6 ff.; cf. *Ch Dogm.*, II, 2, pp. 509 ff.)

3. Certain particularly lucid essays easily amount to this same conclusion, for example, Murry (*The Free Society*, 1948), who

shows that history does not have an intrinsic meaning but that morality consists in the decision to give it one, and the only moral procedure is trial and error; finally, that there is no free society, but only a society which wills to be free. Of course this decision of man to designate what is good is not capricious.

4. Cf. the excellent summation of E. Weil, "Raison, Morale, Politique" (*Critique,* 1948).

5. On the different elements of morality from the theological point of view see, among many others, Reiner "Ethik und Menschenbild," *ZEE,* 1958, No. 5, p. 284.

CHAPTER 6 THE DIVERSITY OF MORALITIES

1. Obviously we cannot mention here all the essays on morality, but we can refer to the remarkable *Traité de l'action morale,* of Georges Bastide, which appeared in 1961. On the problem of the sociology of morality see especially Gurvitch, in Volume II of the *Traité de Sociologie,* and also the articles of Cazeneuve, Ansart, and Michel on the social frames of reference of moral doctrines, in the *Cahiers internationaux de sociologie,* 1963.

2. It is surely one of the many merits of Karl Marx to have demonstrated the contingent character of morality, its connection with economic structures and class relationships, and its role in the interplay of social forces. But, on the one hand his doctrine was considerably deformed by Lenin, and still more so afterward (cf., for example, art. "Ethik," in *Petit vocabulaire philosophique,* by Rosental and Judin, in Russian, 1954; Garaudy, *Le communisme et la Morale,* 1945). On the other hand he does not avoid what he himself accuses the moralists of doing, namely trying to transform into an absolute the relative values of the proletariat and establishing in his turn an ethic of history simply opposed to the ethic of philosophy (cf. Berdyaev, *Christianisme et réalité sociale;* Niebuhr, *Ethics,* chap. I and pp. 122 ff.). (Conversely the other critiques presented by J. Bois, "la crise de la Morale," pp. 82 ff., seem to us ineffectual, as also his effort to validate a natural morality in spite of the Marxist criticisms. He does not succeed!)

3. Let us remember that for certain moralities war is almost a supreme value, and I am not alluding, for example, to a Hitlerian ethic, but to much more ancient concepts. Consider for example this passage from Heraclitus, fragment 53/8, 112: "War is the father of all, the king of all. It shows some to be gods, others to be men. It makes slaves of some and free men of others. One should know that war is the governing principle."

4. This is the constant temptation of every creator of morality.

292   To Will and to Do

Thus in modern times J. Middleton Murry (*The Free Society*, 1948), considering that morality consists in "reasonably wanting freedom for all," comes to the point of declaring that the U.S.S.R. does not acknowledge the moral principle and that, in short, there is no morality in communism. And again, that is the habitual Catholic attitude (so Haering, I).

5. It is a partisan and not a scientific view that leads Gurvitch to say that there is no true morality in fascist societies because the system of modes of the moral life is imposed by force (*Traité de Sociologie*, II, p. 169). In reality that is no more true than for any other authoritarian organization.

6. To say with Haering that the following principles are acknowledged by all peoples: what you do not wish done to you, do not do to others; one must leave with or give to each person that which belongs to him (p. 375), is an obvious mistake! Not all peoples have known the principle of private property, and for the most part the spoiling of the stranger is recommended, etc.! To claim even that monogamy is a universal moral principle is to fly in the face of the largest segment of moralities, and after having made the claim it is well known what theological acrobatics were needed to justify the polygamy of the patriarchs. (Cf. Innocent III.)

Here should be inserted the analyses of Gurvitch on the plurality of *types* of the moral life, which only accentuates this diversity. For moralities differ not only in their content but in the very concept of the structure of the moral life, and Gurvitch rightly distinguishes traditional morality, the morality of the final end, the morality of virtues, of judgments after the fact, of symbolic images, the morality of action, the imperative morality, the inciting morality. But under these circumstances we do not understand how he can say that sociological relativism has nothing to do with philosophic relativism. As a striving for an absolute morality, yes—but as reality!

7. S. de Beauvoir, *Ethics of Ambiguity*.

8. A good example of this is provided by Niebuhr (*Nature and Destiny*) when he constantly returns to the assertion that man attains to the concept of justice and thereby enters upon a true ethic. And from that standpoint he criticizes K. Barth, showing that it is untenable to make of this realization of justice on the part of man a sort of mystery of providence. But as a matter of fact what Niebuhr fails to see is first of all the unbelievable variety of the content which civilizations have attributed to this word justice. Then, second, he fails to see that the concept of justice which he calls "natural," and which satisfies him as a product of a natural society, is in reality justice as understood in

Western society, that is to say a product of the outward Christianization of that society. It is a defective, yet accompanying, elaboration of Christian thought. And it is the Christian by-product which is adopted in the socialist world, as in Africa today. It is not surprising, then, that Niebuhr can establish a relation between this creation which he considers "natural" and the Christian faith!

9. To pretend as does Boisset (in *Le Problème de la Morale chrétienne*, p. 10) that the ideal in itself transcends the notions of the living real is to boast of a completely empty category, and one which each person can fill with whatever he wishes. Hence there is no identification there. And again, to say that the most burdensome moral attitudes obey a single order which is that of obligation (whence is deduced the universal basis of morality) is on the one hand to ignore the whole orientation of morality without obligation and on the other hand simply to postpone the problem, for it remains to explain the whence and the how of this obligation, and at that point one perceives that this notion is manifold and in its turn very diversified according to time and place.

10. Sartre is entirely correct when he writes (on the hypothesis that there is no God) that there can no longer be an a priori good, since there is no infinite and perfect conscience to think it. Nowhere is it written that the good exists, that it is necessary to be honest, that one must not lie, because we are on a plane where there are only men. (See *L'existentialisme est un humanisme*, p. 36.)

11. See also Bonhoeffer's good discussion on the moments when ethics go without saying, and on the moments when there are no ethics at all in society, when it is no longer anything but "problem." (See *Ethik*, pp. 204 ff.; cf. Bon., *Ethics*, pp. 231 ff.)

12. On the ethical phenomenon as an object of reflection cf. Bonhoeffer, *ibid.*

Chapter 7 The Theoretical Moralities

1. Gurvitch is obviously right (*Traité de Sociologie*, Vol. II, p. 147) to raise the question of the sociology of moral doctrines. "One could well ask whether (they) are simply dogmatizations and sublimations of the hierarchy of types and forms of existing moral attitudes." "They could be seen as dogmatic ways of justifying and sublimating a factual situation in the prevailing system of moral attitudes."

2. Bergson has seen clearly that the "heroic" morality was also linked to an environment but conduces to transcending it (*les deux sources*, pp. 30–53; cf. *Two Sources*, pp. 34–58). When we

speak here of theoretical morality we understand not only intellectual morality but also the heroic morality, that which is destined to be embodied in a privileged personality who becomes an
example. Their common ground is that it is always a question of
a morality created by an individual and intentionally. Founders,
reformers of religions, mystics, saints, obscure heroes of the moral
life whom we may have encountered along the road . . . these
are the conquerors. They have broken the resistance of nature
and have lifted humanity to new destinies (p. 48).

3. Cf. Niebuhr's analysis explaining the failure of Kantian
ethics (*Ethics*, pp. 206 ff.).

4. Bergson has correctly seen the problem of lack of application. No speculation will ever create an obligation. The beauty
of the theory is of little account. I can always say that I do not
accept it. And even if I accept it I claim to be free to do as I
please (*les deux sources*, p. 45; cf. *Two Sources*, pp. 47–8. He
is specifically disturbed by the nonapplication of the Stoic morality (pp. 59, 78; cf. *Two Sources*, pp. 60, 77–8) because it remained a philosophy. And he has shown that a morality based
on reason has no chance of ever being accepted and recognized
(pp. 86 ff.; cf. *Two Sources*, pp. 85 ff.), no more than one which
accepts the idealist axiom that the idea of the good possesses an
intrinsic power (pp. 88 ff.; cf. *Two Sources*, pp. 87 ff.). Finally,
the concern to maintain community loyalty, or the concern for
human progress, will not prevail either insofar as it is proposed
by reason (p. 90; cf. *Two Sources*, p. 89). We shall return to
these excellent demonstrations. Cf. also Niebuhr, *Ethics*, pp.
205 ff. The same idea in Mehl: "To every ethic which claims to
be self-sufficient, (one) has the right to object on the grounds
of . . . its inability to move beyond the stage of criticism and the
stage of exhortation" (*Ethique et Théologie*, p. 43).

5. There is the temptation to take the sociology of the moral
life as the base for a moral doctrine, in attempting to know and
prescribe at the same time. Such had already been the attempt
of A. Comte and of Spencer.

On Durkheim cf. Gurvitch, "La science des faits moraux et la
morale théorique chez Durkheim" (in *Vocation actuelle de la
sociologie*).

6. This assumes the elimination of the nonscientific elements
(for example, the sense of sin) for the purpose of setting up an
objective morality (Hesnard's morality without sin, for example), or it may assume that morality will be given a much larger
frame of reference, history for example, and the good is evalu-
ated according to its insertion into history, according to its historical efficacy, etc.

7. This is true also for Christianity, which becomes a mere morality: for example, J. Bois, *Problèmes de la Morale chrétienne;* Peabody, *Jesus Christ and the Social Question.*

8. On this subject cf., for example, Reiner, "Ethik und Menschenbild," *ZEE*, 1958, No. 5.

9. One is familiar with the doctrine of Bergson explaining the application of creative moralities. They must be based on an emotion, on a passion *(les deux sources,* p. 40; cf. *Two Sources,* pp. 40–41) capable of being represented in a mental picture (p. 45; cf. *Two Sources,* p. 43), the religious emotion being an especially favored example. Then this morality must be embodied in an exemplary man, an admired and venerated personality, and what is more, the great moral figures taken together form a sort of heavenly city into which they invite us to enter, and they make their appeal to us (pp. 67, 98; cf. *Two Sources,* pp. 68, 99). But in any event, the realization of this morality presupposes "a society whose state of mind was already such as their realization was bound to bring about" (p. 74; cf. *Two Sources,* p. 74). Thus in all instances it is the life forces which are in play, and whenever one pretends to base morality on reason one reintroduces those forces the moment one attempts to arrive at the realization.

10. Contrary to what is often asserted, that Stoicism was spread among, and by, the slaves, it was in intellectual, legal, and political circles that it had its principal influence.

CHAPTER 8 VALUES

1. At bottom, although he did not use the term, Bergson had earlier voiced the existence of an ethic of values in speaking of "another source of morality," of a morality of aspiration, of call, of impetus *(les deux sources,* pp. 30–53; cf. *Two Sources.* pp. 34–59), of the attitude of the open mind which calls for an effort, an ambition, and which assumes an emotion tending toward the achievement of a moral value which is an urge, a demand for movement, etc.

2. How true Bonhoeffer's observation is when he reminds us that man is first of all a living being and not an ethical subject, and that the moralists too often forget that life is not a series of great ethical decisions, finally that the ethical phenomenon is a limiting case. The "you ought" only comes into play when the duty is unworkable or forgotten *(Ethik,* pp. 204 ff.; cf. Bon., *Ethics,* pp. 194 ff.). It is curious that it should be in connection with the ethics of value and the phenomenologists that a reminder of these primary truths becomes necessary, precisely the phenomenologists who had the intention of starting only with man as a living being. Bonhoeffer sees the facts clearly when he

acknowledges that the phenomenon and the ethical moment exist, but that they are limiting cases. (See *Ethik,* p. 205; cf. Bon., *Ethics,* p. 208.)

3. It is currently the custom to assert the superiority of situation ethics over legal or traditional ethics, but Etienne Borne, in an article in *Force Nouvelle,* has demonstrated perfectly that this situation ethics can lead, in a war situation, to approving any kind of behavior, and that in the last analysis it was in the name of situation ethics that torture was justified in the war in Algeria, or that the O.A.S. outrages were considered legitimate. The tragic thing, he says, is that one should fail to perceive the substitution of one morality for another, and that when all is said and done situation ethics permits all immoralities. (See *Force Nouvelle,* 1961.)

CHAPTER 9   THE LIVED MORALITIES

1. Bergson *(les deux sources,* p. 7; cf. *Two Sources,* p. 14) has the merit of showing how moral obligation rests upon social pressure, yet without that's being an outside pressure because each one of us "belongs as much to society as to himself."

2. See the excellent critique of the morality of French society in 1930 by E. Mournier, "Technique des moyens spirituels," *Esprit,* 1934, No. 26.

3. The well-known description by Bergson still holds *(les deux sources,* pp. 12, 19; cf. *Two Sources,* pp. 18, 19, 20, 25) : it is society that draws up for the individual the program of his daily routine. In the ordinary course of events we conform to our obligations rather than think of them. Habit is enough, and in most cases we have only to leave well enough alone in order to accord to society what it expects from us. We decide naturally on what is in keeping with the rule. Duty is performed automatically, but because of the organic interrelatedness of our obligations these tiny duties add up to a whole. All duties are tinged with the hue taken on exceptionally by one or the other of them. Obligation weighs on the will like a habit, each obligation dragging behind it the accumulated mass of the others, thus utilizing the weight of the whole for the pressure it is exerting. Here you have the totality of obligation for a simple, elementary moral conscience.

4. The reduction of all ethics to an individual morality is very characteristic of the bourgeois period. As K. Marx indeed shows, the bourgeois, because he belongs to the dominant class, and because he does not want to admit that he does belong to a class or that he is engaged in a class struggle, believes, or pretends to believe, that social relations are nothing other than the manipu-

lation of personal relations, and consequently that it is possible to transpose personal morality into social relations.

5. The ethical doctrine of choice rests on a false concept of freedom (for example that of Simone de Beauvoir, *Morale de l'Ambiguïté;* cf. S. de Beauvoir, *The Ethics of Ambiguity,* Citadel, 1962), inserted into an absurd and disjointed world. But then that is no longer a freedom (cf. analysis in Bonhoeffer, *Ethik,* p. 134; cf. Bon., *Ethics,* p. 144). Nor is there any more of a choice *in the presence of* the commandment of God, for the latter is not a proposition which is made to us. It is not one "possibility" among other possibilities. It is the word of God or it is nothing. We understand it in that way or we do not understand it. The freedom which it leaves us with is the freedom to obey, but not the freedom to choose among several possibilities of which obedience would be one. For the commandment is both a "you must" and a "you can," and an "I promise" that such will be the case (cf. Bonhoeffer, p. 220; cf. Bon., *Ethics,* pp. 220–21). All other freedom is an illusion.

But at the same time this freedom should refer the one who is to act back to the one who is the source of his action (not a good, but a person), the one who says, "Apart from me you can *do* nothing" (John 15:5). Ethics in that case fulfills its authentic function because it teaches man this quite simple truth, that the will of God is *revealed* in order to be *done.* That would seem to go without saying, but experience shows that Christians need constantly to be told it.

From the moment man seized the power to decide good and evil, he imagines that he always has to choose between a good and an evil. But we need to take note of the fact that it is only in the degree in which man fails to recognize the word of God, fails to hear the voice of God, that he claims to possess and to exercise this choice. If man hears the voice of the good shepherd he no longer has a choice. If he recognizes that the good is the voice of God there is no more choice. Disobedience, unbelief, no longer have a reason for existence. They have become, in the words of Barth's formula, "the impossible possibility that evil constitutes for God himself."

Disobedience to the word of God is never a choice. It is only the evidence that man is unable to take seriously what God says. It is only the proof that man is listening to every other word but that of God. It is only the proof precisely that man is not free, and that he precisely is not making a choice. From then on we are in the presence of a radical contradiction. For natural ethics (all moralities) choice is the ethical situation par excellence. It is choice which characterizes ethics. Now in the presence of God, to the contrary, we are faced with a concrete decision already accomplished. There are not several possibilities. There are not interpretations of a general law. There is not a choice proposed between a good and an evil. The idea of a possible choice is already in itself the fruit of our disobedience and our unbelief (K. Barth, *Dogm.*, II, 2, 2, p. 167; cf. *Ch. Dogm.*, II, 2, 669). The man who pretends to exercise an ethical choice is simply a liar. Under these conditions there can be no conciliation.

Chapter 10   Man's Stance with Respect to Morality, Moralism, and Immoralism

1. Marx's analysis of ideology may be applicable here, showing that all moral (or immoral) positions are the result of a false conscience. Man's spiritual capacity makes it possible for him to add to his ignorance of the true situation an element of conscious deceit in the attempt to appear loyal to the values or to himself. All this lends itself to the biblical affirmation that ethics is the result of the break with God.

Chapter 11   Technological Morality

1. In this technological morality we include, among others, that morality being developed by human relations agencies in the United States, and that developed in the Soviet Union. This latter is much less dominated by Marxist concepts than by technological principles. Cf., for example, Chambre, *le Marxisme en Union Soviétique*, chap. 6; de Graaf, "Marxismus und Moral in der Sovjetrussischen Literatur," *ZEE*, 1957, No. 5; Delimars, "l'Ethique marxiste et son enseignement en U.S.S.R.," *Cahiers du Bien politique*, 1958.

2. Niebuhr's analysis (*Nature and Destiny of Man*) of the characteristics of the new morality of modern man and of its contradiction with Christian ethics is excellent. Belief in the goodness of man, the search, no longer for virtue, but for a reorganization of society or for a plan of education to solve all moral problems, the validation of the reason as a guide to man, faith in salvation through history (or faith in progress), elimination of the concept of fundamental evil in favor of the idea of particular evils, etc., all of that enters into what we are calling technological morality.

3. Finally, one should evoke the morality which would arise automatically through biological or chemical manipulations. Let us bear in mind the discourse pronounced by Jean Rostand before the Académie Française in 1962, in which he said this: "It is in the direct line of our progress to learn how to control chemi-

cally the deeds of our conduct like the other phenomena of life. It is already possible, through the use of a hormone or a vitamin or an oligo-element, to produce an increase of courage, willpower, maternal love. After the tranquilizers will come the moralizers. We are promised soon to have available drugs to reduce envy and to calm ambition, and how long will it be before we have lozenges for devotion, tablets for gentleness, and pills for self-denial?" This is nothing but an extension of the technological morality, beginning with the moment when it is only a question of securing behavior in conformity with the collective behavior, apart from any individual decision or responsibility.

4. K. Barth, *Dogm.*, II, 2, 2, p. 57 (cf. *Ch. Dogm.*, II, 2, p. 564).

Part III   The Impossibility and
the Necessity of a Christian Ethic

CHAPTER 12   THE IMPOSSIBILITY
OF A CHRISTIAN ETHIC

1. It is important to take note of the fact that the word ethic never occurs in the New Testament, although it was current in the Greek philosophy of the time. Likewise the word duty is never employed in a moral sense in the New Testament. It is often employed in the juridical sense of a money debt. When the Bible speaks of morality it uses such words as "the law," "walking," or "being" in accord with the will of God, or "adhering to" the will of God, and as Crespy observes (*Christianisme social*, 1957, p. 694) these are terms in the sphere of action, of being, of living, not in the sphere of speculation. It is not a theoretical construction of a morality. It should be added that the moral portion of the apostolic letters in the New Testament is always less precise, less organized, than the dogmatic portion. It could be said that there is a complete dogmatic statement in the writings of Paul, but not a complete morality. There are only examples of morality, a description of certain elements of the Christian life, but never a rounded moral doctrine.

2. Niebuhr has produced an excellent critique of ethics derived too easily from "orthodox" theology: an authoritative code which bypasses the problems of modern man, a break between the imperative and the real, irrelevant precepts, a premature identification of a canonical moral code with the transcendent will of God, elimination of the tension between present grace and eschatological promise, suppression of the reality of human history in favor of eternity, acceptance of an authoritarian order for fear of anarchy caused by sin, complacency toward wicked historical forms on the ground that all is ultimately sinful, sup-

pression of the positive aspect of the commandment of love, on the ground that since it cannot be realized its only function is to reveal evil, sin, man's incapacity, etc. (Niebuhr, *Ethics*). All these criticisms are just and formidable.

3. As Niebuhr (*Nature and Destiny*) shows very clearly, that which is finally inadmissable in the multiplicity of moralities is not the diversity of their contents but the pretention of being "the last" and absolute, the association of idolatry and the will to power with the formulation of what ought to be, the rejection of relativity and finitude, the claim to moral autonomy, all of that in ethics is man's effort to deny the determined and contingent aspect of his existence, and it is just that which repeats the very sin of Adam. But it is the same for the Christian. Hence we must be infinitely careful to realize that ethics only exists in the encounter and confrontation of our concrete existence with the command of God, which is a decision not within us but above us. (See K. Barth, *Dogm.*, II, 2, 2, p. 140; cf. *Ch. Dogm.*, II, 2, p. 645.)

Every claim to know this norm of ourselves, every attempt to confer upon our own activity a similarity to the action of God, is a rejection of Jesus Christ, a relapse into disobedience. The ten commandments and the Sermon on the Mount, often interpreted as principles of a Christian ethic, are not so much that as they are commandments, that is, they relate to a given historical reality and can never become general metaphysical notions. Hillerdal shows equally well the contradiction which exists between casuistry and New Testament ethics.

4. Let us add, as Hillerdal emphasizes (*ZEE*, 1957, No. 6), that this opposition is already expressed by the fact that there *apparently* are several different ethics, several models and moral systems in the Bible. The commandments as a whole do not possess that splendid unity which we would like to attribute to the work of God!

5. At the same time, this *hic et nunc* does not entirely correspond to the imminence of the kingdom in Bultmann's "last hour." The existential present, the renewed encounter with the kerygma, is no doubt correct, but it neglects the continuity of God's will and it reduces the whole of the Christian life to obedience in an instant, which it is not. The kingdom of God is not only the transformation of each instant into a last hour. It is also a glory which really comes. It is wherever Jesus Christ reigns, and it is the revelation of this reign at an actual last hour.

6. How can that be good which man has chosen for himself? In the face of the response of God we no longer have the possibility of asking what the good is and how it is to be accom-

plished. (See K. Barth, *Dogm.*, II, 2, 2, p. 10; cf. *Ch. Dogm.*, II, 2, pp. 517–18.)

7. K. Barth has clearly shown that it is absolutely out of the question to grasp in its reality the form in which the commandment of God ordains as permission *and* establishes a law as gospel. Every attempt at systematic definition can only end either in *legalism* or in *antinomianism,* that is to say, either the setting up of a system of duties apart from grace or the negation of all duty, of all commandment. That, in fact, is what experience demonstrates, and it teaches us the impossibility of constructing a Christian ethic. (See K. Barth, *Dogm.*, II, 2, 2, p. 96; cf. *Ch. Dogm.*, II, 2, pp. 593 ff.)

8. Yet even though it is always a matter of particular commandments the command of God never degenerates into a sort of incoherent chaos of special and contradictory directives addressed to ever different individuals. Man in the presence of God's command does not dissociate into a series of situations without common ground with his fellows and without continuity, for the command comes from God and God himself is consistent. Moreover, since this commandment is the decision of the goodness of God, it is not confused and does not create chaos. To the contrary, it is the very commandment of God which gives authentic continuity to man's life. This fundamental unity of the commandment, often emphasized by K. Barth, prohibits our turning ethics into a body of good prescriptions, a catalog of moral or economic religious laws. This distortion of the commandment of God destroys the commandment itself.

9. The whole of the Christian life in its essence and origin is contained in the gift of grace given to it, and by which God justifies it. Such, then, is the life of this man. Grace is the final reality of his life. There is no method for obtaining it nor for holding onto it. What presumption, then, to imagine that one can construct an ethic on it or out of it (cf. Bonhoeffer, p. 75; cf., Bon., *Ethics*, p. 79) ! The "out of it" is already significant, for it assumes that one has departed from it. There is no Christian principle to be deduced from it. There is no commandment which reduces this gift to a formula. An ordinance assumes the possibility of carrying it out. Grace is fulfilled outside of our possibilities. The problem remains intact (to talk like the theologians) of the relation between justification and sanctification. It is false to confuse the one with the other. But how make them meet (except intellectually and theoretically)? On the impossibility of Christian principles see our book, *Présence au Monde Moderne.* The commandment of God is neither a general rule nor a categorical imperative, nor a principle of action. (Cf. K.

Barth, *Dogm.*, II, 2, 2, pp. 159 ff.; cf. *Ch. Dogm.*, II, 2, pp. 661 ff.)

10. K. Barth (*Dogm.*, II, 2, 2, p. 173; cf. *Ch. Dogm.*, II, 2, p. 675) reminds us that there could not be principles for a biblical ethic to the very degree to which we have only to do with commandments of God. The important personages in biblical history teach us that in the command of God we are dealing with God himself and his action, not with principles, or more exactly, the only principle possible in a biblical ethic is the very person of the one who gives the commandment.

Crespy (*Christianisme social,* 1957, p. 827) likewise considers that the content of Christian morality could not be determined by general principles, by axioms, as with moralists like Spinoza or Kant. Such principles, he says, are established through speculation on the concept of duty or of the good. That path is entirely foreign to Christian reflection. For the latter, as a matter of fact, the heart of all reality is not the idea, but rather the historic revelation of God. In the face of this revelation principles have only a verbal reality.

But when we say that there are no Christian principles we of course do not mean that there is no "spirit" in contrast to the letter. We certainly are not going back to the *"Gesinnungs Ethik"* and the theology of Ritschl. But, as Bonhoeffer says, the problem of the life of the Christian is that of incarnating the work of Christ in ourselves. Christ is not a model, nor an ideal, etc. He is the one who comes in us, and who makes us to be crucified and risen again with him. Jesus Christ makes it possible for man to become that man whom God became. There are no Christian principles because nowhere does scripture tell us that God became a principle. It tells us that he became a man. Nowhere are we presented with ideas, with principles, but with God acting in reality. So much is this true that ethics does not have to ask the question: What are the Christian principles?, but rather the question: How can Christ be incarnate in us? One understands readily that a formal, inclusive, theoretical answer is impossible! (See Bonhoeffer, pp. 27–8; cf. Bon., *Ethics*, pp. 23 ff.)

11. K. Barth, *Dogm.*, II, 2, 2, p. 55 (cf. *Ch. Dogm.*, II, 2, p. 562).

12. Prunet, *La Morale chrétienne, d'après les Ecrits Johanniques,* p. 51.

13. We are well aware that these different texts do not have equal historical value in the sense of modern historical science, but if some of them testify to a very ancient custom enjoying actual usage, all show what was the vision of Israel, the chosen people, concerning this custom. They show that Israel inserts the interdiction into the sphere of Jahweh, and their significance lies precisely in that fact.

14. Soë, sec. 16.

15. K. Barth, *Dogm.* (German edition), III, 4, sec. 52 (cf. *Ch. Dogm.,* III, 4, sec. 52).

16. Bonhoeffer, *Ethik,* pp. 136 ff. (cf. Bon., *Ethics,* pp. 150 ff.).

17. K. Barth, *Dogm.* (German edition), III, 4, sec. 52.

18. As H. Roux has well said (*Commentaire des épîtres pastorales*), one does not go beyond the grace of God. One cannot add a law or a science of morals to the gospel of God, nor again, complete the faith by a morality.

19. Niebuhr well shows (*Ethics,* p. 20) how a Christianity which takes on a purely historical dimension (for whatever reason, be it liberalism or a transcendental theology out of contact with the real) is in fact dependent upon the corruptions of its own peculiar "ethos" and of its culture. Morality plays a corrupting role within the church in the last analysis.

20. We haven't the presumption to summarize the theological doctrine of the Holy Spirit, of which there are numerous interpretations and an infinity of nuances. We confine ourselves to indicating, in propositional form, the elements which we have had in mind as necessary for an understanding of the problem of ethics.

God neither governs the world nor directs the lives of Christians through the ministry of the church, but through the action of the Holy Spirit. Hence it is not up to the church to formulate an ecclesiastical ethic, still less "commandments" (Soë, sec. 9).

Sanctification is the work of the Holy Spirit within us (de Quervain, I, 75) and the Keswick movement was right in its strong reminder of the fact (see, for example, Cruvellier, *la sanctification par la foi,* 1930). We must not give way to any spiritualism, but neither should we deny the specific action of the Holy Spirit. That is to say that the Christian life has no other reality than that given to it by the Holy Spirit.

The Holy Spirit never identifies himself with our person. He is not a part of us. He performs a work upon us. He is never given over to us. There is no method for obtaining him. The good which he makes known to us is never an objectified datum. The point is to lead a life in conformity with the requirement of the commandment of God, and *then* the Holy Spirit can act through the instrumentality of our lives.

In responding to the action of the Holy Spirit only faith makes it possible to accept what the Holy Spirit demands (which, apart from faith, is folly or useless) and also to take in its urgent and personal quality. Hence, apart from faith there could be no ethic derived from the commandment, and which could be received. In this sense it has to be said that a Christian ethic is necessarily an ethic of faith. But faith itself is still a gift from God (de Quervain, I, 82).

The good is never our personal work. It is always the work of the Holy Spirit within us (Soë, sec. 20). It is the Holy Spirit who causes us to know the good, who causes us to recognize a good in an event, who gives a decision its positive qualification, and who makes God's commandment alive and current for us. Hence no *independent* morality is possible. No virtue is described in the Bible as having an intrinsic value. All virtue has value only in relation to Jesus Christ, thanks to the action of the Holy Spirit. The Holy Spirit can bring about a "suspension of ethics." As Prunet rightly says, John pushes to the extreme the paradox of the fulfillment of ethics through the suspension of ethics (see the entire section on the Holy Spirit in *Théologie Johannique*).

But all the preceding propositions do not imply a personal conduct directly inspired by the Holy Spirit at every moment, nor a disjointed ethic sometimes defended on the basis of the text "The Spirit blows where it wills." In this, K. Barth criticizes Soë, who gives in a little too much to inspiration *hic et nunc* (III, 4, sec. 52; cf. *Ch. Dogm.*, III, 4, sec. 52), and Hillerdal rightly reminds us of the kerygmatic character of ethics (*ZEE*, 1956).

The Holy Spirit is not a pure mystery. We know that he is a spirit of justice, a spirit of truth, a spirit of love (cf. Prunet, *loc. cit.*), that he addresses to man no other truth than Jesus Christ himself, and that he has no autonomy with respect to the Trinity in the guidance of men.

The Holy Spirit only speaks to man through the word of Jesus Christ. He makes that word alive for each one. He makes the gospel contemporary and causes it to be perceived in the law itself. He opens our ears so that the command of God may be received for what it is. Hence he refers back to something enduring, to an objectivity, to an event, and he never ceases to send us back to it (K. Barth, *loc. cit.*).

The action of the Holy Spirit does not do away with the personal decision of the individual, with his independence and his ethical responsibility. Man's independence is respected by God, and God always awaits his free decision of willing obedience in love. God does not in anything mechanize man by the overwhelming intervention of the Holy Spirit. Hence sanctification is not to be understood as a putting into play of spiritual automation, nor as a series of acts which are "holy" because commanded by the Holy Spirit. It is a matter of the regeneration of one's being through the appropriation of the work of Christ by the mediation of the Holy Spirit, but this transformation is assumed to be expressed in our personal and free decisions. From then on, as K. Barth says (*loc. cit.*), the task of ethics consists rather in pursuing the history of the relations between God and man, a history in which the ethical event takes place.

21. According to the powerful formula of K. Barth, the object of theological ethics is not the word of God which man has seized upon, but rather the word of God which lays hold upon man (*Dogm.*, II, 2, 2, p. 39; cf. *Ch. Dogm.*, II, 2, p. 546). This shows better than anything the impossibility of calling a morality "Christian." It cannot even be a commentary on the Bible! And likewise we need to recall here (K. Barth, *Dogm.*, II, 2, 2, pp. 148 ff.; cf. *Ch. Dogm.*, II, 2, pp. 653 ff.) that it is the divine decision which is the norm of our actions. Now this decision is not an idea, nor a principle, nor a system. It is only a decision, established in the covenant and taken in Jesus Christ. Hence it cannot be elaborated by us. It can only be, in its turn, the source of our decisions. Ethical reflection, then, will be the knowledge which accompanies each one of our decisions in relation to those which preceded it or are to follow it, but nothing more!

22. To a certain degree what we find here is the conflict between the infinite requirement and the finite commandment emphasized by Ricoeur (II, 2, pp. 58 ff.; cf. *Symbolism*, pp. 54 ff.), and what he describes as the dialectic of the Jewish ethic seems to me inevitable as well for a Christian ethic. The commandment, the value, cannot be saved except by continual reference to the most holy God, and this requirement can only be expressed in an ethic, yet the latter never ceases to betray that which it expresses.

23. K. Barth, *Dogm.*, II, 2, 2, pp. 134 ff. (cf. *Ch. Dogm.*, II, 2, pp. 641 ff.).

24. K. Barth, *Dogm.*, II, 2, 2, p. 275 (cf. *Ch. Dogm.*, II, 2, p. 781).

25. On this see Von Rad, *Théologie de l'Ancien Testament* (cf. Von Rad, *Old Testament Theology*, New York, Harper & Row, 1962).

26. Bonhoeffer, *Ethik*, pp. 75 ff. (cf. Bon., *Ethics*, pp. 82 ff.).

27. Bonhoeffer reminds us forcefully (*Ethik*, pp. 149 ff.; cf. Bon., *Ethics*, pp. 166 ff.) that the Christian ethic demands to be lived, or indeed it is nothing. The law of God asks to be done, not to be interpreted. It is done or it is forgotten (James 1:25). Man can retain the revelation only if he lives it. The word of God is only grasped in the action performed, in the process of carrying it out.

28. It is obvious that all this is registered in the doctrine of the determination of man by election, which nevertheless does not rule out this man's self-determination (on all this K. Barth,

Dogm., II, 2, 2, p. 3; cf. *Ch. Dogm.,* II, 2, p. 510).

29. On this importance of invention see, among others, Crespy, *Christianisme social,* 1957, p. 832.

30. Hillerdal, *ZEE,* 1957, No. 6.

31. K. Barth, *Dogm.* (German edition), III, 4, sec. 52 (cf. *Ch. Dogm.,* III, 4, sec. 52); Niebuhr, *Ethics,* pp. 45, 105, 166, 187.

32. Hillerdal, *ZEE,* 1957, No. 6.

33. Apart from the intrinsic impossibility of a Christian ethic, it is also necessary to ponder the special problem brought about by the extreme diversity, plurality, and inconsistency of the ethical systems in Protestantism alone. That should make us think. The *morality of repression* of sin (invincible, besetting, which man at most can repress but from which he will only be delivered in the kingdom); *Pelagianism* (our natural powers suffice for complete obedience to the law); *perfectionism* in its various forms (Roman, Arminian, liberal . . .); (baptism, or conversion, or the message of Christ, are the seed from which obedience to God grows. It is no longer the law [which is disparaged] nor the result of an action which is important, but the current work and progress); *thesis of the repression of sin* (Wesley); *thesis of ethical relativism* and of indifference toward works or toward the distinction between degrees of perfection, etc.

To be sure, we shall not go into a systematic description and critique of these diverse systems, for we do not pretend here to be presenting a treatise on ethics. We shall make only one observation: just as the diversity of theologies is explained in the last analysis by the fact that one has departed, in one way or another, from "scripture alone and the whole scripture," so also the diversity of Christian ethics is explained by the fact that one claims to separate the ethical problem from theology and to put ethics in the foreground. It is the attempt to consider the fact, the phenomenon, the problem, the value of ethics *in itself* and *preferentially* which leads to all the errors.

What is needed, obviously, is to reduce ethics to its humble station and consequently to begin afresh with Christ and his work. Christ is the whole of the moral life of the Christian. The law of the Christian is nothing other than the Christ in his person. It is in him that life is given to us, and hence also the law of our life. This diversity is not in the same category with the normal diversity of which we shall speak later on. It is, in reality, normal that ethics for the Christian should change according to places, times, and cultures. No argument against this ethic can be deduced from that diversity. But what we are here pointing out is the deleterious diversity of moralities stemming from a seduction of morality itself, which drags man from his faith-relation with God in order to put him into relation with morality, on the outward side of the sphere of ethics.

CHAPTER 13 HISTORIC FORMATION
OF CHRISTIAN MORALITIES

1. The "ethical question" cannot be avoided. K. Barth defines it as "the search for the rationale and the possibility of fixed principles, laws, rules, habits, and constants, which control the multitude and variety of human actions." (See *Dogm.*, II, 2, 2, p. 6; cf. *Ch. Dogm.*, II, 2, p. 513.)

2. See, among others, the excellent analysis of Ricoeur, II, 2, pp. 119–34 (cf. *Symbolism,* pp. 118–39).

3. The interest in classification appears clearly in the *Didache* with the distinction of the two ways, that of the good and that of perdition, with the teaching of the virtues and the catalog of vices.

4. It would seem that it is in Clement of Alexandria that one finds for the first time the idea that wherever a true morality is found it means that Christ is at work. Objective morality becomes the criterion and sign of God.

5. Morality in the narrowest sense of the word solidifies under the influence of the penitentials (sixth to eighth centuries) in Ireland, then in France and Germany. These are directives furnished to confessors for the imposition of penances in accordance with the offenses committed. Detailed lists are drawn up of all the sins with their penalties. Casuistry, which was well on its way from the time of Ambrose, finds in the penitentials its place of crystallization.

6. The discussions on probabilism and probabiliorism in the seventeenth century are characteristic of this endeavor as being the inevitable and ultimate refinement of casuistry. Far from resolving the problem, Alfonso de Liguori only plunged the church deeper into it. Even Haering is forced to acknowledge that one gains the impression that true religious morality has lost much of its vigor in these sterile debates (I, 78; cf. *Law of Christ,* Vol. I). But it must be emphasized that these discussions cannot be avoided once one is determined to make "Christian morality" applicable to everybody.

7. Without entering into the question of the relation between ethics and dogmatics, it is necessary at least to point out the unavoidable relation between truth and ethics. We have already seen that heresy and bad conduct are frequently shown to be related to one another in the letters. Likewise Roux, *Epîtres pastorales,* p. 44, emphasizes that it is impossible to live otherwise than according to the truth which is in Jesus (Ephesians 4). In

other words, the Christian notion of truth is not merely a dogmatic notion. It is also the basis for ethics. He who has received
the revelation of the truth is called upon to persevere in the
things which have been taught him. They are normative for him,
and that is why the different aspects of ethics are linked in the
letters to different aspects of the revelation. For example, as
Roux indicates, the ethical exhortation of the first letter to
Timothy is envisaged from the point of view of the doctrine of
the incarnation. The second letter to Timothy sets forth an
ethic of service based on the lordship of the risen Christ. Finally,
the ethic indicated in the letter to Titus is a baptismal cate-
chetical instruction based on the doctrine of justification. Furthermore, it is well known that K. Barth throughout the whole of his
dogmatics has shown the ethical implication of each theological
proposition step by step in its development.

Elsewhere Roux, *Epîtres pastorales,* p. 194, lays stress on another relation between heresy and the choice of an ethic. Every
discussion, he says, in the church concerning ethical questions
which are not located on the true ground, that of grace and of
the freedom of the new man, should be abolished. At bottom,
heresy is precisely a moral or dogmatic choice which engenders
division. In the absence of a recognition of the ethical consequences of justification by faith in Jesus Christ, one can only end
up with a bad doctrine of the moral life and of sanctification.

8. This is what Niebuhr (*Ethics,* p. 9) rightly attacks when he
speaks of the identification which Christian orthodoxy makes between the transcendent will of God and a canonical moral code.

9. Nineteenth-century Protestant theology followed the orientation which had been given by St. Thomas in constructing a
speculative ethics (cf. de Quervain, *Die Heiligung,* pp. 28 ff.)
severed from scripture and unrelated to the lordship of Jesus
Christ. It represented, moreover, the continuation of the legalistic doctrine of the seventeenth century.

CHAPTER 14   THE NECESSITY
FOR A CHRISTIAN ETHIC

1. We shall only be speaking here of the fundamental and permanent necessity for a Christian ethic, and not of
the necessity for our own times. It is indeed true that there appears to be an immense lacuna in our society, that of Christian
ethics. We refer for example, among many other studies, to what
Bonhoeffer says in the opening paragraphs of his *Ethics,* or to
Piper ("Mittelbarkeit der christlichen Ethik," *ZEE,* 1947, p. 125) ,
or Dippel ("Christliche Existenz in der modernen wissenschaft-
lichen und technischen Welt," *ZEE,* 1958, p. 129) . And this lacuna is more obvious in French Protestantism than elsewhere.

2. Crespy (*Christianisme social,* 1957, p. 691) stresses precisely that the problem of a Christian morality is not only raised by the existence of the other moralities but by the very character of the Christian faith. The latter, he says, drifts into metaphysical idealism if one takes away from it its ethical consequences. Neither Luther nor Calvin separated the law from faith. Morality should conform to the content of preaching. It is, in short, the logical and reasonable worship of which Paul speaks in Romans 12.

3. Hillerdal (*ZEE,* 1957, No. 6) on this subject is right to remind us that the necessity for a Christian ethic rests on the two following constant factors: the biblical commandments are not so clear and especially do not constitute an obvious ensemble, there are large ambiguities; second, it is not easy to find objective criteria for applying the promises, values, and commandments of the Bible to present concrete situations. Cf. also Soë, sec. 18.

4. K. Barth, *Dogm.* (German edition), III, 4, p. 36 (cf. *Ch. Dogm.,* III, 4, p. 31).

5. K. Barth, *Dogm.,* II, 2, 2, p. 29 (cf. *Ch. Dogm.,* II, 2, pp. 536, 539).

6. Bonhoeffer, *Ethik,* p. 206 (cf. Bon., *Ethics,* p. 219).

7. K. Barth, *Dogm.* (German edition), III, 4, p. 31 (cf. *Ch. Dogm.,* III, 4, p. 25).

8. Haering, I, p. 41 (cf. *Law of Christ,* Vol. I).

9. Roux, *Ep. Pastor.,* p. 80.

10. K. Barth, *Dogm.,* II, 2, 2, p. 70 (cf. *Ch. Dogm.,* II, 2, p. 577).

11. *Ibid.*

12. K. Barth, *Dogm.,* II, 2, 2, p. 140 (cf. *Ch. Dogm,* II, 2, p. 645).

13. K. Barth, *Dogm.* (German edition), III, 4, pp. 11 ff. (cf. *Ch. Dogm.,* III, 4, pp. 15 ff.).

14. Soë, *Eth.,* sec. 17.

15. Bonhoeffer, *Ethik,* pp. 176 ff. (cf. Bon., *Ethics,* pp. 117 ff.).

16. Bonhoeffer, pp. 136 ff. and 149 ff. (cf. Bon., *Ethics,* pp. 151 ff. and 166 ff.).

17. Bonhoeffer, pp. 147 ff. and 182 ff. (cf. Bon., *Ethics,* pp. 164 ff. and 201 ff.).

18. If God wants something of man, if he asserts his will, that is never in order to give an inconsistent, arbitrary order which someone could perform who is ultimately above God. No, what God wants of man is only revealed to us in what he wants and has himself already done *for us* (K. Barth, *Dogm.,* II, 2, 2, p. 55; cf. *Ch. Dogm.,* II, 2, p. 538).

On ethics as expressing man's belonging to God see de Quervain, *Die Heiligung,* pp. 9 ff.

19. Bonhoeffer is doubtless right when he says that the au-

thority and the possibility of ethical discourse stems from the fact that God himself has formulated his will in the form of a commandment. But it is not clear (pp. 204–22; cf. Bon., *Ethics,* pp. 222 ff.) whether he is speaking exclusively of Christian ethics or whether, as the opening paragraph seems to indicate, he is speaking of all ethical research.

20. The point is to seek with respect to each particular situation that which pleases the Lord, he who is the unerring judge of the good, of justice, and of truth. . . . No systematic nor intuitive analysis of a given situation, no matter how penetrating, can ever replace this examination (K. Barth, *Dogm.,* II, 2, 2, p. 133; cf. *Ch. Dogm.,* II, 2, pp. 634–5). This reminds us that ethics cannot be predetermined, and second, that in order to think ethics it is necesary to take the requirement of God as the *point of departure,* and not the tangible given of the situations in which we are placed.

21. It is not a matter of distinguishing in the Bible that which is law from that which is gospel. All is law, as de Quervain (pp. 255 ff.) rightly says (but also it is all gospel; cf. K. Barth). So true is this that ethics must be based on the totality of scripture and not on this or that text which seems more "moral"!

22. Hillerdal quite correctly has been able to assign a three-fold task to ethics (*ZEE,* 1957, No. 6): the description of the ethos of the New Testament, the method of interpreting biblical ethics for current preaching, and the analysis of the contemporary scene in which the man who is to live the faith finds himself. It is in the conjunction of these three elements, in fact, that ethics acquires its *truth* and its reality.

Niebuhr (*Ethics,* p. 9) is perfectly right in indicating that the whole validity of an ethic depends on the quality of the tension which it sets up between the transcendent and the historic. And he shows exactly (pp. 19 ff.) how that can only be the fact of a transcendence, and how the utopias and religious naturalisms end in a moral laxity from the moment the goal is reincorporated into history.

23. K. Barth, *Dogm.,* II, 2, 2, p. 29 (cf. *Ch. Dogm.,* II, 2, p. 535).

24. On the fact of an ethic which is descriptive and not normative see Piper, "Die Mittelbarkeit der christlichen Ethik," in *ZEE,* 1957, pp. 125 ff.

25. K. Barth, *Dogm.,* II, 2, 2, p. 31 (cf. *Ch. Dogm.,* II, 2, p. 537).

26. *Ethics,* p. 202.

27. Cf. F. J. Leenhardt, "Existe-t-il un système chrétien?," *Le Semeur,* June 1950.

Demco 38-297